Cooking Without Recipes

BOOKS BY HELEN WORTH

Cooking Without Recipes
Damn Yankee In a Southern Kitchen
Down-on-the-Farm Cook Book
Hostess Without Help
Shrimp Cookery

COOKING WITHOUT RECIPES

by Helen Worth

GRAMERCY PUBLISHING COMPANY
NEW YORK

To my mother and father,
who taught me the pleasure of learning

Contents

Acknowledgments

Assisting me in writing this book were many accomplished people, including Ann Burtt and other members of my staff whose uncanny faculty for being inside my head has eased the writing of this work immeasurably. I also am grateful to my students, whose discerning questions forced me to present the facts of cooking with ever greater precision.

Cooking Without Recipes

I

How to Use This Book

Since civilization began, cooks have made love to their families with food. Your kitchen makes you a part of that past—and opens the door to a future where you too can set your table with meals that comfort and sustain, delight and cheer.

To cook successfully, you need knowledge plus experience. Because, as with any skill, it's easy—but only when you know how. Actually, cooking is an art based on a science, and what is presented here is an *understanding* of cooking—the reasons behind the recipes —and the myriad variations that make cooking an art.

This is the book I wish I could have read before my first unsure tilt with dinner. If I had known then that the making of a soufflé* wasn't a secret locked tightly in a chef's cap, and that its preparation required neither a certificate in abracadabra nor the soul of an artist, walking into my kitchen would have been a pleasure immediately. Since I learned the hard way, my purpose is to remove the mystery from food preparation, thereby easing cooking for you.

The idea behind this book, a result of many years of intensive study and research, is that, although recipes are legion, the fundamental cooking principles are few. For instance, whether a recipe is called "Boeuf Bourguignon," "Chicken Cacciatore," "Hungarian

* This symbol indicates that the recipe and/or further information on the subject is detailed elsewhere in this book. Check the Index.

Gulyas," or "Irish Stew," it is based on the same cooking technique: braising.

An intrinsic grasp of the fundamental principles will make successful cooking as natural as your ability to walk and talk and breathe. Also it will mean you will be able to produce impeccable food—from the simple perfection of a baked potato to the haute cuisine elegance of crêpes suzette.

For instance, to suit the varying degrees of tenderness of the raw food, cooking is arbitrarily reduced to two techniques—dry heat for tender food, moist heat for tough food. Once you understand that the degree of tenderness limits the method, you have mastered one of the important cooking absolutes. With this understanding you are free to experiment confidently and to adventure creatively, using the foods you prefer, rather than rigidly following recipes by rote.

Remember that, no matter what you prepare, your primary concern is flavor. A wise cook considers nutrition, economy, speed and ease, too, but food prepared solely with those in mind is neither economical, nutritious, nor time-saving. Because it probably will— and rightly—go back to the kitchen uneaten.

Trial-and-error recipe following robs you too—again of time and energy, and, as important, of money spent for food and of pride. To benefit from this book, don't attempt a recipe until you know and understand the reasons behind it. I have tried to tell you, as much as it is possible, how to do what, when to do it, and, most important, why.

To get the most from this book, realize that important procedures are specified. For example, you are told when to cover a pot or skillet, when to sift flour. Procedures that vary from the normal are also specified. You are told when *not* to blanch almonds, when *not* to peel onions.

Because the physical and chemical sciences are part of cooking, the directions you find here are scientifically accurate. They include the latest principles and methods developed by the food specialists working in the laboratories of the United States Department of Agriculture.

Many of the pattern recipes and the methods for putting them together are revolutionary. They are my adaptations of what I have found to be unnecessarily complicated and often senseless directions for preparing famous international specialties. In these adaptations the flavor is equal to, and often an improvement on, that produced by the classic methods. These changes also fit today's food and contemporary equipment. As the hundreds of students I have taught know, they work. One—the Shaker-Jar Method*—allows flour-thickened sauces to be prepared rapidly. Another—the braising technique —is almost effortless.

Many of the recipes call for Brown-Quick, a precooking aid I developed for fast browning. Its use also reduces shrinking and toughening of meat and poultry. Brown-Quick intensifies the flavor of food too. Although its use is optional, it is one of the few products I wouldn't willingly cook without. Throughout the text it is referred to as a "quick-browning aid." If you can't find it in your own stores, it may be ordered by mail from New York City specialty shops such as B. Altman, 34th Street and Fifth Avenue; Bazar Français, 666 Sixth Avenue; Bloomingdale's, Lexington Avenue and 59th Street; or Charles & Co., 340 Madison Avenue.

In this book, whenever possible, amounts for a single serving of a dish have been given. This will allow you to increase the pattern recipes ad infinitum, without resorting to slide-rule computation, and also will enable you to practice with a minimum amount of food.

I urge you to think of cooking as an art based on a science, and to make your kitchen your laboratory. Until you're sure, test small quantities. For instance, cut a slice of beef liver into cubes and practice frying, broiling, and the tap-test for doneness. For your first essay at pie crust, prepare a half or a quarter recipe.

Practice chopping a carrot with a cleaver or chef's knife to gain facility in dicing foods. In fact, to speed any of the routine tasks, drill yourself in them, just as you would to perfect a tennis stroke or a dance step.

A final benefit—because *Cooking Without Recipes* teaches you *how* to cook, you'll recognize the way the fine dishes you enjoy in good restaurants have been put together so you can consider dining out inspiration for your own adventures in the art of cooking.

In using this book, *you* have a responsibility: to understand the principles before you try the recipes, and to trust and follow the techniques as given, even when they differ radically from directions in other books. I ask for your trust with the full knowledge that I am calling upon your time, your energy, and your pocketbook.

You will have to turn pages at first, but without the cross-references this would have been only another collection of repetitive recipes. And just as food should not be wasted, I have tried not to waste words.

When the principles set forth become knowledge, you will have fewer and fewer pages to turn. And finally you will be able to say to a friend, "Just tell me the ingredients—I don't need a recipe." At that point, you will know you can really call yourself a cook.

Watching a professional cook in action will enable you to handle equipment and food with skilled celerity, but as with any other learning, in the last analysis, only you can teach yourself to cook. The reason you need experience as well as knowledge is variability. A few of the cooking inconstants are your utensils and your range, the weather, and the food itself—its variety, age, and size. These are what make cooking an exciting challenge and why the only answer to the question "How long will it take?" is "Approximately." Understand that any time schedule can serve only as a guide, and check food frequently toward the end of cooking. In addition, realize that "about 20 minutes" means the food can take anywhere from 15 to 25 minutes to finish cooking; "about 2½ hours" means from 2 to 3 hours, etc.

When preparing a recipe, read it through first. Next, assemble all the ingredients and equipment at the cooking area in order of use if space allows. For speed, keep frequently used recipes on index cards, and note on them the required equipment.

You'll avoid an overcrowded file if you analyze the basic technique of a recipe you want to clip from a newspaper or magazine and record only the ways it differs from the normal. For example, in a recipe for fried chicken that suggests rolling the poultry in Parmesan cheese as well as in bread crumbs, add the specified amount of each to a master card headed "Fried Chicken."

To "extend" limited counter space, put staples away as you use them. To speed cleanup operations, cut and peel vegetables on wax paper, and rinse and stack used equipment in the sink or dishwasher immediately after use. To avoid repeated washings, rest spoons used for occasional stirring of sauces on a paper towel, and to keep your counter clean invert pan covers when you remove them. Wipe up spatters and spills as you go along, and as you work remember the old proverb: "It's easier to keep clean than to make clean."

I hope the information given here will be so helpful you'll never make a mistake. But first-aid directions are offered in case anything goes wrong. If it does, remember that acrobats often falter on purpose so the cheers accompanying their final success will ring louder. If you need further encouragement, think of your present skills—driving a car, for instance—that in the beginning were so difficult, and that you now exercise with confident ease.

Finally, be proud of the memorable meals you serve, and, as you work be glad your table is shared.

II

How to Be a Successful Cook

Cooking is a giving art. It blesses you, and rewards everyone at your table. And, although you may not always walk into your kitchen with glad cries, once there you'll want to produce food that is welcomed, enjoyed, and appreciated.

Don't let the size of your kitchen trouble you. Just realize that a midget-small kitchen will necessitate preliminary organization to avoid running out of space; while a king-size room will call for step-saving planning to avoid running out of breath.

Before you begin cooking, it's a good idea to understand the principles for planning a perfect menu. Once they are learned, break them at will—but know why you are doing so. For example, one principle is variety, and the shore dinner, composed of several kinds of seafood, flagrantly but delectably flouts the rule that no food should appear more than once at the same meal.

However, in general, for menu variety do not serve tomato salad if tomatoes are part of the stew; blueberry pie if blueberries appear in the fruit cup. To avoid repetition, you also must know recipe ingredients. For instance, cheese soufflé and ice cream don't belong at the same meal because they're both made of milk and eggs.

A second menu-planning principle deals with contrasts—color, flavor, texture. Foods of the same color such as white fish, mashed potatoes, and raw turnip are a ghastly combination, and colors that clash—beets, tomatoes, and shrimp—must be avoided too.

As far as flavor and texture are concerned, realize that a menu should not be composed of all rich foods or all lean, all bland or all spicy, all soft or all crisp.

An eye for balance and proportion is important, too. Consider the charm of a strawberry on a grapefruit half as opposed to the awkwardness of a peach; the way a huge baked potato dwarfs cubes of meat broiled on a skewer.

Think in terms of the character of the food, too—baked beans should not precede crêpes suzette; baked Alaska would be ridiculous as a finale for hot dogs. And choose foods with regard to the type of meal and the guests. Sirloin steak has no place at an elegant luncheon for ladies, nor dainty sandwiches at a meal for men.

Finally, because we "feast with our eyes first," visualize your menu as a whole. If it would make a gorgeous still-life painting, your meal will have the added enhancement of beauty.

Coordinating menus so everything is ready when needed will in time become intuitive. Until then, rough out a menu schedule. For example, when dinner's at 7:00, put potatoes for baking into the oven at 6:00, lamb chops to broil at 6:35, peas to boil at 6:40, etc.

PLAYING WITH FIRE

Even before you boil water, it's wise to get acquainted with your range and its capabilities. It should simplify things for you to realize that whether the heat is to be used in the oven, the broiler, or on top of the range, and that whatever the cooking method is called—roasting, frying, boiling, etc.—the heat adjustments can range only from low to high and variations thereof—moderate, moderately high, moderately low.

To understand this best, light a top-of-the-range flame. Turn it on full for a high flame (*extremely hot* in oven or broiler). Cut it down halfway (a medium-size flame corresponds to *moderate* in the oven; *medium* in the broiler). Then turn it as low as you can (*very slow* in an oven).

In addition to holding a correct temperature and conserving fuel, thermostatic controls on oven and broiler save you from visually choosing these low, medium, or high temperatures. Because a thermostat can go out of order, keep a small thermometer in the oven for checking to be sure the settings are accurate.

For best and most effective use of your range, read, understand, and follow the manufacturer's directions. The cooking and baking temperatures given throughout this book apply to gas ranges. Although they are similar to those used on electric equipment, when they differ, follow the temperature given by the manufacturer.

DESCRIPTIVE TERMS FOR HEAT OF LIQUID

Lukewarm (Tepid): A drop on the inside of your wrist will feel neither warm nor cold.

Scalding: Bubbles appear around the edge of the pan.

Simmering: Only an occasional bubble rises to the surface. When necessary to slow cooking, keep pan cover tilted slightly to allow cold air to rush in.

Boiling: The liquid bubbles in the center.

NOTE: During cooking food absorbs heat and because there are just so many BTU's (British Thermal Units) available at any temperature, realize that the more food you cook at one time the longer it will take. For example, 2 chickens will take slightly longer to roast than 1 chicken; 4 eggs will take longer to soft- or hard-cook than 1 egg. Variables make it impossible to determine beforehand the exact difference in time.

FREEZERS

A freezer filled with good things is a tribute to your managing ability and to your intelligent use of surpluses. It also will let you greet unexpected guests with pleasure rather than with panic.

Freezers are marvelous time and work savers, too. The ice-cube compartment of your refrigerator is, of course, not as spacious or as cold, but will perform approximately the same functions as a freezer. Simply remember that food cannot be stored there as long. For most economical management use foods fairly soon.

These icy chambers also speed what was formerly a lengthy procedure: when a recipe directs that food be refrigerated 2 hours or overnight, the same results can be accomplished in about a half hour of freezing; about an hour in the ice-cube section. Remove when the food has "set."

SUGGESTION: Freeze decorated cakes or frozen desserts unwrapped to keep all the curlicues and gewgaws intact. Cover closely as soon as the decorations have hardened.

Should frozen foods thaw before needed, they may, under certain conditions, be safely refrozen, because the process of thawing and refreezing doesn't make foods unsafe. However, once thawed, they spoil more rapidly than fresh foods, and must be refrigerated promptly.

Foods may be refrozen if they have not completely thawed, or if they have been thawed for a short time, and held in the refrigerator. But thawing and refreezing usually causes loss of the juices which account for flavor and food value. In addition, refrozen vegetables may toughen; refrozen fruits become soft and mushy.

COOKING EQUIPMENT

Pots and pans are available in many materials, but no one material fills every cooking need. Thin, lightweight equipment will give you speedy heat, but it's difficult to control. Heavy skillets and pots make for slowpoke but even cooking. Enamel-on-iron casseroles are marvelous because they serve more than one purpose. They can be used on top of the range as well as in the oven, are handsome enough to be brought to table, and their weight means foods keep hot longer.

Warped pans are not only annoying to use, but also give poor results. Sturdy, easy-to-clean utensils (few seams, rounded corners, smooth edges) equipped with tight covers cannot be considered luxury items, because unlike fine feathers they'll be in almost constant use and will rarely need replacing.

COMMON COOKING OPERATIONS

Manual dexterity plays an important part in good cooking. Practice for expertise.

BEATING

This operation is used to aerate a single food or a combination of foods, and may be done with an electric mixer. By hand, use a vigorous rotary motion. For efficiency, tilt the bowl so you are beating or whipping the mass, rather than following the bowl contours. A rubber spatula makes an effective tool.

BLANCHING

Blanching is simpler than peeling a quantity of peaches or tomatoes, and is always used to remove almond skins.

Bring water to a boil, then turn off heat and immerse food to be blanched. (For ease, immerse small quantities in a sieve.) Allow food to remain in water until skins loosen, about 5 minutes. Remove from water and slip skins off, pinching almonds at the pointed end.

PRECAUTION: To sliver almonds, cut them immediately after blanching.

BLENDING OR MIXING

These directions mean combining mixtures with a stirring motion.

CHOPPING, CUBING, DICING, MINCING

A cleaver or scissors are ideal tools for these cutting operations, and partially frozen foods are easier to cut.

Chop means cut coarsely. Cube means cut small even cubes, and the size is usually indicated. Dice means cut in cubes of approximately ¼ inch. Mince means cut very fine.

CREAMING

Creaming makes solid food, such as butter, easier to spread (as in sandwiches) and fluffy enough to incorporate readily with other foods.

Food is easier to cream at room temperature; an electric mixer will do the job to perfection. If you lack one, a rubber spatula is an excellent tool because it also enables you to keep the sides of the bowl scraped down. Cream food until light and fluffy by forcefully pressing it against the sides of the bowl. Push away and repeat, using a circular motion.

FOLDING

Airy mixtures such as soufflés and angel-food cakes are combined by folding, because beating would break down air bubbles. A rubber spatula makes the ideal tool. To fold, tilt bowl and draw the spatula through mixture in a clockwise direction from bottom to top of bowl, using as few strokes as possible.

KNEADING

Doughs are kneaded in some cases to develop gluten. During kneading, air is incorporated, too, making bread and the like lighter and larger in volume. Kneading also makes certain doughs flaky.

To knead, cover a wooden board or porcelain or marble table

top with a thin film of flour. If necessary, add more flour during kneading, but remember that as the dough is worked stickiness will disappear. Press the dough with your palm to make a hollow, and with your hand in the same position use your fingertips to pick up the back edge of the dough and fold it toward you, enclosing the hollow. Give the dough a quarter turn at the end of each stroke. Don't press heavily on the dough. Knead at rhythmic even speed.

PURÉEING

Soft foods such as bananas, or food cooked until soft such as diced vegetables, often require pressing through a sieve so they form a pulp. Good electric mixers have attachments for puréeing. A blender, food mill, or grinder also may be used.

STIRRING

Use a whisk or spoon and move the mass in the shape of a figure 8 to reach all areas.

MEASURING INGREDIENTS

When a recipe calls for a teaspoon of herbs or seeds, it's not a matter of great moment if more or less is used, or even if they're omitted entirely. However, in baking, for best results, standard measuring equipment and accurate measurements are required. To be sure of accuracy, place cups on a level surface and check measurements at eye level.

DRY INGREDIENTS

To save dishwashing measure dry ingredients, then use the same cup for liquid.

Flour: A long, hard look has been taken at the blanket rule that says flour must always be measured after sifting. Because flour packs down on standing, the rule was in the interest of accuracy. Sift first if you like. However, if you measure gently as indicated below, you probably will not be taking up an excess amount. To be sure, when not sifting, use 2 tablespoons less per cup than the amount called for. Recipes in this book specify flour measured after sifting. Sift or not, as you like.

To transfer flour easily, sift onto wax paper, then spoon lightly into a dry measuring cup. Do not shake the cup. Cut off excess with the flat of a knife.

Spices, Baking Soda, etc.: Use measuring spoons, and cut off excess by running the flat of a knife over the spoon. To avoid washing spoons repeatedly, measure dry and light-colored ingredients first.

Cereals: For accuracy, aerate by stirring before measuring.

SOLID SHORTENING

The following water displacement method simplifies measuring a fraction of a cup of solid shortening and is the most accurate way: Pour cold water into a measuring cup, leaving unfilled enough space for the amount of shortening called for. (For example, if using a 1-cup measure when a recipe calls for ¾ cup of shortening, add cold water to the ¼ cup mark.) Add fat by spoonfuls—be sure it's completely submerged—until the water reaches the 1-cup mark. Drain the water and turn shortening out on a paper towel to absorb any clinging moisture.

Butter is easy to measure accurately if you remember that there are 8 tablespoons to a quarter pound of butter, or that a tablespoon of butter measures about ⅜ of an inch on a quarter-pound bar.

PRECAUTION: Don't trust marked wrappers—they're not always put on straight.

LIQUID INGREDIENTS

Use Liquid Measuring Cups.*

CUPBOARD AND REFRIGERATOR NEEDS AND NICETIES

"The whole can never be better than the sum of its parts" is a cliché that applies to cooking. And although a cupboard *can* be bare of kickshaws like delicate wine vinegar, tangy capers, redolent cloves, the food that comes from that kitchen will lack the excitement of variety. The following lists the necessities Mother Hubbard couldn't keep in supply, plus niceties that will help you create savory and spirited dishes.

BAKING POWDER

Baking powder has gas-forming properties which make it a leavening agent. It loses potency with time, so date the can on purchase and discard it at the end of a year. Keep cans tightly covered, too, because the moisture in the air can cause loss of gas.

There are three varieties—tartrate, phosphate, and sodium-aluminum-sulphate phosphate (commonly known as S.A.S.-phosphate). In tartrate powder, the action begins as soon as the powder is touched by liquid. Phosphate powder reacts in the same manner, but the gas is released more slowly. The leavening action in S.A.S. powder, sometimes called "double-acting," isn't fully liberated until the mixture containing it is heated.

Because of the different varieties, the amounts required vary, so check the label on the can for the correct amount to use. The recipes contained here are written for tartrate baking powder. If you choose a different variety, check the directions on the label.

FLOUR

For good nutrition, buy enriched flour.

Bread flour is excellent if you bake bread frequently. It is interchangeable with all-purpose flour.

All-purpose flour is the kind to use when recipes simply call for "flour." It is a little less strong than bread flour.

"Instant" flour, which requires no sifting, is more expensive than all-purpose flour.

Cake flour is soft and is not interchangeable with other flour except in a cupboard-is-bare emergency, when all-purpose flour may be substituted for cake flour, and vice versa, as follows:

1 cup cake flour equals 1 cup all-purpose flour minus 2 tablespoons.

Self-rising flour contains leavening and salt. Read label directions before use.

NUTS

Nuts contain protein, but are composed mainly of fat. They may be added to or subtracted from recipes at will, except in the case of certain tortes, cakes, or cookies where ground nuts are substituted for part of the flour.

Buying and Storing Nuts: Shelled nuts are more costly than nuts in the shell, and don't keep as well. (Even nuts in unopened vacuum-packed containers become limp and rancid with age.) Unsalted nuts keep better than salted nuts, and filberts, almonds, and peanuts keep better than pecans and walnuts.

Store all nuts in the refrigerator or, for longer storage, in the freezer. Tightly covered shelled nuts will keep a year in the freezer.

SEASONINGS AND FLAVORINGS

It will never be known for sure if seasonings and flavorings became a part of the art of cooking in a desperate effort to mask decay, or if their use was born when a Neolithic lady, absently chewing a green blade, suddenly said, "Hey!" Whichever or both, the tang and piquancy they give to food are ours to enjoy, and they come from all over the world.

Although seasonings vary with personal preference, food should have authority. When seasoning to taste, allow yourself only three tastes. After that, you'll have what is technically known as "palate fatigue." Then wait about 15 minutes before taste-testing again. And realize that the direction "season to taste" is not a mysterious operation. You've been practicing it at table for years when you instinctively add the right amount of sugar to your coffee, pepper to your potato.

Incidentally, a touch of salt always improves a sweet dish, but in increasing dessert recipes that call for salt, don't increase the salt proportionately. A touch of sugar also often perks the flavor of non-sweet dishes. A touch, a dash, a dot, or a pinch are all approximately a sixteenth of a teaspoon.

ACIDS

In approximate order of decreasing sharpness, the cooking acids are *vinegar*—white, cider, malt, etc., *wine vinegar, lemon* or *lime juice,* and *dry wine*—white or red. They're interchangeable, depending upon the amount of acidity required. Taste before using, so you'll know how much to add.

Wine vinegar is the most flavorful and delicate vinegar. Be sure to buy a non-pasteurized variety. Then when dry wine, white or red, sours, simply add it to the bottle and you'll never have to invest in wine vinegar again.

Flavorings such as a crushed clove of garlic may be added to your bottle of wine vinegar, as may fresh or dried herbs, seeds, and the like. However, to avoid having a cupboard bulging with different varieties and to have more authoritative flavor, add your choice of flavoring directly to salads, barbecue sauces, marinades, etc.

CHOCOLATE

Chocolate is available in a variety of forms.

Unsweetened chocolate, often called "bitter" or "baking" chocolate, is most frequently used for cooking. It comes marked or wrapped in 1-ounce portions, sometimes called "squares," and also is available already melted.

Semisweet chocolate often is called sweet chocolate. Chocolate bits, dots, etc., are precut semisweet chocolate.

Chocolate scorches and changes flavor when melted over direct heat. So set it on a pilot light, a warm radiator, or use the top of a double boiler with hot, rather than boiling, water below. If chocolate lumps when melted alone or with other ingredients, smooth it, preferably with a whisk, before proceeding.

Milk chocolate is difficult to melt because it contains very little fat and a great deal of sugar.

Chocolate is difficult to cut, grate, or shave unless fresh. Covered candy dishes are functional because chocolate will absorb off-flavor from cardboard boxes. Chocolate may be frozen. Refrigeration grays it but doesn't alter flavor.

Cocoa: This is chocolate with half or more of the fat removed. The two types are natural and Dutch process. Chemicals have been added to the latter. "Breakfast" cocoas must contain at least 22 percent fat and are richer than natural cocoa. Unless specified in recipes, cocoa and chocolate are not interchangeable.

Store cocoa in a tightly covered tin box because it absorbs odors.

FLAVORING EXTRACTS

These concentrated flavors are composed primarily of alcohol. All are interchangeable and they may be used singly or in any combination. *Vanilla* is the most common; others are *almond, orange, lemon,* etc. To preserve their strength, cover extracts tightly and store in a dark place.

Vanilla Beans: Recipes often call for these instead of for vanilla extract. To substitute, use 1 teaspoon vanilla extract for a 1-inch piece of bean. In making custards and the like, add the bean to the milk and remove it when the milk is heated. It then may be rinsed and dried for reuse.

For lovely aroma, store a split vanilla bean in a shaker of confectioners' sugar and another with your cocoa.

To make French vanilla ice cream, etc., halve the bean lengthwise, and scrape out and add to the mixture the inner pulp—tiny black seeds.

HERBS

Herbs have a long and fairly rakish history. Once they were used (unsuccessfully) as ingredients in love philtres; now we enjoy their fragrant, inspiriting zest in food. As innocuous as grass, they're a welcome addition when salt or spices must be eliminated, and doctors don't normally forbid their use even in special diets.

Herbs may subtly flavor dishes or be downright dominant. Personal taste, rather than rule, governs their use.

Buying Herbs: Some markets carry fresh herbs in season, and many stores sell dried herbs. Dried herbs lose strength with age, so buy them in small quantities, store them in tightly covered glass jars, and check their strength after about six months.

PRECAUTION: Buy whole-leaf rather than powdered herbs, because crushing allows the flavoring oils to evaporate.

Preparation and Cooking of Herbs: For cutting fresh herbs, scissors are better and easier to use than a knife, and a blender is best of all. To cut with scissors, discard stems, bunch leaves tightly, hold between first three fingers and thumb, and snip.

It's not necessary to steep dried herbs before use. Simply crush or not, as desired, before adding them to soups, stews, salads, etc.

Drying Herbs: This is an exceedingly simple process. As with autumn leaves, the major problem is to keep them *from* drying. For best flavor, pick just before they flower. Small leaves don't require cutting, but cut large leaves coarsely. Spread on wax paper in a single layer, and they'll dry overnight at room temperature.

Depending upon age, 1 teaspoon dried herbs equals about 1 tablespoon fresh herbs.

Here are a few of the most commonly used herbs:

Basil: This is often called the "soulmate" of the tomato because the two make such a fine flavor pair.

Bay Leaf: Strong-flavored, this is best with lusty food and is almost invariably used with dill pickles.

Capers: These flower buds of pungent flavor are available salted or in brine. Salted capers (usually found in Italian markets) have better texture and keep indefinitely. When using them, rinse or reduce the salt in your recipe. Capers give salads *élan* and are often added to Beurre Noir.*

Celery: The leaves have more flavor than the stalks and, when dried, can be used as an herb.

BUDGET MEMO: Cut coarsely and dry a quantity to have on hand.

Chervil: An herb doted on by the French, this is an almost invariable component of their *fines herbes* mixture. More subtle than parsley, chervil tastes to some people like licorice.

Chives: Frail sister of the onion, this herb shines as a garnish. Cut spears fine.

Dill: Fresh dill is pretty as a picture and especially delectable with seafood. "Weed" is the name given to the green top when dried.

Fines Herbes: This French term refers to combinations of herbs chopped fine. Equal parts parsley, chervil, and chives are an example. Dried herbs or a combination of fresh and dried may be used.

Garlic.

Horseradish: Sold grated and preserved in vinegar (happily, because dicing an onion pales before it as a tear-jerking job), preserve this lusty condiment's strength by storing it in the refrigerator.

Marjoram: Sweet marjoram is a good salad herb. Wild marjoram is less sweet; the Italians call it orégano and add it to many of their dishes.

Mint: Of the many varieties, spearmint is most commonly used. Constant companion of juleps, fruit, and iced tea, it is delicately flavorful. Some cooks add mint to a green salad with wonderful results.

Orégano (see Marjoram).

Parsley: There are three varieties: The curly is stronger than the flat-leafed, which is sometimes called Italian parsley. Both stems (they're milder) and leaves are useful in cooking. Curly parsley makes a more attractive garnish. Chinese parsley, actually coriander, has a marvelous sprightly flavor, and is also used by Spanish cooks, who call it *cilantro.*

Rosemary: Rather strong-flavored, often accompanies poultry, pork, and lamb in the Italian cuisine.

Sage: Dried sage is almost an American cliché, especially in poultry stuffings, where it unfortunately overpowers poultry's bland flavor. Fresh sage makes a delicate and delicious addition to many foods.

Savory: Both summer and winter savory are members of the mint family. Summer savory is milder in flavor.

Tarragon: Should be used sparingly because of its bold anise flavor. Wonderful in salads, it also enhances poultry and seafood.

Thyme: American cooks use this almost as frequently as they do sage. It has distinctive bouquet, and a constant habitat is clam chowder.

Watercress: The peppery leaves of this relative of the mustard family are used chiefly to enliven salads.

SPICES AND SEEDS

Like herbs, powdered spices stale rapidly. Therefore, buy small quantities and check their potency after a year. For freshest flavor, however, pulverize whole spices in a blender or in a mortar and pestle as you need them. Seeds add pleasing and unusual flavor to recipes, and also perkily garnish salads, cookies, and the like.

The following varieties are generally not hard to find. Because palates vary, and it's almost impossible to describe a flavor, taste each to learn your preference. Then use as desired—singly or in any combination, ground or whole.

Allspice: A spice so named because it tastes like a mixture of cinnamon, cloves, and nutmeg.

Anise Seeds: These are small and licorice-flavored.

Caraway: The seeds are almost invariable in rye bread, and can inspirit any lusty-flavored food.

Cardamom: A member of the ginger family, but with a tang of its own. A thin pod contains the seeds.

Cassia: Like cinnamon in flavor but from a different plant, it is what we buy as cinnamon. Available ground or in sticks, the color varies from light to dark brown.

Celery Seeds: These taste like celery (which is grown from them), but have a slightly bitter pungency.

Chili Powder: This combination of herbs and spices is available sweet, semisweet, or hot. Orégano is usually an ingredient of chili powder. Mexican cooks use chili extensively.

Cinnamon: The only true cinnamon comes from Ceylon and the Malabar coast of India. It is very light in color and rarely available here. See Cassia.

Cloves: These are the unopened flower buds of an evergreen tree. East Indians chew them after meals to sweeten breath.

Coriander: Furnishing an herb (see Parsley) and seed, this is a double-barreled delight.

Cumin Seed: Like chili powder, this is an almost invariable ingredient in Spanish cooking (where it's called *comino*) and is often added to mixtures of chili powder.

Curry Powder: Like chili powder, this is a combination of herbs and spices and also may contain seeds. East Indians literally "roll their own" for each dish to suit family preference, the food being served, and for variety.

Mustard Seed: The ground seeds make dry mustard. Hot!

Nutmeg: Once you've smelled and tasted this freshly ground, you'll discard the powdered variety promptly.

Paprika: Unless otherwise specified, use sweet paprika in recipes. It's also available semisweet and hot. Hungarian paprika is superior to Spanish. To retain color and flavor, store paprika in the refrigerator. The sugar paprika contains makes it a fine browning agent. Simply sprinkle on foods before broiling, baking, or frying them in shallow fat, or add enough to give a good red color to the flour for coating foods to be fried in deep fat.

Pepper: Choose peppercorns (hot), cayenne (hotter), chili pods (hottest).

White pepper is black pepper without a coat—the black outer surface of the berry. It's specified for use in clear soups and light-colored sauces because the grains of black pepper are unattractive.

Liquid pepper: Liquid pepper contains chili peppers steeped in vinegar, and makes an excellent substitute. Two recipes for a delectable homemade version follow.

Pepper Sherry

Half fill a 6-ounce bottle with chili tepins or chili pequins. Add dry sherry to cover. Allow to stand 2 weeks, shaking occasionally. Add sherry and chili tepins as necessary to original bottle. If desired, decant into an attractive bitters bottle and use it at table, too.

Cognac Pepper

Crack 4 tablespoons peppercorns coarsely and add ½ cup cognac. Prepare and decant as above.

Poppy Seeds: Stores catering to a Central European trade grind the seeds for their customers. They are then simmered with sweetening and spices and used as fillings for *kuchen, strudel,* and the like. Whole seeds add charm to green salads, bread, crackers, etc. Refrigerate to prevent rancidity.

Saffron: Made from the stigma of a special kind of crocus, this is almost as costly as a corsage. The soul of *bouillabaisse* and many of the Near Eastern rice dishes, it tints food golden, and has a hauntingly subtle flavor. Turmeric may be used as a color, but not a flavor, substitute.

Sesame Seeds: Delicate nutlike flavor makes these a popular topping for crackers and bread. Toss with salads, toasting them first if desired, or sprinkle on food before broiling or baking. Refrigerate to prevent rancidity.

Turmeric: The root of a plant of the ginger family, it bears no flavor resemblance to ginger. Actually turmeric has little savor, but it colors foods yellow, and is an inexpensive color (but not flavor) substitute for saffron.

FLAVOR INTENSIFIERS

Monosodium Glutamate: For centuries the Orientals have intensified food flavors with monosodium glutamate. Msg is the common abbreviation, and Ac'cent is its best-known trade name.

To learn how to use msg, taste to recognize its flavor. Then when you prepare a sauce, taste the sauce both before and after adding the msg. You'll bless it for the finish and rounding it gives to soups, meat, poultry, fish, vegetables, salads, and stuffings.

A shaker of msg is essential to good cooking, and may be used before, during, or after food preparation. Because it doesn't dissolve in fat, when preparing recipes such as salad dressing, mix the msg with the acid, rather than with the oil.

Generally allow about ¼ teaspoon msg for 6 servings of food.

Soy Sauce: Composed essentially of msg, this too intensifies food flavors. The least expensive is not necessarily the best buy, as it comes in varying grades.

Brown-Quick: This quick-browning aid is used before broiling, frying in shallow fat, or pan-broiling meat, poultry, fish and shellfish, etc. A blend of herbs and spices and nutritious soy sauce of excellent quality, it intensifies the flavor of foods on which it is used, and eliminates the need for preliminary salting. Brown-Quick makes cooking easier and faster too, because preliminary browning of stews, pot roasts, and meat balls becomes unnecessary.

SHORTENING

The words "shortening" and "fat" are synonymous, and except in recipes for baked products, liquid and solid fats may be substituted for one another, measure for measure. They also may be used in combination. (Butter and olive oil often are paired for frying.)

BUTTER

This is made by churning sweet and/or sour cream, and is notable for delicate flavor. Refrigerate butter in a covered container. It will keep about three months in the freezer.

Butter burns at low temperature and contains liquid, which spatters, making it a poor frying fat unless it is clarified.

Clarifying Butter: Melt butter over a low flame. As soon as it melts, remove from heat and skim, discarding the foam. Allow to cool (for speed, refrigerate or freeze) and remove and use the hardened butter, discarding the milky liquid that has settled to the bottom. Store in refrigerator or freezer and use for browning meat, poultry, or seafood.

Making Butter: To be able to assure guests you're serving "the best butter," you might enjoy making your own. Knowing how is imperative if you've turned your back at the wrong moment while whipping cream—overbeaten cream begins turning to butter, and cannot be rescued.

Beat heavy cream with a rotary beater or electric mixer until it forms a solid mass. Drain the liquid and refrigerate. When the mass hardens, knead to press out any additional liquid (whey). If you don't like sweet butter, add ¼ teaspoon salt for each pint of cream. Mold attractively.

MARGARINE

Contains vegetable oil, skim milk, salt, and artificial coloring. Made to taste like butter, it is similar in food and caloric value, and makes an excellent economy substitute. It takes longer to melt than butter, and, like it, burns readily.

HYDROGENATED VEGETABLE SHORTENING

Does not require refrigeration. Made of flavorless vegetable oils, it has no flavor either.

LARD

This rendered and refined pork fat, with sweet, delicate flavor, is excellent for cooking and baking. Difficult-to-obtain leaf lard is the finest quality. This is the richest of all fats; if it is being substituted, use 2 tablespoons less per cup than the quantity of other fats called for.

OTHER SOLID SHORTENINGS

Markets now carry completely flavorless shortenings that combine lard and vegetable oil.

LIQUID SHORTENINGS (OIL)

The following are the most commonly used: corn and cottonseed (which have no flavor), olive, peanut, and soya. Sesame seed oil, used by the Orientals and in parts of the Balkans, is a costly magnificence.

Vegetable oils should be refrigerated to avoid rancidity. Smell and/or taste before use to be sure they're fresh. The cloudiness caused by refrigeration disappears when oils warm to room temperature, even if frozen. (If oil freezes, your refrigerator may be set at an excessively cold temperature, which is wasteful of current.)

Unless prescribed by your doctor, it's inadvisable to use the calorie-less mineral oil, because it interferes with digestion and the absorption of vitamins.

DEEP-FAT FRYING

Almost any food may be fried in deep fat. Hors d'oeuvre tidbits such as *tempura*, Chicken Maryland,* and pineapple fritters dappled with confectioners' sugar are only a few of the delectables that emerge from a kettle of sweet hot fat. The choice of foods is almost limitless, and they may be fried with or without a cloak. *À l'anglaise* is what the French call foods dipped in egg and crumbs, and Cover Batters* and Fritter Batters* also may be used. Perfection is achieved when the fried food is not greasy, has a crisp, golden-brown exterior, and is cooked throughout. Good results are obtained with the fats listed below, because they can be heated to a high temperature without burning. (Burning fat smokes and becomes unpleasant in flavor, as will any food cooked in it.)

BUDGET MEMO: Roast beef drippings are superb for deep-fat frying.

Oil gives fried food a glossy appearance. Because it's liquid, the correct amount to use is easy to gauge. Corn and cottonseed oils have no flavor. Oils other than the flavorless corn and cottonseed add delicate flavor to foods fried in them.

Lard requires preliminary melting, which is time-consuming, and until it melts it is almost impossible to gauge the correct amount to use. However, it has a sweet, delicate flavor, and gives foods a handsome non-greasy finish. *Hydrogenated vegetable shortening* may be used for deep-fat frying.

Success in deep-fat frying lies in bringing the fat unhurriedly to the correct temperature and maintaining that temperature throughout. Fat that is not hot enough soaks into food, and will overcook it before it browns. Fat that is too hot burns food on the outside before the interior cooks through.

The best utensil for deep-fat frying is a deep pan with small diameter and straight sides. For foods such as doughnuts and fritters that expand, fill it about half full. With too little fat, food burns on the bottom; with too much, fat may bubble over.

PRECAUTION: Keep baking soda at hand to douse any flames.

Because thermostats may not be impeccably accurate and also gang aft agley, you must be able to judge the temperature of the fat, even if using thermostatically controlled deep-fat frying equipment. A deep-fat thermometer is a convenient means for determining correct temperature. Lacking one, test the fat with bread cubes. Generally a moderate temperature of 375° F. produces satisfactory fried foods. At this temperature, a 1-inch cube of day-old white bread becomes light brown in about 40 seconds. To test without bread cubes, drop a dot of the food into the fat and listen for the singing sound.

PRECAUTION: Do not test with a drop of water—the spattering fat may burn you.

If additional fat is needed during frying, add it to the kettle and heat to the correct temperature before adding more food.

Overcrowding a kettle lowers the temperature of the fat and prevents expansion of foods such as fritters and doughnuts.

For best results, turn foods fried in deep fat only once. Use a slotted spoon, because a fork can puncture the crust and allow fat to soak in. Remove cooked food from the fat and drain on absorbent paper.

Unless the fat has burned, it may be strained and reused. However, remember that it smokes (burns) at a lower temperature each time. To reuse fat after frying strong-flavored foods, fry a few slices of raw potato in it to absorb off-flavors. Cover used fat tightly and store it away from heat and light.

The loose crumbs that drop from coated meat or poultry have crunchy goodness. Take advantage of them by pouring the fat off and either making gravy in the pan or stirring cooked potatoes or dumplings in the crumbs.

SUGGESTION: To add confectioners' sugar to fried foods easily, place the food in a paper bag with the sugar and shake until coated. The same trick works with salt, and also may be used to flour-coat.

Egg-Crumb Coating

Food is coated with eggs and starchy materials before frying to encrust it and also to absorb the surface moisture that would thin the fat and cause spattering.

Egg is superior for encrustation because it hardens instantly upon contact with heat and also acts as an adhesive. For best results, refrigerate coated foods about 20 minutes before frying to allow the egg to dry.

> 1 egg
> 1 tablespoon water
> ½ teaspoon salt
> ⅛ teaspoon pepper
> Coating material
>   Crumbs (bread or cracker)
>   Cornmeal (white or yellow)
>   Flour
> About 1½ pounds food for coating.

Beat egg and water in a soup plate only until blended, and add seasonings. Spread coating material on wax paper. Dip food in coating material, egg mixture, then coating material, and redip until all the egg is used, ending with coating material. Fry in fat heated to moderate, 375° F., until the exterior browns and the interior is completely cooked.

NOTE: Combinations of the coating materials may be used and grated cheese may be substituted for half of any of them.

SUGAR

Granulated: When a recipe doesn't specify a particular kind of sugar, use granulated.

Sift granulated sugar before use if it's extremely lumpy. Spoon gently into a dry measuring cup. Do not shake the cup, and cut off excess with the flat of a knife.

Very Fine: Finer than granulated sugar, but not as fine as confectioners', this has a number of aliases; berry sugar, fruit sugar, veri-, super-, and ultra-fine sugar. Measure as for granulated sugar. The virtues of this sugar are many. It dissolves quickly in cold beverages; it melts more readily when caramelizing is called for; and because of its fineness it interferes less with the air bubbles when beaten into egg whites.

Brown Sugar: Hardens as it loses moisture. For best keeping, enclose in transparent plastic wrap and store in a tightly covered glass jar. It may be substituted for granulated when measured as follows: Pack firmly enough into the measuring cup so it holds shape when turned out. If a small quantity of brown sugar has hardened, smooth lumps with a rolling pin; place a large quantity in a very slow oven for a few minutes to soften. Dark brown sugar has fine, authoritative flavor. Light brown sugar is an anemic substitute. Granulated brown sugar will not harden but presents other problems.

Maple Sugar: Proceed as for Brown Sugar.

Confectioners' Sugar: Sometimes called powdered or icing sugar, this is the finest grind of white sugar. The more X's on the box, the finer the grind. Confectioners' sugar lumps readily, so sift before use, except when adding it to beverages. Because it contains cornstarch, it makes beverages cloudy, so for clarity, choose very fine sugar. Frosting sugar, as fine a grind, does not contain cornstarch.

TOMATO PRODUCTS

The only requisite for adding tomatoes to foods is enjoyment of their flavor. They can appear in soups, sauces, gravies, main dishes, vegetables, salads, and salad dressings. Fresh tomatoes are expensive out of season, but fortunately many substitutes of varying cost and excellence are available. Tomato paste is usually the most costly. Other flavorful substitutes are canned tomatoes and tomato purée, and, at lowest cost, tomato juice. All of the following are canned, and therefore cooked.

Canned Tomatoes: These have been peeled. Canned plum tomatoes, sometimes labeled "Italian," contain a larger proportion of pulp to liquid, and speed cooking when recipes direct that sauces be cooked until thick.

BUDGET MEMO: Cans of perfect whole tomatoes are an unnecessary extravagance for sauces, soups, or gravies.

Tomato Juice: A liquid tomato product made by pressing cooked tomatoes through a sieve.

Tomato Purée: Made by puréeing cooked tomatoes, its flavor is stronger than canned tomatoes, but not as strong as tomato paste. Already thickened, it speeds the preparation of tomato sauces.

Tomato Paste: Tomato pulp cooked until very thick. Sometimes herbs and spices are added. It may be diluted but, in the interest of extra flavor strength, need not be. Taste and see. A small amount undiluted thickens and flavors sauces.

Ketchup and *Chili Sauce:* Highly seasoned, sweetened condiments, these may not be substituted for the tomato products listed above.

III

Meat for Memorable Meals

Meat is precious. It's the food most likely to light up the eyes of a man. It's the backbone of menus because it determines their character. And it's precious economically because a quarter of every food dollar is spent on it.

BUYING MEAT

With meat, good cooking begins at market. Butchers are sometimes irascible, often with good reason, because cooking ignorance can ruin perfect meat, and when blame is erroneously laid at their door they have every right to snarl.

Earning your butcher's respect means you will be pampered with the best he has to offer. You are well on the way to that respect when you know that some cuts of meat are *tender,* and some are *tough.* The tougher the cut, the more flavorful it is. For example, tough meat, ground for tenderness, produces the savory hamburger and meat loaf.

Meat, a protein, is composed mainly of lean and fat. The fat offers juiciness and flavor, so nod happily when the butcher offers a cut with streaks of fat running through the lean. This is called "marbling." A lavish exterior covering of fat also indicates high quality. The butcher's own phrase, "No waste, no taste," means the fat for which you've paid melts away during cooking. Chefs and good butchers often "bard" (top with a layer of fat) certain cuts of meat to prevent drying, to act as basting, and to add richness. Thanks to our well-fatted meats, larding—pulling strips (lardoons) of fat through it—is unnecessary.

The round purple federal inspection stamp protects you from buying unwholesome meat. Grade stamps indicate quality. The government grade for the finest meat is *U.S. Prime*. In decreasing order of cost and flavor come: *Choice, Good, Commercial,* and *Utility*. Don't bother cutting off the grade stamps; they're harmless and disappear during cooking.

QUANTITY OF MEAT PER SERVING

This depends upon the meal itself, the number and richness of accompanying courses, and the possibility of unexpected guests. Appetites are another consideration: a gentleman who has just whipped his weight in wildcats will eat more than a desk worker. And it also depends on the meat—the same person who is satisfied with a quarter-pound of hamburger may want a pound of steak.

Allowances on U.S. Department of Agriculture charts are minimal—one-quarter pound boneless meat, three-quarters pound meat with bone per serving—but can act as a guide.

WASHING MEAT

Nutritionists frown, and rightly, on this unnecessary exercise, because cooking kills bacteria, and water washes away flavor and food value. If you must, simply wipe meat with a dampened paper towel.

STORING MEAT

Always remove cardboard—meat absorbs its flavor—and butcher paper, which is an insulating agent.

Refrigerator: Cover raw meat lightly; cooked meat tightly.

Whole pieces of raw meat and cured or smoked meats keep about a week; cubed raw meat, four to five days; ground raw meat and variety meats such as liver, about two days.

Cooked meat and cold cuts keep about four days, smoked or corned meats about two weeks.

Ice-Cube Section or Freezer: Cover both raw and cooked meat tightly.

PRECAUTION: Wrap chops, hamburgers, etc., separately for easy removal.

Most meat may be stored safely in the refrigerator ice-cube section about three weeks, in the freezer six months to a year. The larger the cut, the longer it will maintain quality. The exceptions are ground raw and variety meats—store them only half as long—and smoked and cured meats, which will keep only about two weeks in the ice-cube section, about a month in the freezer.

It's best not to refreeze thawed meat, because the drip lost through thawing contains flavor and food value. However, if it hasn't spoiled, refreeze, realizing it won't be as juicy or as nutritious.

BUDGET MEMO: Stock your freezer with butcher-shop bargains, and remember that freezing helps to tenderize meat.

COOKING MEAT

There's nothing complicated or mysterious about cooking meat. In addition to fat, it is composed of fibers and connective tissue. Heat melts the fat, firms the fibers, softens the connective tissue. The more exercised parts of animals that produce the tough cuts are high in connective tissue; the tender cuts have very little. The cooking method must fit the cut; therefore, moist heat is used for tough cuts, dry heat for tender.

Whether meat is tough or tender, two important basic rules apply to all proteins and produce flavorful, tender, nutritious meat. They are: *Use the lowest possible heat for the method* and *Do not overcook.* Well-done meat has less juice, less flavor, and less food value.

Seasonings for Meat: These penetrate very little. Salt is almost invariably—and erroneously—sprinkled on meat before cooking. Erroneously because salt extracts juice and interferes with browning (it's almost impossible to brown a wet surface). So stay the salt shaker, and remember that because perfectly cooked meat has retained its own salty juices, it requires little, if any, additional salt.

Pepper and other spices, herbs, and seeds may be added to meat before, during, or after cooking. They're fairly ineffectual on roasts because flavor penetration is so slight.

Dredging meat with flour may aid browning, but it also makes it stick to the pan. Precooking aids such as Brown-Quick or soy sauce speed or eliminate the necessity for browning and also enhance flavor.

Fats for Cooking Meat: The most economical fat is the meat's own.

SUGGESTION: The most flavorful beef fat comes from around the beef heart or kidney and tastes much like marrow.

"Drippings" (the melted fat left after roasting beef, frying bacon, etc.), are fine refrigerator possessions and also may be frozen. Store different kinds separately.

To Make Drippings: Cut a small amount of solid fat into small pieces and melt in a covered pan over a low flame. Melt a large quantity over hot water. The process is known as "rendering" or "trying out."

Drippings are used for flavoring or for frying any compatible food. For instance, roast beef drippings are wonderful for potatoes; bacon drippings for frying eggs, fish, etc.

MARINATING MEAT

Marinating means allowing meat to bask in a flavorful liquid composed basically of oil and acid. The trick was developed by canny cooks in countries where meat was tough and flavorless. The acid acted as a tenderizing agent, and other additions—garlic and spices—not only added flavor, but also often masked spoilage.

Today, marinating is done only for variety, so a 20-minute bask is sufficient, although marination can continue for a couple of days. There's nothing sacred about the proportion of oil and acid; it depends upon their strength, your palate, and the food being marinated. For instance, strong-flavored foods such as game will benefit from more and sharper acids. Simply increase or decrease amounts to taste.

Marinating can be a preliminary to broiling, roasting, frying, or braising.

Basic Marinade

    3 parts flavorful oil—olive, peanut, etc.
    1 part acid—vinegar, lemon juice, dry wine

Added enhancements—garlic, herbs, spices, seeds.

Cooking Time for Meat: Time charts for cooking meat can only be guides. Well-aged meat cooks more quickly than unripened meat; short, chunky roasts cook more quickly than oblong roasts; small roasts require more time per pound than large roasts; and fat

—an insulating agent—slows cooking. The weight of the roasting pan, the height of its sides, and the insulation and accuracy of the oven are additional factors that influence cooking time. Despite these variables, the following will give you the skill of a professional.

Testing Doneness: Chefs test doneness in tender foods by tapping. To learn how, tap the fleshy part of the inside of your arm *lightly*. Note that it springs back. Tap-test meat the same way. You will find it feels soft when raw, springy when medium done, firm when well done (and, alas, when overcooked).

Practice this test with beef liver cut in 1-inch cubes. Broil or fry one cube at a time until your touch judgment corresponds with the desired degree of doneness when the meat is cut. Incidentally, cooked meat has a characteristic aroma, so use your sense of smell, too, to help judge doneness.

In a roast, a meat thermometer is the only accurate method for testing doneness. Insert the thermometer halfway down in the center of the meatiest portion of the roast, being sure it doesn't touch bone or fat. With a frozen roast, wait until cooking has thawed the meat sufficiently for insertion.

The common test for tenderness of tough meats is to pierce them with a fork. Unfortunately, punctures allow juice to escape, so use an ice pick rather than a fork, or even better, pinch off and chew a bit of the meat to judge tenderness.

Frozen Meat: In the interest of flavor and food value, cook meat either frozen or just thawed. In broiling frozen steaks or chops there's a further advantage. Because cooking time is increased, a crusty brown exterior is easier to achieve—but broil frozen meat at a lower temperature or the exterior may burn before the interior finishes cooking.

Allow about five minutes longer for broiling or frying small cuts such as chops; about 10 minutes more per pound for roasts.

DRY HEAT METHODS FOR COOKING MEAT

Dry heat is the name for the important basic cooking technique used for naturally tender cuts of meat, and as the name implies no liquid is added.

Dry heat cooks but does not tenderize.

There are four variations of dry heat: *roasting* (sometimes referred to as *baking*), *broiling, pan broiling,* and *shallow-fat frying* (sometimes referred to as *sautéeing*). Meat is not usually fried in deep fat.

ROASTING

Despite the U.S. Department of Agriculture's significant discoveries proving that constant low temperature is superior to searing (cooking at a high initial temperature), disagreement is still as heated as a restaurant oven. But most modern cooks go along with science, because tests show that a constant low temperature produces juicier meat. In addition, searing shrinks roasts about 50 percent, a grave disadvantage when the high cost of meat is considered. With constant low heat, shrinkage is only about 15 percent.

Additional joys—roasts cook and brown more uniformly, don't toughen, and retain more food value. Pans and oven are easier to clean because there's no fat spatter, and fuel is saved. Temperatures can range from very slow, 275°, to moderate, 350° F. The cooking time is, of course, longer at 275° F., but the lower the temperature, the less the shrinkage.

For uniform cooking, set a roast on a rack to allow heat to reach all sides. (Bones of prime ribs of beef make their own rack.) For even cooking and a beautifully browned surface, use a pan with low sides, choosing one as near the size of the roast as possible. (Skillets, cake, or pie pans are all acceptable.) Set a monster roast on the broiler pan. If your broiler has no sides, make a boat with aluminum foil to hold the juices.

Roasts require no liquid—adding it steams the meat, as does covering the pan. A roast set in the pan fat side up requires no basting—the melting fat does a much better job than you could. There is, in fact, a disadvantage to basting—when the oven door is opened, cold air rushes in, increasing cooking time.

Always give a roast time to "repose." This French term (and chef's trick) means to remove the roast from the oven at least 20 minutes before it's to be carved and served. Place on a platter and set the platter on or near the warm range. The obvious advantages are that guests are never kept waiting, latecomers are not a matter of concern, the gravy can be prepared, and the roasting pan washed and put away. Less obviously, and as important, the juice begins to gelatinize so very little is lost, and the roast is easier to carve.

If you're worried about keeping the roast hot, realize that a large piece of meat won't cool rapidly, that it's impossible to serve a smoking hot piece of roast meat, and that hot gravy (and plates) will warm the slices. If you are still concerned, invest in a hot tray.

SUGGESTIONS: Roasts weighing less than 3½ pounds shrink excessively. If you must cook a small one, allow at least two hours in all.

Boned rolled roasts ease the carver's chore but the slices are not as handsome. In addition, bones conduct heat so a boned roast cooks more slowly and is therefore not as juicy or as tender.

To keep a roast crusty, avoid baking foods that create steam—puddings and the like—along with it.

To keep juice from escaping when turning chops or steak, either insert a fork in the fat or use tongs. A good carver uses his fork sparingly, and you'll notice that a good waiter scoop-serves meat with a spoon and a fork.

Pattern for Roasting Meat

1. Insert a meat thermometer in center of the meatiest portion of the roast.

2. Place on a rack in a shallow pan, fat side up, and roast until done.

3. If desired, prepare Gravy* with pan liquid.

BROILING MEAT

Again science has come up with some new rules for this second variation of dry heat. To produce plump, succulent steaks and chops, broil at approximately 450° F., a medium-high flame. Lower the temperature by about 25° if meat is frozen or if cut especially thick.

Place cuts of meat 2 inches thick about 3 inches from the flame. Raise the broiler pan about an inch for thinner cuts; lower it about an inch for thicker cuts. Use the chef's test for turning broiled meat —it is ready when the juices begin to flow to the surface. If the broiling temperature is correct, it will then be brown enough to turn. It is unnecessary to grease broiler or pan, and equally unnecessary to use a rack or to preheat the broiler. To make cleaning easier, cover surfaces with aluminum foil.

SUGGESTION: When broiling small steaks or just a few chops, use a small pan with low sides (skillet, pie pan, etc.), setting it on the broiler pan.

If your broiler and oven are thermostatically controlled, leave oven or broiler door open slightly to permit cold air to rush in, thus maintaining the medium-high flame required for broiling. (In a closed oven the thermostat cuts the size of the flame when the oven reaches the temperature at which it has been set.)

Should the fat catch fire (an unlikely possibility with a temperature of 450° F.), smother the flame with a pan lid or douse with salt. (Brush off excess salt before serving the meat and, because there is so little penetration, the meat will be edible.)

Pattern for Broiling Meat

1. Place meat on a pan or broiler.
2. Use a medium-high flame, 450° F., and broil until brown.
3. Season, turn, and brown second side.
4. Broil to desired degree of doneness and season second side.
5. If desired, prepare Gravy* with pan liquid.

PAN-BROILING MEAT

This method is another variation of dry heat. It differs from frying only in the omission of fat, so people on fat-free diets welcome it. When the pan is heated to the correct temperature, even liver won't stick. If the pan is too hot, the meat will stick and will shrink and toughen; if not hot enough it will stew rather than brown and the resulting moisture will make browning impossible. Should this happen, pour off but save juices for gravy, etc. There should be a pleasant sizzling sound when the meat is added. Maintain that temperature throughout browning by raising or lowering the flame.

A heavy pan is required. (Skillets coated to prevent sticking are usually too light in weight for successful pan-broiling.) If the pan is metal, test the temperature by sprinkling the surface with a few drops of cold water. When it is heated sufficiently they will bounce violently and dry almost immediately. Test the temperature of an enamel-coated pan by holding your fingertips on the outside edge next to the handle. The heat will be bearable for 2 to 3 seconds when the pan is ready.

Use the chef's test for turning the meat—it is ready when the juices begin to flow to the surface. If the temperature is correct it will then have browned sufficiently.

Pattern for Pan-Broiling Meat

1. Heat a heavy skillet over a medium-high flame.
2. Place meat in skillet and brown. Season, turn, brown second side, and season. (At this point a piece of meat about ½ inch thick will be done.)

3. For cuts about 1 inch thick, reduce heat to low after browning, cover pan, and cook to desired degree of doneness.

4. If desired, prepare Gravy* with pan liquid.

FRYING MEAT

The only difference between this last variation of dry heat and pan-broiling is the use of fat. The method is often called "shallow-fat frying," or "sautéeing," to distinguish it from Deep-fat Frying.* Frying is the cooking method that is most destructive of food value.

Use only enough fat to cover the bottom of the skillet, and heat it *to* the smoking point. (Smoking fat is burning, tastes terrible, and so does any food cooked in it.) With a metal skillet, test the temperature as you would an iron—wet your finger and quickly touch the outer edge of the skillet next to the handle and listen for the sizzle. In an enamel-coated pan use the test suggested in pan-broiling.

Fats for Frying Meat: For flavor and economy, use fat cut from the meat itself or drippings. Oil also may be used. Olive oil is superior; peanut and soy oils are good. The flavorless corn and cottonseed oils, and hydrogenated vegetable shortening add no savor.

Butter and margarine burn before meat browns and spatter excessively, and their delicacy of flavor is overpowered by emphatically flavored meat fats such as beef. Clarified Butter* or equal parts butter and olive oil are, however, excellent for veal.

As a preliminary to browning, herbs, spices, and seeds, singly or in combination, may be tossed in the fat, uncovered, for about two minutes or until aromatic. Vegetables such as diced onion, diced green pepper, crushed garlic, or combinations may then be simmered in the fat for about 5 minutes. If you like them soft, cover the pan.

Pattern for Frying Meat

1. Add just enough fat to cover bottom of pan.

2. Heat fat over a medium-high flame *to* the smoking point.

3. Place meat in skillet and brown. Season, turn, brown second side, and season. (At this point, a piece of meat about ½ inch thick will be done.)

4. For cuts about 1 inch thick, reduce heat to low after browning, cover pan, and cook to desired degree of doneness.

5. If desired, prepare Gravy* with pan liquid.

MOIST HEAT METHODS FOR COOKING MEAT

This is the name used for the important basic technique for cooking tough cuts of meat. Liquid and the steam it produces when heated act as tenderizing agents. There are two variations of moist heat: *braising* and *water-cooking*. For variety and for speed, tender cuts are often braised or water-cooked. This is an especially useful method when they are cuts with little flavor of their own.

BRAISING MEAT

Within a few months, a steady diet of roasts, steaks, and chops loses its charm. Fortunately, because lusty pot roasts and stews are the dishes that will become the pride of your repertoire and give you the greatest flavor value for your meat dollar. Their sauce means that braised foods must be served in deep containers, so for language glamour call them casseroles.

Cubed meat produces a stew; a large piece makes a pot roast. A perfect braised dish consists of an accumulation of flavors, none of which predominates. The multitude of foods that can cook with the meat make the complications and produce the many recipe titles. This variety means you can create your own recipes, using foods you enjoy, those at their seasonal best, or those on hand.

When the liquid is a flavorful stock or wine, when aromatic herbs and spices and colorful vegetables cook along with the meat, the delectable result will add stars to your cooking crown.

It takes time to cook meats by moist heat, but as opposed to the almost constant supervision needed for frying, pan-broiling and broiling, the waiting need not be watchful. A stew or pot roast can be put together while you're preparing another meal, simmer while you're dining, and be completely cooked by the time the dishes are washed.

There's an even better reason than convenience for making these dishes ahead—they're more savory after an overnight rest in the refrigerator. As the French say, "The flavors have a chance to marry."

Braising calls upon your imagination and your prettiest casseroles. When these can be used on top of the range as well as in the oven, your work is pleasantly eased. You can cook in them, store them in the refrigerator, then reheat and serve from them.

Braising may be done on top of the range or in the oven. You conserve fuel by oven braising when the oven is in use for other foods, and, although moderate, 350° F., is a good general temperature, food may be braised from moderate to very slow, 250° F. Simply remember that at the lower temperature it will take longer. If the food is prepared in a casserole that can go over a flame, you can speed things by bringing the liquid to a boil rapidly first.

Whether in the oven or on top of the range, the technique is unvarying: cover the pot and simmer gently until the meat is tender. The low temperature prevents toughening of meat fibers during the long period needed for breaking down the connective tissue. Realizing that overcooking toughens meat (the fibers become firmer), cook only until tender.

Many recipes direct that meat be browned by pan-broiling or frying as a preliminary to braising. This is an optional procedure, but, in addition to taking time, frying shrinks meat and toughens the outer layer. Meat brushed with a precooking aid does not require browning.

Meats for Braising: A rack (usually flavoring vegetables) goes into the pan first and, acting as a buffer, keeps the meat away from the intense heat.

For even cooking, arrange meat cut for stew in a single layer, fat side up. It should just fill the pan. If the pan is small, stir meat halfway through the cooking. Place pot roast in pan fat side up and if necessary turn halfway through cooking.

Fats for Braising: See fats suggested for frying. Olive oil is almost mandatory for Italian dishes; combinations of olive oil and butter for Italian or French; peanut or soy for Oriental.

Braising Liquids: Too much liquid results in an insipid sauce so avoid using a pan that is too large. For stews, add only enough liquid to reach a depth of about ¼ inch in the pan. Add about an inch of liquid for pot roasts.

Should the liquid evaporate, and this is unlikely at a simmering temperature, add stock or water to keep it at that level. If cooking is too rapid, even with flame at its lowest, tilt the pan cover to allow cold air to rush in.

The more flavorful the liquid, the more delicious the result. Any of the following may be used alone or in combination:

WATER. The least desirable—having no flavor, it contributes none.

VEGETABLE LIQUIDS. Garnered from cooked or canned vegetables, these have some flavor and some food value.

TOMATO PRODUCTS.*

STOCK. This can be homemade, canned, bouillon powder, or cubes.

DAIRY PRODUCTS. France chooses cream. Sour cream is often used for Central European dishes. Our own New England and South use milk and buttermilk.

SPIRITS. Don't worry about the alcohol in these—it evaporates at 172° F. Dry wine has the happy capacity of adding flavor and enhancing the savor of other foods. If the finished sauce tastes of wine, too much was used. In general choose a dry red wine for beef or lamb; dry white wine for other meats. Vermouth and sherry are further choices.

Bourbon, gin, etc., are not flavorful enough to add much except cost to a braised dish. Brandy, the most expensive spirit, is the exception. Sometimes meat is brandy-blazed before other braising liquids are added.

Vegetables for Braising: The many vegetables that can go into a braised dish make for variety. When possible, compute the required amount of vegetables by the piece, rather than by cup or pound. In other words, if you enjoy mushrooms and they're medium-sized and at peak season, allow three per serving.

PRECAUTION: Potatoes add no flavor to braised dishes and absorb a large quantity of liquid, so cook them separately, or for ease and speed use canned potatoes.

FLAVORING VEGETABLES. Only those that can cook for a long time without developing strong flavors are put in the pan with the meat. Some examples are onion, carrot, celery, tomatoes, mushrooms. Cut them (halve, slice, dice), to extract more flavor.

SHORT-COOKING VEGETABLES. These must finish cooking at the same time as the meat. Leave whole, slice, dice, or cut julienne and judge time accordingly. For instance, add peas about 15 minutes before the meat finishes cooking, carrot sticks about 25.

Use any from this list or others of your choice and add singly or in combination:

Beans, lima or snap	Celery (use some leaves too)—dice
Cabbage, white—quarter or shred	Corn kernels
Cabbage, Chinese—cut in 1-inch rounds	Eggplant—slice or dice
Carrot—for maximum food value, cut sticks	Leek—cut 1-inch rounds
	Mushrooms—use whole or slice

Okra—usually cut in rounds
Peas
Peppers, green or red, sweet
or hot—tear or dice

Squash, summer—slice
Turnips, white or yellow—
slice or dice

Fruits for Braising: These most often find their way into East Indian or Oriental dishes. As with vegetables, they too must finish cooking at the same time as the meat. Cut if necessary. Apples, bananas, canned pineapple, and dried fruits are a few suggestions.

Herbs, Spices, Seeds for Braising: Parsley is the most obvious of the herbs; pepper of the spices. Any others, plus seeds, add interest and flavor. As far as amounts are concerned, taste preference and experience must be your guide.

Pattern for Braising Meat

Cubed meat for stew
> 1½ pounds boned (2 pounds with bone)
> *or*

Pot roast
> 1 to 3 pounds boned (1 to 5 pounds with bone)
> Quick-browning aid, optional
> 2 to 4 tablespoons fat, optional
> 1 or more Flavoring Vegetables*
> *and/or*
> 2½ cups Short-Cooking Vegetables*
> 1 cup liquid, approximately
> ½ teaspoon salt
> ¼ teaspoon pepper
> Dash msg
> Herbs and/or seeds and/or spices

1. Brush meat with quick-browning aid. To brown, use a large heavy pan and fry in fat or pan-broil. (If not browning, or if pan-broiling, omit fat.)

2. Make a bed of flavoring vegetables and top with meat, preferably in a single layer.

3. Add only enough liquid to reach a depth of ¼ inch in pan for stew; 1 inch for pot roast.

4. Add seasonings (salt, herbs, etc.) to liquid.

5. *Top of range:* Bring liquid to a boil rapidly, reduce flame and simmer only until meat is tender.

Oven: Simmer covered in a slow, 250° F., to moderate, 350° F., oven until meat is tender.

6. Remove meat when tender and strain liquid if flavoring

vegetables are not to be served with it. Add short-cooking vegetables so they will finish cooking (or heating if canned or frozen) at the same time as meat.

7. If desired, thicken pan liquid as for Gravy.*

8. Season to taste. Makes 4+ servings.

Day-Before Preparation of Pot Roasts: Place cooked meat in bowl, pour strained pan liquid over, cover and refrigerate. Next day remove congealed fat and save for use in gravy if desired. Slice meat and arrange overlapping layers in an attractive casserole and distribute any vegetables such as roasted peppers, cooked carrots, etc., between layers and on top. Season liquid to taste, first thickening it as for Gravy* if desired. Pour over, cover casserole and reheat as directed below.

Freezing Braised Meat: Cooked stews and pot roasts freeze beautifully, and a pot roast sliced before storing will taste better because it freezes more rapidly and also reheats with less danger of overcooking.

For freezer storage, it's convenient to foil-line the casserole to be used for reheating. Add the cooked stew or pot roast and cover with foil overlap, allowing about an inch of room for expansion. When it is frozen, remove the foil-covered meat from the casserole, wrap it securely, and note the date and the number of servings. Return it to the freezer; the casserole to the cupboard. To reheat, remove the foil (for ease hold it under running water for a few seconds) and fit the meat back into the casserole.

It's best to just-thaw pot roasts and stews in the refrigerator before reheating. If cooking directly for freezer storage, undercook meat and vegetables slightly; omit salt and pepper, because salt contributes to rancidity, pepper may turn bitter.

PRECAUTION: Both refrigeration and freezing diminish seasoning, so always correct seasoning before serving.

Reheating Braised Foods: Whether in the oven or on top of the range, moderate heat (350° F. or a medium flame) is best. Rapid enough to prevent food from drying, it is not so rapid food will burn on the bottom before the center heats. Allow about a half hour at moderate heat. Decrease the temperature if guests are dawdling over their drinks; increase if they look toward the dining room yearningly.

WATER-COOKING MEAT

This variation of moist heat is primarily used to cook tongue, corned beef, etc. Although it is almost a preliminary requisite in countries where the meat is very tough, ours is generally of such high quality it may be braised. The disadvantage of water-cooking is that most of the flavor is leached out, hence the spicy sauces and accompaniments used in India and the Orient to mask the fact that the meat has given its flavor-all to the liquid. When the meat is cubed, even more flavor is lost.

As with braising, this cooking method takes time, but when the foods are put together you are free for other pleasures or chores.

Water-cooking is the name of the method used, because of the quantity of liquid. Fancy vocabularies term it "poaching," but the word "boiling" is a misnomer because at high temperatures meat loses flavor and food value, toughens, and shrinks.

For even cooking, place the meat on a rack or make a rack of flavoring vegetables. The liquid is brought to a boil to speed cooking and to retain flavor and the meat is turned halfway through to insure even cooking. The cooking liquid will be flavored by the meat so save it for sauces or soups.

Many recipes direct that ham, tongue, or corned beef be soaked as a preliminary to cooking. This was necessary when there was less control over the salting, smoking, and corning processes. However, today these meats often are extremely bland. To be on the safe side, taste the water after the first hour of cooking. If it's exceedingly salty, drain and replace with fresh water.

Liquids for Water-Cooking Meat: In fine French cooking, often a flavorful stock makes the liquid, but otherwise water is used. Other available savory and nutritious liquids may be added at will. Examples are liquid from cooked or canned vegetables. Acids (dry wine, wine vinegar, etc.) add flavor and also act as tenderizing agents. Use about 2 tablespoons acid for each quart of water.

Flavoring Ingredients for Water-Cooking Meat: The addition of vegetables and herbs adds savor to the liquid. Lusty varieties that do not develop strong flavor with long cooking (onion, carrot, garlic, cloves, bay leaf, etc.) are best. Cut, halve or slice vegetables to extract most flavor.

Pattern for Water-Cooking Meat

1. Place meat on a rack in a kettle.
2. Add 1 tablespoon salt (except for smoked or salted meats) and any desired vegetables and/or seasonings.
3. Bring liquid to a boil and add enough to almost cover meat.
4. Cover pot and return liquid to a boil rapidly.

5. Reduce flame and simmer covered until meat is tender, turning it halfway through cooking.

BEEF

In admiring beef, we demonstrate our British heritage. Signs of excellence are cherry-red flesh that is smooth and fine-textured. Beef should be well marbled (streaks of fat running through the lean), and the fat should be creamy white and firm. Red, porous bones, signs of youth, also indicate good quality.

Beef Tenderloin

The technique for roasting this admirable and costly cut of beef varies from the usual. Its tenderness, lack of fat, and long narrow shape necessitate fast cooking at high temperature.

Have butcher bard one 6-pound beef tenderloin with beef fat or salt pork. (Or ask for enough diced fat to cover top.) Brush with quick-browning aid if desired and place on a rack in a pan with low sides. Roast in a preheated very hot, 450° F., oven, allowing about 45 minutes for rare, about 60 minutes for well done. Makes 8 servings.

Beef in Red Wine

This delectable stew illustrates braising, with wine as the liquid. If you use a French Burgundy, the recipe title becomes *Boeuf Bourguignon*. An American Pinot Noir is an excellent substitute, and other dry red wines may be used.

    2 tablespoons diced salt pork
    2 pounds beef, cubed
    2 tablespoons quick-browning aid (optional)
    1 large onion, sliced
    1 cup dry red wine, approximately
    1 teaspoon salt
    1/8 teaspoon cayenne pepper
    1 teaspoon thyme
    12 medium mushrooms, sliced

Render salt pork; brush beef with quick-browning aid and brown if desired. Proceed as in the Pattern for Braising Meat.* Makes 4+ servings.

Variations

Substitute a pot roast for cubed beef.
Substitute 8 whole small white onions for onion slices.

Consommé with Boiled Beef

This illustration of water-cooking a large cut of meat is a lusty way-to-a-man's-heart treat.

1 large unpeeled onion, quartered
2 large carrots, quartered
5 stalks celery, cut coarsely
1 parsnip, cut coarsely (optional)
1 one-pound can tomatoes
4 sprigs parsley
1 teaspoon basil
1 teaspoon thyme
1 bay leaf
1 clove garlic, crushed
1 tablespoon salt
1 teaspoon peppercorns
2 pounds beef bones
4 pounds beef, flank or brisket
3 quarts cold water, approximately

Place vegetables, herbs, and seasonings in a large kettle. Add bones and top with beef. Prepare as directed in Pattern for Water-Cooking Meat* and cook until beef is tender, about 2½ hours.

Strain stock and if time allows refrigerate beef in strained stock. The next day skim off fat. Slice beef, season stock, and heat meat slices in it. Serve in a tureen, or pass meat separately. Makes 6+ servings. Horseradish Cream* is an almost imperative accompaniment.

Pot Au Feu

This version of *Pot au Feu* is prepared by water-cooking beef in beef stock. It proves that water-cooking of beef cut in chunks is adequately savory, if done this way.

Substitute 4 pounds beef shin or rump cut into chunks for the flank in the preceding recipe, and use marrow bones cut in 2- to 3-inch sections. Prepare as directed in Pattern for Water-Cooking Meat.*

After refrigeration, skim off fat, remove meat, and bring stock to a boil. Add 2 turnips quartered, 3 carrots cut in wedges, 6 peeled small white onions (stick with cloves if desired), 1 teaspoon thyme, and boil 10 minutes. Add beef and marrow bones and cook until vegetables are tender. Marrow spread on black bread is the cook's reward. Makes 6+ servings.

VEAL

Veal is infant beef and as such has little fat or flavor. Similar to young chicken, the two are interchangeable in recipes. Signs of good-quality veal are smooth, fine-grained, grayish-pink flesh. The lack of fat makes veal too dry to broil or pan-broil, but it combines splendidly with rich foods. For instance, bacon or salt pork is often laid over roasts. When veal is fried, more than the usual quantity of fat may be used, and cream—sweet or sour—makes an excellent braising liquid.

Veal Scaloppine

Braising a tender meat demonstrates that variety is the spice of life and offers speedy cooking, most of which is accomplished by frying. Avoid overcooking as veal dries and toughens readily. *Escalope* is the French word for the Italian *scaloppine*. Have the butcher cut thin slices from the leg, then pound them—"to rags" is his phrase. This breaks down the connective tissue and allows for rapid cooking.

    12 pieces veal cut for scaloppine, about 1½ pounds
    Quick-browning aid (optional)
    2 tablespoons butter
    2 tablespoons olive oil
    ½ cup wine: dry vermouth, dry or medium sherry,
       marsala
    Salt
    Pepper
    Msg
    Parsley, cut fine

Brush meat with quick-browning aid. Melt butter in a skillet, add olive oil and, using a medium-high flame, heat *to* the smoking point. Fry meat in the fat until lightly browned, about 2 minutes on each side. Add wine, cover pan, reduce flame, and simmer about

5 minutes, or until meat is done. Season to taste with salt, pepper, and msg, and garnish with parsley. Makes 4+ servings.

Variation

One-fourth cup diced pimento, and/or 1 tablespoon capers added with the wine gives Veal Scaloppine colorful charm.

Veal Paprika

This admirable dish illustrates braising in sour cream. For speed, it's usually made with veal steaks or chops, but cubed veal shoulder may be used.

> 4 tablespoons fat: butter or bacon
> 1 large onion, sliced
> 1 teaspoon salt
> 1 tablespoon paprika
> 1 cup (½ pint) commercial sour cream
> 2 pounds boneless veal
>   or
> 4 pounds veal with bone

Melt fat in a skillet, and add onion, salt, and paprika. Use a medium flame and brown onion, stirring as necessary to prevent burning. It will take about 20 minutes. Gradually add sour cream that is at room temperature, and top with veal. Cover pan, and simmer until meat is just done, about 30 minutes. If desired, thicken pan liquid as for Gravy.* Season to taste. Makes 4+ servings.

Veal Cacciatore

Follow recipe for Chicken Cacciatore,* substituting 2 pounds boneless veal or 4 pounds veal with bone for chicken, and cook about 30 minutes, or until done. Makes 4+ servings.

LAMB

A government survey on eating habits indicates that people who enjoy lamb are intelligent and/or mature. To prove you are the former, choose pinkish-red flesh that is fine-grained and smooth. Look for fat that is firm, brittle, and flaky, and either pinkish or white.

Lamb becomes mutton, a lusty, flavorful meat, on its first birthday and then resembles good beef in appearance. Because lamb comes from a young animal, all cuts except the shank are tender. Lamb when overcooked is dry, with a strong, unpleasant flavor. It should be served either rare or medium-rare.

"Spring" lamb was born in fall and held until spring for slaughtering. "Genuine" spring lamb is just a few months old and is available from March through May. More tender and less flavorful than spring lamb, it is also more expensive.

Garlic Lamb Roast

> 1 6½- to 7½-pound leg of lamb
> 4 cloves garlic, peeled and slivered
> Quick-browning aid (optional)
> 1 tablespoon dried mint

Using a sharp knife, "plant" garlic slivers in the lamb every 3 or 4 inches. Brush with quick-browning aid. Sprinkle lamb with mint and refrigerate overnight. Place in roasting pan with 1 medium potato and 1 medium onion per serving if desired, and roast until lamb is medium rare, 165° F. (Meat thermometers indicate only the internal temperature for lamb cooked to the well-done stage. For rare, remove the roast when the thermometer registers 160° F.) Makes 6+ servings.

Lamb Provençale

If you compare this braising recipe with Beef in Red Wine* and the Pattern for Braising Meat,* you will see that although ingredients change, amounts and techniques do not.

> 1 clove garlic, diced
> 1 teaspoon salt
> 2 tablespoons olive oil, optional
> 2 tablespoons quick-browning aid (optional)
> 2 pounds lamb shoulder, cubed
> 1 large onion, chopped
> 1 medium eggplant, cubed
> 1 teaspoon basil
> ¼ cup tomato purée
> 1 cup dry red wine, approximately
> ¼ teaspoon sugar

Crush garlic to a paste with salt. Heat oil in a large skillet and add garlic mixture. (Mix it with tomato purée if omitting oil.) Cook until aromatic, about 2 minutes. Brush lamb with quick-browning aid and brown if desired. Otherwise, arrange onion, eggplant, and basil in skillet in a single layer. Continue as in Pattern for Braising Meat.* Makes 4+ servings.

PORK

All pork is rich and succulent. For superior quality, choose fine-grained flesh, firm white fat, and bones of a pinkish color.

Pork must be cooked until well done (but not overdone) to kill any parasites (*Trichinella spiralis*) it may be harboring. When cooked to an internal temperature of 160° F. on a meat thermometer, rather than the 185° F. formerly recommended, it is safe to eat and will of course be juicier.

Bacon

According to nutritionists, the only food difficult for a normal stomach to digest is well-done bacon.

Broiled: This is a good method of cooking a quantity of bacon because turning isn't required, but watch out for burning. Broiled bacon will be tougher than fried bacon. Separate the strips and broil at 300° F., about 3 inches from the flame, approximately 3 minutes. The bacon has finished cooking when the fat is clear and shows no white. Drain on absorbent paper.

Fried: Place strips in a cold pan. Cover pan and fry, using a low to moderately low flame. Do not pour off fat during cooking—its heat cooks the bacon. Turn once or twice if necessary, and cook to desired doneness.

SUGGESTION: For bacon "bits" or squares, cut bacon with scissors and fry as above.

Pork Sausage

Broiled: Cook until done, allowing 20 minutes for sausage ½ inch thick.

Fried: Place sausage links or patties in a single layer in a heavy skillet. Cover and cook over a low flame about 10 minutes, depending upon size. Uncover, increase heat to medium, and cook until browned.

PRECAUTION: If skillet is not heavy, add enough water to cover bottom when frying sausage.

Ham

Roasting: For speed and to avoid shrinkage, when possible, roast ham with the skin on. Make a small incision in the skin for inserting the roast meat thermometer.

In buying a half ham, remember that the butt end has more bone in proportion to lean meat, is a little more tender than the shank end, and also is more expensive.

Country-cured or home-cured hams should be soaked 8 to 12 hours in cold water to cover before roasting. Water-cooking is often a requisite for good flavor. To improve appearance, hams may then be baked, if desired. Allow about 20 minutes per pound. Virginia-style hams are treated similarly, unless purchased fully cooked.

Fully cooked hams can be heated before serving (allow 20 minutes per pound) to improve flavor and texture.

Ham is often basted with wine, ginger ale, fruit juices, cider, honey, maple syrup. They penetrate very slightly; add glamour in the telling rather than in the tasting.

Toppings such as canned pineapple or whole cloves are often used to decorate ham. They come under the category of unnecessary but nice.

If using a topping, skin the ham 30 minutes before it finishes baking. With a sharp knife, score, by cutting the fat (but not the meat) into diamond or other shapes. Pat the surface with brown sugar, if desired. Place the decorations in the fat, using toothpicks to secure them (remove before serving), if necessary. Continue baking ham until it is glazed and brown, basting once or twice.

BUDGET MEMO: Ham slices are expensive, bought as such. For economy, have one or two slices cut off when you buy a half ham. Cut diagonal gashes in fat every inch or so, to prevent curling while cooking.

VARIETY MEATS

If you enjoy liver, kidneys, sweetbreads, brains, etc., your menu range will be wide indeed. Many variety meats are economical too, and liver is highly respected nutritionally.

LIVER

All liver is tender. As with any protein, overcooking is what toughens it. Beef and pork liver are more nutritious than calves' liver, and far less costly.

KIDNEYS

Veal kidneys are treasured by epicures. Their fat, which tastes much like marrow, is what makes them magnificent. Today they are sold ready to cook, and soaking and parboiling are unnecessary.

Depending upon their size and your preference, leave kidneys whole, split, or cube them. Overcooking toughens them as it does liver, so except for pork cook medium rare.

HEART

Although usually braised or water-cooked, heart cut in pieces is wonderful broiled. One beef heart makes about 6 servings; veal heart 2 servings; pork and lamb heart 1 serving.

GROUND MEAT

Grinding tough meat makes it tender, thus allowing it to be prepared by any of the dry-heat methods. This means speedy cooking, economy, an enlarged culinary repertoire, and the extra savor tough cuts afford. Whether it is crumbled as in meat sauces or shaped as in hamburgers and meat loaf, ground meat is a theme with a host of variations in every country.

Beef is most commonly used and good cuts are *chuck, round,* and *flank.* Packages labeled "ground beef" are perfectly acceptable meat, but are likely to have a high percentage of fat. Flavor variety is added when pork is combined with the beef.

Ground meat may be shaped, then pan-broiled, broiled, or fried as in hamburger, baked as in meat loaf, or braised as in meat balls. It also makes a stuffing for baked vegetable shells such as green pepper, tomato, eggplant. Other ingredients add the interest of variety.

Handling Ground-Meat Mixtures: Place ingredients in a bowl and combine, using a kneading motion with fingers held apart. The air enclosed makes the mixture light and it has been kneaded sufficiently when it holds together and leaves the bowl clean. Shape the mixture lightly rather than packing it.

SUGGESTION: For browned-all-over crustiness place meat loaves in a pan as for a roast. Otherwise fill a baking pan about two-thirds full.

One pound ground meat makes 4 servings when shaped into a loaf, or into 4 large meat balls.

Egg in Ground-Meat Mixtures: This acts as a binding agent and is used primarily in meat balls and meat loaves. Use 1 egg to a pound of meat.

Fat in Ground-Meat Mixtures: If lean flank steak is used, add 2 to 4 tablespoons flavorful fat for each pound. Steak or roast beef drippings add superb flavor.

Liquid in Ground-Meat Mixtures: This adds moisture, therefore juiciness, and is used primarily for meat balls and meat loaves. A quick-browning aid (use it to brush surfaces, too), sweet or sour milk or cream, stock, gravy, dry wine, water—the more of these you add, the juicier the finished product will be. About a tablespoon is a good beginning for a pound of meat. It will absorb an amazing amount but don't add so much the mixture won't hold shape.

Extenders for Ground-Meat Mixtures: One pound of meat stretches to about 6 servings when any of the following are included: 1 cup cooked rice; 1 slice stale bread soaked in water about 10 minutes, then squeezed dry (rye bread offers the flavor dividend of caraway seeds); ½ cup fine dry bread or cracker crumbs (soak in 1 cup milk or cream about 20 minutes, or until all the liquid is absorbed).

Flavoring Ingredients for Ground-Meat Mixtures: For 1 pound, choose any or all: a raw onion, chopped fine; ¼ cup parsley sprigs torn coarsely, or other fresh herbs; a clove of diced garlic; 1 teaspoon dried herbs; ½ teaspoon seeds.

IV

Perfect Poultry

Everybody benefits when poultry makes the entrée. The first advantage, of course, is flavor. Distinctive enough to require no embellishment, as in crisply broiled chicken or crackling-skinned roast turkey, most poultry is also so delicate that a galaxy of foods and sauces companion it gracefully.

Finally, poultry is nutritious. Chicken and turkey offer an added advantage—they're low in calories as well as high in protein. Incidentally, dark meat has more food value than light, and in a correctly cooked bird the difference in flavor is practically indistinguishable. (With overcooking, white meat loses succulence, dark meat develops strong flavor.)

BUYING POULTRY

Poultry is usually less expensive in autumn and early winter. Because a large bird has proportionately more meat to bone it's a better buy. If there is no indication of age and only the *kind* of poultry appears on the label, it must be a young bird.

Poultry may be purchased three ways (1) live weight; (2) dressed (actually undressed, because it's been plucked); and (3) ready-to-cook (eviscerated).

Government-graded poultry is your assurance of quality. Because poultry is impossible to inspect on the inside unless the viscera (giblets) have been removed, only ready-to-cook birds are graded. Government grades, in decreasing order of cost, are A, B, and C, and all are wholesome. The main difference lies in plumpness and amount of meat to bone. In addition, Grade A birds will have handsome conformation; Grade C birds may have torn skin, a crooked wing, etc.

BUDGET MEMO: Choose Grade C birds for the stew pot, where appearance is not important.

In buying poultry look for plump, short-bodied birds with broad meaty breasts and fleshy drumsticks. Evidences of youth are pinfeathers, pliable wings, soft feet. Fair skin indicates a well-fatted, therefore succulent, bird. Weight isn't always an indication of advanced age—certain breeds grow quite large rapidly. Nature endows lady poultry with more fat and breast, so in an older bird choose a hen.

QUANTITY OF POULTRY PER SERVING

It's almost impossible to give exact amounts, because added ingredients such as stuffings extend the bird, and rich sauces also make it go further. In addition, variation of meat to bone is great. However, approximately 1 pound of a small bird is adequate for 1 serving; ¾ pound of a large bird because there's more meat to bone.

When chicken is disjointed (cut for fricassee), it makes more sense to compute the number of pieces per serving. Two of the meaty pieces—choose from drumsticks, thighs, and quartered breast —make a normal serving. (Guests have trouble coping with the bony pieces, so unless you cook for people who love finger food save these parts for use in stock, pilaf, etc.)

A 4- to 5-pound bird yields about 4 cups meat after cooking.

CLEANING POULTRY

Ready-to-cook birds are exactly that, and as with meat, washing simply washes away flavor and food value. If you buy poultry live or dressed, your butcher will accomplish the most unpleasant cleaning tasks. However, if he hasn't removed the oil sac on top of the tail, cut under it deeply with a sharp knife. Pluck any feathers with a tweezers and singe pinfeathers by holding the bird over an open flame (or a candle if your range is electric).

STORING POULTRY

Poultry is perishable, so refrigerate or freeze it promptly, storing the giblets separately. Wise cooks freeze the liver separately too and save up enough to make a paté or to splurge at brunch.

Remove butcher wrappings as noted in Storing Meat.*

Refrigerator: Cover raw poultry lightly; cooked poultry tightly. Raw poultry keeps about two days; cooked poultry about five days. Stuffing should be removed and stored separately.

Ice-Cube Section or Freezer: If freezing sectioned poultry, be sure to wrap pieces individually for ease in separation. Cover both raw and cooked poultry tightly. Either keeps in the refrigerator ice-cube section about two weeks; about six months in the freezer.

COOKING POULTRY

The two basic cooking methods—Dry Heat* and Moist Heat*—apply to poultry as well as to meat. Because poultry is a protein, the most important rule is: *Use the lowest possible heat for the method and do not overcook.*

Err on the side of under- rather than overcooking, and to please a gourmet serve tender poultry medium done. Incidentally, the pink color next to the bone in completely cooked birds doesn't indicate undercooking or affect flavor. It's caused by the same chemical reaction that produces redness in ham.

As with meat, piercing allows juice to escape, so turn birds cut for fricassee with spoon or tongs, whole birds with towel-protected hands.

DRY HEAT METHODS FOR POULTRY

Dry heat methods—roasting and broiling—are used for cooking tender birds. Poultry isn't normally pan-broiled. Because chicken is about the only bird that lends itself to frying, complete information on that technique is detailed in the section on Chicken.*

ROASTING POULTRY

Poultry is roasted exactly like meat, but birds should be trussed. The reasons: they hold their shape and balance better in the pan. In addition, the tied legs protect the thin layer of breast and help keep it from drying out. About 15 minutes before the bird is done, cut the twine so the protected layer can cook completely.

To truss, fold the wing tips back on the wings and tie the drumstick ends tightly together with twine.

Place poultry breast up on a rack in a pan with low sides, and roast in a preheated oven. Add no liquid and do not cover. Depending upon the size of the bird and whether or not it has been stuffed, temperatures can range from very slow to very hot (250–450° F.). Except for birds weighing over 6 pounds, turning is unnecessary, as is basting. Like roast meat, a roasted bird should be allowed to repose before carving. A large bird removed to its serving platter and kept near or on top of the range will still be warm at the end of 45 minutes.

For stuffings and information on roasting stuffed poultry, see the section on Stuffing* at the end of this chapter.

Seasonings and Fats for Roasted Poultry: Unlike meat, poultry has little depth, so various seasonings penetrate the flesh fairly effectively. Powdered ginger, favored by both German and Oriental cooks, adds a clean, tangy note. Paprika enhances color. A quick-browning aid brushed on adds flavor. The bird then may be spread with fat—butter, margarine, a flavorful oil such as olive, or bacon drippings.

Testing Doneness: A bird has finished cooking when the meaty part of the drumstick feels firm when tapped lightly, when the drumstick joint moves easily, and when the juices that run out at the tail are colorless. (Lift and tilt the bird to see.)

If these signs fail to convince you, pierce the meaty part of the drumstick with an ice pick. When the bird is done, any oozing juice from here will be colorless too. No oozing juice is another indication of complete cooking (or, unfortunately, of overcooking).

BROILING POULTRY

Birds for broiling can weigh up to 3½ pounds. With shears separate halves of birds by cutting down back and breastbone. For small birds split at breastbone without separating halves, and spread open for broiling.

No preliminary seasoning is necessary, but for a brown crust and extra savor, brush birds with a quick-browning aid. If you're not counting calories, add a final brush with any of the fats suggested for roasting above.

When using a marinade or flavoring sauce, brush both sides of the bird when turning. Vegetables and/or fruits may be broiled on the rack with the poultry. Halves of tomatoes, bananas, or spiced peaches are delectable examples.

Pattern for Broiling Poultry

1. Place bird on a pan or broiler rack, skin side down, about 3 inches from flame.
2. Broil at medium-high temperature until brown, allowing more time for cooking fleshy side.
3. Turn and broil skin side until done. Lower flame if skin is browning too rapidly.
4. If desired, thicken pan drippings as for Gravy.*

MOIST HEAT METHODS FOR POULTRY

BRAISING POULTRY

Chicken is the variety of poultry most likely to be cooked by braising, and whether the dish is called Chicken Cacciatore* or Paprikascsirke,* braising is the basic method on which the recipes are patterned. The numerous recipes are due to the fact that every country, using chicken in combination with other indigenous ingredients, has its own distinctively titled specialties.

Meaty stewing chickens are usually chosen for braising because they are most savory, but for variety and speed small tender birds may be used.

Strong-flavored vegetables such as cabbage, emphatic herbs such as bay leaf, and lusty stock such as beef tend to overpower poultry's delicate flavor.

Follow the Pattern for Braising Meat.*

WATER-COOKING POULTRY

The meat from elderly chicken is delectable for salads, chicken and dumplings, chicken pie and the like. Very old tough birds must be tenderized by water-cooking. As for meat, more liquid is used than in braising, and about 2 tablespoons of dry wine may be added to each quart of liquid. The by-product, of course, is stock, which is saved for soups, sauces, and gravy. Stewing chickens are the birds usually water-cooked. For greater succulence and for large attractive slices, cook birds whole. If cut for fricassee, remove the quicker-cooking white meat sections as soon as done, and for even tenderness, if necessary, turn a whole bird halfway through cooking.

Follow the Pattern for Water-Cooking Meat.*

CHICKEN

Once you've learned the various terms for chicken, and they are legion, you'll be able to choose the best bird for the cooking purpose. The dividends are flavor and economy. It's as foolish to buy a roasting chicken for soup as it is to purchase prime ribs of beef for hash.

Formerly only infant birds weighing less than 2 pounds were tender enough to broil. Scientific breeding and feeding, however, have produced plump young chickens weighing up to 3½ pounds. Sometimes called "broiler-fryer," sometimes labeled as to use— "fryer," "broiler," or "roaster"—it also may be marked "young." The official title is "small all-purpose bird" because it can be cooked by any of the dry heat methods or for variety and speed by moist heat methods. Cost per pound is approximately the cost per serving.

> BUDGET MEMO: If roasting chickens cost more than twice as much a pound, small all-purpose birds will be a better buy, and more chickens in the roasting pan means everyone gets a drumstick.

A 5- to 8-month-old chicken weighing over 3½ pounds is called a *roaster*. *Capons* (castrated males) are rich, meaty, succulent, and expensive examples of scientific meddling. Seven to 10 months old, their weight begins at 4 pounds. Their destination is the roasting pan.

Stewing chickens are over 10 months old and can weigh up to 6 pounds. Those that come to market are not truly tough—as a barnyard bird would be. A stewing chicken (sometimes called a fowl or old hen) may be braised or water-cooked.

ROASTING CHICKEN

Roast a small all-purpose bird at hot, 400° F., about 45 minutes in all. Add about 30 minutes more for a stuffed chicken.

Roast a chicken 4 pounds or over at moderate, 350° F., about 20 minutes a pound. Allow about 10 minutes more per pound if chicken is stuffed. If the skin looks dry, baste with any of the fats and for variety choose from any of the seasonings detailed under Seasonings and Fats for Roasted Poultry.*

Chicken Tarragon

Called *Poulet à l'Estragon* in France, this is one of the classic French dishes. It is an illustration of roasting and the recipe's simplicity is proof that elegance need not be complicated. Brush with a quick-browning aid and/or fat if desired. Then simply insert 5 or 6 sprigs of fresh tarragon in the cavity of a small all-purpose bird or roasting chicken, or rub the cavity with about a teaspoon of dried tarragon and roast as directed above.

BROILING CHICKEN

Broil chicken at medium high, 450° F., about 25 minutes.

FRYING CHICKEN

Choose a plump young chicken weighing up to 3½ pounds. It may be fried either in shallow fat as an optional preliminary to braising, or in deep fat.

Shallow Fat: Have a small all-purpose chicken cut for fricassee, or quarter a very small bird. Because it is lean, use enough fat to reach a depth of ⅛ inch in the pan. Fats may be lard, poultry fat, butter, oil, or a combination. If butter alone is used, it should be clarified.*

For best results use a heavy skillet just large enough to hold the chicken. Heat fat *to* the smoking point, using a medium-high flame, and adjust flame as necessary to keep the fat sizzling hot without smoking. Place pieces in the pan skin side down, cover, brown, and turn to brown second side.

Deep Fat: In this technique, the chicken is fried until done. Have a small all-purpose chicken cut for fricassee (quarters are too large to cook through). Place in a bag with dry ingredients such as flour, cornmeal, bread or cracker crumbs, or a combination, and shake until pieces are well coated. Allow about ¾ cup dry ingredients for a 3½-pound chicken. Or coat with Egg-Crumb Coating.*

In a deep heavy pot, heat about 1 inch of lard or oil to medium high, 375° F. Avoid overcrowding when adding chicken—the fat should come up around each piece. Put in the meaty pieces first because they take longer to cook. Keep pot covered and turn to brown both sides, allowing about 20 minutes in all for meaty pieces. Drain on absorbent paper.

SUGGESTION: If pan space is limited, fry a few pieces at a time until almost brown, about 3 minutes on a side, remove to a shallow pan, and bake in a hot, 400° F., oven about 10 minutes, or until done. Although this method saves time, results will not be as flavorful.

Ann's Southern Fried Chicken

This almost unbelievably simple method can make your reputation as a cook. It comes from a Georgia peach, and, a variation on deep-fat frying, results in juicy, flavorful chicken with a crisp skin that tastes like cracklings. It's so good two people can finish a small all-purpose bird even if neck, gizzard, heart, and liver are fried too.

> ½ teaspoon salt
> ⅛ teaspoon pepper
> 1/16 teaspoon msg
> ½ cup flour
> 1 three-and-a-half-pound small all-purpose bird,
>   cut for fricassee
> Lard

Season chicken with salt, pepper, and msg. Place flour in a bag. Add chicken and shake until coated, and fry as directed for deep fat, above. Makes 2 servings.

NOTE: The cooked chicken may be frozen, then reheated uncovered in a pan in a single layer. Allow about 10 minutes in a preheated extremely hot, 500° F., oven.

Francine's Chicken Maryland

Proceed as for Ann's Southern Fried Chicken above, but dip chicken pieces in 1 cup milk before coating. Reserve milk. Prepare Gravy* in pan in which chicken was fried, using 1 tablespoon of the frying fat, 1 tablespoon flour, and the reserved milk. Be sure to scrape up (and don't remove) the chicken crumbs—they're delectable. Season to taste.

OVEN-FRYING CHICKEN

The small all-purpose chicken has given rise to a constellation of recipes, all based on this simple-to-do oven technique. Sometimes it's called oven roasting; sometimes oven baking. The method produces a crisp brown skin similar to that achieved by frying.

Because the chicken is quartered or cut for fricassee, it gets full benefit from any seasonings and fats used to coat it. The fat prevents the bird from drying, and about 4 tablespoons is the amount to use for a 4-pound bird. Bake in a preheated hot, 400° F., oven about 30 minutes. The following is a lovely buttery example.

Chicken Baked in Herb Butter

4 tablespoons butter, softened
1 tablespoon paprika
1 teaspoon salt
½ teaspoon pepper
Dash msg
1 teaspoon grated lemon rind
1 teaspoon rosemary
1 teaspoon thyme
1 three-and-a-half-pound small all-purpose chicken
1 lemon, cut in wedges
Parsley sprigs

Cream butter with seasonings and herbs and rub on all surfaces of chicken, cut in quarters or for fricassee. Arrange in a single layer in a pan with low sides and bake as directed above, basting once with juices in the pan after first 15 minutes of cooking. If chicken hasn't browned sufficiently, increase heat last 10 minutes. Garnish with lemon wedges and parsley. Makes 2+ servings.

Variations

As long as the general rules for oven-fried chicken are followed, any compatible additions add savor and increase your repertoire. For instance, you may substitute any other herb, or combination, replace the herbs with seeds, substitute other spices, brush with barbecue sauce, dip in milk and coat as for Francine's Chicken Maryland,* etc.

BRAISING CHICKEN

Sections of young chicken will be done in about 35 minutes. Sections of a stewing chicken will be tender in about 2 hours.

Chicken Cacciatore

This Italian version of stewed chicken translates to chicken "hunter's style." In France, hunter's style reads *chasseur*.

2 tablespoons olive oil, approximately
1 clove garlic, diced
½ teaspoon salt
½ teaspoon orégano
½ teaspoon basil
⅛ teaspoon hot red pepper
1 medium onion, diced
2 tablespoons quick-browning aid (optional)
1 four-pound stewing chicken, cut for fricassee
8 to 12 medium mushrooms, cut in ⅛-inch slices
1 small green pepper, torn into 1-inch pieces
½ cup tomato purée
¾ cup dry wine, white or red, approximately

Use just enough olive oil to cover bottom of skillet. Crush garlic with salt, orégano, and basil. Add to oil with hot red pepper and onion and cook over a medium flame about 2 minutes, or until aromatic, stirring occasionally. Brush chicken with quick-browning aid and if desired brown it. Then make a bed for chicken with mushrooms and green pepper. Add tomato purée and enough wine to reach a depth of ¼ inch in pan. Proceed according to Pattern for Braising Meat,* simmering gently about 2 hours, or until chicken is tender. If substituting a small all-purpose bird, cook until done, about 40 minutes. If desired, thicken pan liquid as for Gravy.* Season to taste. Makes 4+ servings.

Paprikascsirke (Paprika Chicken)

Substitute 4 pounds chicken cut for fricassee in the recipe for Veal Paprika.* Allow about 2 hours for a stewing chicken, about 40 minutes for a small all-purpose bird. Makes 4+ servings.

WATER-COOKING CHICKEN

Time for water-cooking an old chicken is about 2½ hours; allow about 40 minutes for a small all-purpose bird. In either case, follow the Pattern for Water-Cooking Meat.*

Chicken in the Pot

Poulet au Pot is the French name for this example of water-cooked chicken. (In haute cuisine restaurants, the chicken is cooked in chicken stock.)

1 four- to 5-pound stewing chicken, disjointed
1 large carrot, cut coarsely
3 stalks celery and leaves, cut coarsely
1 clove garlic, crushed
1 large onion, cut in eighths
4 sprigs parsley
1 teaspoon dill seeds
1 teaspoon dill weed
2 tablespoons salt
½ teaspoon peppercorns

Cook chicken, vegetables, and seasonings as directed in Pattern for Water-Cooking Meat* about 2½ hours or until tender. Preferably, prepare a day ahead and refrigerate chicken in strained stock. Before serving remove fat, and heat chicken in stock, adding any desired vegetables, dumplings, noodles, rice, etc. Serve as a big soup meal. Makes 4 to 6 servings.

TURKEY

America's notable contribution to poultry is the Thanksgiving bird, and few foods crown the table as regally at *any* time. Because breeders are producing small plump birds, turkey can even appear at dinner for two but the small birds have very little flavor.

Usually only tender turkeys are marketed so they're normally prepared by dry heat. For variety, they may be braised and water-cooked as may birds labeled mature, old, or yearling.

To prevent drying of the outer layer, just-thaw a frozen turkey in the refrigerator. A bird weighing up to 10 pounds will thaw in about a day, over 10 pounds in about two days.

ROASTING TURKEY

For best flavor, choose a turkey weighing 10 pounds or over. Roast turkeys, turkey halves, or quarters weighing less than 6 pounds as directed for Chicken.* If your pan is too small for a large bird, make an aluminum foil boat and place it on the broiler pan.

Allow about 1 pound turkey for each serving. Decrease amount by about ¼ pound for birds weighing 20 pounds or over.

For even cooking, a bird weighing more than 6 pounds may need turning halfway through roasting. If necessary, turn from breast up to breast down, and for handsome appearance, finish breast up. Touch-test, etc., to determine doneness, as described in Roasting Poultry.*

Roast turkeys weighing up to 9 pounds at slow, 325° F., about 2½ hours. Decrease the temperature by 25° and add an hour of roasting time for every additional 4 pounds. Roast turkeys weighing from 17 to 30 pounds in a very slow, 250° F., oven 6 to 9 hours. In either case, add about 10 minutes per pound if turkeys are stuffed.

Turkeys may be brushed with a quick-browning aid, then with oil or fat before roasting. If the skin of a large bird looks dry, anoint with fat once or twice more during roasting.

Turkey Parts: Halves and quarters may be roasted or oven-fried as for Chicken.* Turkey steaks (the whole bird is sliced from breast to back) will be more succulent if oven-fried or broiled.

DUCK

Even at 35 cents a pound, duck is a luxury, because there's so little edible meat. The carcass is large, and during cooking the savory fat that makes duck so good melts and melts. These drippings are superb for frying, and may be stored in the refrigerator or freezer.

Allow about 1½ pounds duck per serving.

ROASTING DUCK

Score with a sharp knife, being careful not to cut into flesh. Follow directions for Roasting Poultry.*

Roast in a preheated slow, 325° F., oven, allowing about 1¼ hours for rare; 1½ hours for medium; 2 hours for well done. If necessary, increase heat to moderate, 350° F., the last ½ hour to melt excess fat and aid browning. If duck has been filled with a starchy-base stuffing, increase time by about 30 minutes.

Basting isn't required, but various additions, such as honey, fruit juice, orange marmalade, may be added or brushed on for variety about ½ hour before the duck finishes cooking.

Duck may be braised.

GOOSE

Like duck, goose is extremely fat, therefore succulent. Although normally roasted, it's often combined with dried beans to make unctuous specialties such as the French *cassoulet.*

ROASTING GOOSE

Follow directions for Roasting Poultry.*

Using a preheated slow, 325° F., oven, allow about 20 minutes per pound unstuffed, 10 minutes per pound additional if filled with a starchy base.

Refrigerate or freeze the delectable drippings for frying and the like.

Allow about 1½ pounds goose for each serving.

POULTRY DIVIDENDS

Using poultry giblets—livers, hearts, gizzards, necks, and, when available, feet—gives you a budget plus. These extras enrich a stock pot, or may be cooked in a small quantity of water and used as the base for sauce or gravy.

Livers make a delicious hors d'oeuvre spread, and sautéed or broiled accompany omelets and scrambled eggs with distinction. Braised as for Veal Paprika* (livers will cook in about 10 minutes), they're an epicurean specialty.

STUFFINGS

Stuffings are used to extend meat and poultry, to add interest to vegetables, and to make fish go further. Birds need not be stuffed for roasting. But stuffings taste good, stretch your food dollar, and also majestically puff the bird's breast.

However, food finishes cooking in the inner center last, so a lower roasting temperature is required and roasting time must be increased. This means that the thin layer of meat may overcook before the stuffing is done. In addition, because stuffings are made with starchy bases, they absorb much of the bird's juice.

To avoid the disadvantages and have your stuffing too, bake it separately in a casserole or in muffin tins.

Roast stuffed chickens weighing up to 2½ pounds at slow, 325° F., for about 1½ hours; up to 4½ pounds at slow, 325° F., about 2½ hours.

If desired, you can subtly enhance the flavor of an unstuffed bird by filling the cavity with a peeled, quartered onion, branches of celery, sprigs of parsley, or an herb bouquet. Duck and goose taste good filled with tart fruits—apple wedges, cooked cranberries, peeled orange slices, etc.

Filling a Bird: Stuffing swells, so fill birds only ¾ full—and with a light hand, because packing results in a soggy mass. Stuff body cavity and, if desired, neck skin. Close openings with toothpicks, or lace with poultry pins and twine, or sew.

Fold neck skin toward the back even if it hasn't been stuffed, and tuck under the wing tips or, if it won't hold, close opening as above.

Research indicates that it is unwise to stuff a bird until just before roasting. Adding the stuffing hot will speed cooking. To prevent sogginess, do not stuff a frozen bird until it thaws.

There are two varieties of stuffing, dry and moist. Basically, both are composed of a *starchy base*, a *savory fat*, and *flavoring ingredients*.

STARCHY BASES FOR STUFFINGS

Bread: White, corn, whole wheat, or pumpernickel (not the sour variety), or combinations may be used. It should be at least a day old. For moist stuffing, very stale bread is best.

SUGGESTION: Fresh bread may be spread in a pan in a single layer and dried in a very slow, 250° F., oven.

A 1-pound loaf of bread (about 18 slices) makes approximately 10 cups cubed or pulled bread; 5 cups crumbs.

CUBES. Remove crusts and cut in ½- to 1-inch pieces. Prepare a day ahead if desired.

CRUMBS. Halve the loaf, fork out the soft inside and pick it into ⅛-inch crumbs. Prepare a day ahead if desired.

PULLED. Pull into small even-sized pieces, removing crust if desired.

Cooked Rice: Whether brown, white, or wild, this makes a delicious stuffing.

Potatoes: Raw grated white potatoes combined with onion and a flavorful fat taste like potato pancakes. Some people enjoy cooked mashed white or sweet potatoes for stuffing.

Allow 1 cup starchy base a pound minus 1 cup, if a bird weighs under 10 pounds; minus 2 cups if over 10 pounds. Because rice swells, allow 1 cup less than the measure of bread or potatoes.

FATS FOR STUFFINGS

Butter, margarine, poultry fats, or a combination may be used. Depending upon the richness of the bird and the flavoring ingredients (nuts require less, oysters more), use 1 to 2 tablespoons fat for for each cup starchy base.

FLAVORING INGREDIENTS FOR STUFFINGS

These include vegetables, fruits, and meats. Use any you enjoy in any combination, following the Pattern for Dry Stuffing,* below.

SEASONINGS FOR STUFFINGS

Allow about ¼ teaspoon each any dried herbs and/or seeds per cup of starchy base.

Pattern for Dry Stuffing for a 4-Pound Bird

    1 small onion, diced
    4½ tablespoons fat
    3 cups starchy base
    ½ teaspoon seasonings: herbs and/or seeds
    ½ teaspoon salt
    ¼ teaspoon pepper
    Dash msg
    ¾ cup Flavoring Ingredients

Cook onion in melted fat in a skillet 5 minutes. Mix with starchy base and seasonings. Add any desired flavoring ingredients from the list below and season to taste.

Flavoring Ingredients

If celery, green pepper, or mushrooms are used, dice and cook them in the fat with the onion. Break or chop nuts coarsely. Chop dried fruit coarsely (if it's very dry, soften as directed in Dried Fruit*). Heat oysters gently in their liquor about 5 minutes, or until edges ruffle, and add with their liquor.

Allow about 1 tablespoon salt pork, bacon, or pork sausage for each cup starchy base if choosing them as flavoring ingredients. (Dice salt pork; cut bacon into bits, and fry gently in a covered skillet until done; crumble pork sausage after cooking.) Add any of these with their fat, and omit fat called for in the above pattern.

MOIST STUFFINGS

Place stale pulled bread in a sieve or colander and allow water to run over it until just softened. Squeeze to extract excess moisture and add 1 slightly beaten egg for each 2 to 6 cups starchy base. Proceed as directed in Pattern for Dry Stuffing* above.

V

Delectable Seafood

People who turn their backs on fish and shellfish usually have never tasted it cooked with loving care. When perfectly prepared, it is delicate in flavor and succulent. Fish has other advantages. Naturally tender, it cooks in a hurry. Because there are over 30,000 species (fish is the largest of any class of vertebrates), there's menu variety and to spare. It's fairly inexpensive and—a final nutritional advantage—both fish and shellfish are proteins; contain vitamins and minerals. Shellfish offers the same advantages as fish but is comparatively expensive.

The word "seafood" will be used here as an inclusive term for both fish and shellfish with specific references to fish or shellfish indicated.

BUYING SEAFOOD

Seafood is least expensive in late spring and early summer, and size is no indication of quality. The actual amount of meat obtained from fish and many shellfish is small. For instance, the edible portion of a 1¼-pound lobster is only ¼ pound.

BUDGET MEMO: A large fish has proportionately more meat, so

it's a better buy. Some varieties of fish are more fashionable than others. Because demand raises prices, for economy choose the unfashionable types, such as porgy, smelts, etc. Local seafood in season will be a best buy.

Freshness and fine flavor go hand in hand. In fish, choose firm bodies with tightly clinging scales and bright unsunken eyes. Neither fish nor shellfish should be slimy, and both should have what is delicately known as a "fresh but characteristic odor."

QUANTITY OF SEAFOOD PER SERVING

One pound whole fish (as it comes from the catch).

Three-quarter pound drawn (entrails removed).

One-half pound dressed (drawn, with scales removed, and usually head and tail).

One-third pound steaks (slices cut from large fish, such as tuna).

One-third pound fillets (boned, dressed halves of fish too small to be cut into steaks).

FROZEN SEAFOOD

Ready to cook, this is usually next best in succulence and flavor to fish from your own hook. Unfortunately, unless thawed it will overcook on the outside before it finishes cooking throughout, so just-thaw and cook immediately.

CANNED FISH

Already cooked, this lacks the full flavor of fresh or frozen fish. For maximum food value, don't discard its liquid and/or oil.

BUDGET MEMO: When perfect whole pieces are unnecessary— for instance in making sandwich spreads, salads, etc.— buy the less expensive variety, labeled "flaked" or "grated."

STORING SEAFOOD

Because it's perishable, hasten fish home from market. Discard store wrappings and wash it if you must. Refrigerate in an odor-proof container or cover tightly and freeze. Seafood will keep as follows:

Refrigerator: Fresh fish, shellfish, lightly salted smoked fish, 1 to 2 days. Cooked fish, shellfish, chowders, bisques, etc., opened canned fish, about 3 days. Heavily smoked, dried, and pickled fish, 2 to 3 months.

Ice-Cube Section: Fresh fish and shellfish, about 2 weeks. Cooked fish, shellfish, opened canned fish, chowders, bisques, etc., about 3 weeks. Heavily smoked, dried, and pickled fish, about 4 months.

Freezer: All varieties keep at least 3 months, but with long storage their appearance becomes unattractive.

It's best not to refreeze thawed fish, because the drip lost through thawing contains flavor and food value. However, if it hasn't spoiled during thawing, you may refreeze with the realization that it won't be either as juicy or as nutritious.

CLEANING SEAFOOD

Markets scale and clean fish, and upon request remove large bones, fins, and skin.

SUGGESTION: To remove fish odor from your hands, rub them briskly with a quantity of salt. Rinse in cold water, then wash in hot. Follow the same procedure to remove odor from dishes in which fish has been cooked or served.

GARNISHES AND SAUCES FOR SEAFOOD

Most seafood is lean and delicate in flavor. All seafood is soft and fairly colorless. To compensate, choose from accompaniments that are rich, piquant, and that offer texture and color contrast.

Acids: Dry wine, vinegar, lemon, or lime juice offer piquancy.

Almonds: Add texture contrast and richness. Usually blanched, they may be slivered and also may be toasted.

Capers: An elegant and piquant addition to broiled or sautéed fish, sauces, or salads.

Cucumbers: Unpeeled spears offer color and texture contrast.

Fat: Butter, margarine, pork drippings, flavorful oils such as olive, soy, peanut, and the costly but magnificent sesame seed oil add delectability. Bacon or salt pork strips may cover seafood before baking or broiling.

Grapes: Green grapes add color contrast and fresh flavor. Huge bunches of purple grapes decorate platters handsomely.

Herbs, Spices, Seeds: Parsley for color, chives for color and piquancy, dill seed and/or weed for flavor, paprika for color, ginger for pungency.

Lemon or lime: For color and piquancy, cut thin slices (the rind may be peeled off) or wedges. Dip in paprika and/or finely cut parsley or chives.

Marinades: See Marinating Meat.*

Olives: Black, pimento-stuffed, green, or green tree-ripened all add color contrast and richness; green and pimento-stuffed add piquancy.

Pimento: Offers sweetness and color contrast.

*Tartare Sauce:** Offers richness (mayonnaise) and piquancy (pickles, horseradish, etc.)

COOKING SEAFOOD

There's an unfortunate prejudice against cooking seafood—its aroma. But the blame is usually the cook's—the smell comes from overcooking. As with most proteins, it's better to err on the side of under- rather than overcooking.

Because all seafood is naturally tender and delicate in flavor, the different varieties are used interchangeably in recipes. Simply adjust cooking time to accommodate the varieties in size. The test for doneness is the same as for meat: seafood is springy when medium-done; firm when done. It also will be opaque rather than transparent and gelatinous. If you must, twist a fork in the thickest portion of fish— it will flake easily when done.

Although some fish are fatter than others, fat content varies seasonally, so be grateful for the added richness rather than worrying about using more or less fat when substituting varieties in recipes.

Seafood is naturally tender, so it's cooked by dry heat: baked (the synonym for "roasted"), broiled, and fried in either shallow or deep fat. Because it's lean, pan-broiling is not a recommended method.

For variety, seafood also is cooked by moist heat methods.

DRY HEAT METHODS FOR SEAFOOD

BAKING (ROASTING) SEAFOOD

A whole baked fish on a platter is a delight to behold. It also will be juicier than if head and tail have been removed. Often whole fish are baked on and served from a handsome wooden plank to avoid breaking during transfer to a platter.

A baked fish looks more attractive and shrinks less when slashed. Cut at a 45-degree angle almost to the bone at 1-inch intervals on both sides.

Bake whole or dressed fish in a very hot, 450° F., oven about 5 minutes a pound. Allow about 20 minutes in all for small fish, steaks, or fillets.

BROILING SEAFOOD

Brush small whole fish, shellfish, fillets, or steaks cut about an inch thick with fat or cover with bacon or salt pork strips. (If using a quick-browning aid brush it on first.) Slash whole fish as for baking. Broil flesh side up 2 inches from flame at very hot, 450° F. Turning is unnecessary. Fillets or steaks take about 10 minutes.

Broil large whole fish, thick fillets, or steaks about 2 inches from the flame at moderate, 350° F., about 20 minutes in all, turning halfway through cooking.

FRYING SEAFOOD

Small whole fish, fillets, thin steaks, and shellfish respond best to frying and either shallow or deep fat may be used.

Shallow Fat: Coatings aren't obligatory and won't adhere if the seafood is dry, but a dip in milk, pre-cooking aid, or water will make a coating cling. Like chicken, seafood is lean, so whether fried as an optional preliminary to braising, or until done, the amount of fat—a depth of about ¼ inch in the pan—is the same. The fats may be lard, oil, or a combination of butter and oil. Frying fish differs from frying chicken in that the pan is not covered. In a skillet, preferably heavy, heat fat *to* the smoking point, use a medium-high flame, and fry uncovered until done, adjusting flame as necessary to keep the fat sizzling hot without smoking and turning to brown both sides. If seafood is to be braised, add liquid when browned. Otherwise, fry until done and drain on absorbent paper.

Allow about 5 minutes for fish cut ½ inch thick.

Deep Fat: Coat and fry any of the seafoods mentioned above in about 1 inch of lard or oil heated to 375° F. Drain on absorbent paper.

Leftover fried fish is delicious cold. Serve with a sharp sauce such as Horseradish Cream,* Horseradish Mayonnaise,* Tartare Sauce,* etc.

MOIST HEAT METHODS FOR SEAFOOD

BRAISING SEAFOOD

Rapid cooking is required to prevent seafood from toughening, so braising becomes a semi-frying technique. Choose from fish fillets, steaks, or shellfish.

WATER-COOKING SEAFOOD

Any seafood may be water-cooked. "Poaching" is the fancy term for this method, which provides shrimp for cocktail, whole salmon for the buffet table, etc.

Tie a whole fish in cheesecloth so it can be removed to the platter without breaking. Make individual cheesecloth packages of steaks or fillets. (If they are tied together, the outside will toughen before the inside cooks.) When poaching small shellfish such as shrimp, tie the vegetables in cheesecloth (see Court Bouillon*).

The cooking time varies with the size of the fish. Steaks or fillets cut 1 inch thick will poach in about 10 minutes; a large whole salmon in about 30 minutes.

Salted water can be the cooking liquid, but Court Bouillon* or Chicken Stock* adds flavor and may then be used in a sauce for the seafood.

CLAMS

Quahogs or large hard-shell clams require chopping and end up in chowders. The smaller hard-shell clams, littlenecks or cherrystones, are eaten raw, or cooked as in recipes for oysters. Soft-shell clams are steamed or fried.

A live, therefore fresh, clam has a tightly closed shell. Avoid any with broken or open shells. Markets open clams upon request. If you dig them out yourself, there's work ahead.

Preparation and Cooking: Wash under cold water. Open shells as follows: Hold clam in your palm with shell hinge inward. Insert a very strong sharp knife between shells and quickly cut around clam and through muscle that holds the halves together. A slight twist of the knife pries the shell open. Cut meat from opened shell, or serve as is.

SUGGESTION: To open clams painlessly, wash and freeze. Remove from freezer an hour before serving and immerse in cold water until shells are partially opened. Pry open with a paring knife and scrape clam and juice from shell.

Allow 6 to 12 clams per serving, depending on size; one quart shelled clams makes 2 to 3 cups chopped, 6 servings.

Bake or grill clams on the half shell or in a pan about 10 minutes;

Broil clams on the half shell about 5 minutes;

Fry clams in deep fat about 4 minutes.

Steamed Clams (Steamers)

Place clams in ½ inch cold water in a large kettle. Cover pan and cook over low flame about 15 minutes, or until shells open. Strain liquid through several thicknesses of cheesecloth and use as a dip for the clams, then drink it if desired.

CRABS

Both hard- and soft-shell crabs are of the same species; the hard crab, shedding its shell, becomes a softie during molting. If you are buying live crabs, to get your money's worth, be sure the large claws are intact.

Allow about 3 blue crabs—hard- or soft-shell—per serving. About 26 hard crabs yield 1 pound meat; make about 4 servings.

Preparation and Cooking:

Soft-Shell: Kill by thrusting a sharp knife between the eyes. These are between the large claws. Rinsing is the only preliminary preparation necessary, but, if you wish, lift each of the pointed ends of the top shell and scrape away the spongy substance between shell and body on each side. Place crab on its back and cut off tail.

If the muscle contraction, which continues after death, bothers you (and why not!) chill crabs thoroughly before cooking.

To *broil*, brush with fat, and allow about 15 minutes under the broiler.

Fry in deep or shallow fat, about 15 minutes.

Hard-Shell: Prepare Court Bouillon.* Plunge live crabs into boiling stock head first, and simmer about 15 minutes, or until done.

When cool, remove claws and legs and crack shells. Break off and discard segment that folds under the body from the rear. Hold the crab with its back toward you, slip your fingers under the top shell, and pull the body downward without breaking it to release the top shell. (The shell may be saved for baking shellfish mixtures.)

Split crab along center crease, and cut hard membranous covering along outer edge. With a nut pick remove the tender, sweet meat from each cavity, being careful not to break pieces of shell into it.

Flake the meat for use in soufflés, salads, with sauces, etc.

LOBSTER

Lobsters from the Atlantic seaboard have claws. The "spiny" lobster from the Pacific is equipped with protruding antennae, but no claws. Rock lobsters (South African tails are superior) have coarse flesh, but are delicious and relatively inexpensive. All varieties of lobster are cooked by the same methods and for similar periods of time.

Preparation and Cooking—Atlantic Coast Lobsters: Buy alive to insure sweet fresh flavor. Pegs inserted in the claw protect you from attack, but in the interest of safety always pick a lobster up behind the claws. A lobster just out of the refrigerator will be sluggish, therefore easier to handle.

To split, place lobster on a paper-protected board with the hard shell toward you. Insert the tip of a long, sharp, heavy knife behind the eyes and cut quickly from head to tail. Open lobster and discard stomach sac near the head and black intestinal vein running from head to tail.

The green tomalley (liver) is a delicacy. A female lobster often contains roe—sometimes called coral, because of its bright red color. If the lobster is to be broiled, don't remove the roe. For lobster in sauce, remove both tomalley and roe to add to the finished sauce.

A 1-pound lobster (¼ cup meat) makes 1 serving.

Bake: Split, separating halves completely if desired. Brush flesh with melted butter and place on a shallow pan in a single layer, cut side up. Bake in a very hot, 450° F., oven about 15 minutes, or until done.

Broil: Split, separating halves completely if desired. Brush flesh with melted butter and place on a shallow pan in a single layer, cut side up. Broil 2 inches from a moderately high, 375° F., flame about 15 minutes, or until done.

Water-Cook: Plunge live lobsters head down into prepared boiling water (1 tablespoon salt and 1 tablespoon acid per quart). Cover pot (you may have to hold it down the first few minutes), and simmer about 15 minutes, or until done.

To remove cooked meat, split lobster from head to tail and pull the "tail" meat out. Crack claws and pull meat out. If you have patience, pull feelers off and pick out meat. Use the meat for sauces, salads, etc. Lobster "medallions" are round slices cut from the tail.

MUSSELS

Clams and mussels, cleaned the same way, are interchangeable in recipes.

OYSTERS

Oysters may be bought shucked or in the shell. Shells should be tightly closed (indicating live freshness) or should close at a touch. Choose plump, shiny, shucked oysters with clear liquor, and no off odor.

BUDGET MEMO: Choose the smaller, less expensive oysters for stew, pies, or creamed dishes.

Preparation and Cooking: For ease in opening, freeze as in instructions for clams. Otherwise rinse under cold water and insert a firm, sharp knife in oyster. (If this is impossible, hit the unhinged side sharply to make a hole.) Insert knife and cut through muscle that holds the two halves together.

To remove bits of shell, slip oysters through your fingers and strain the liquor.

Oysters have cooked sufficiently when their edges begin to ruffle.

Allow about 6 medium oysters; ¼ pint for 1 serving.

Bake (Roast) on the half shell or in a pan about 10 minutes. (Instructions often direct that oysters on the half shell be baked on a bed of rock salt. The purpose is to hold them firmly upright and to retain heat.)

Broil on the half shell or in a pan, about 3 minutes.

Fry shucked oysters in deep or shallow fat, about 3 minutes.

SCALLOPS

Small bay or cape scallops are superior in flavor to the large sea scallops. For freshness, choose clean, odorless, creamy-colored (rather than dead-white) scallops.

One and a half to 2 pounds—or 1½ pints to 1 quart—scallops makes about 6 servings.

Cooking time in all cases depends on size.

Bake about 15 minutes.

Broil about 10 minutes.

Fry in deep or shallow fat about 5 minutes.
Braise about 5 minutes.
Water-Cook about 5 minutes.

SHRIMP

Raw shrimp is relatively inexpensive. Store-cooked shrimp is usually tough, flavorless, and costly.

BUDGET MEMO: Choose small and therefore less expensive shrimp for stews and the like, where appearance is unimportant. About 35 small shrimp, 15 large, make a pound.

Allow about ½ pound raw shrimp per serving.

Preparation and Cooking:

Peeling. Hold shrimp with feelers down and crack like a peanut from feet to back. Slip shell off from feelers up. (It's easier to peel shrimp before cooking.)

Cleaning. It isn't necessary to remove the sand vein. If you feel you must, cut along the outside curvature with a knife and remove vein.

Bake, broil, fry, braise, or *water-cook* (preferably in Court Bouillon*) and shell or not as preferred, as described for scallops, above.

FROGS' LEGS

The small, more delicately flavored legs are a delight to people who enjoy finger food; the large legs—called jumbo—are meatier and require knife-and-fork work.

Preparation and Cooking: The legs are available skinned and cleaned. If you catch your own, cut the legs off close to the body, wash and pull skin off from top to bottom. (Only the hind legs are used.)

To avoid muscle contraction, treat as for crabs.

Allow about 12 small frogs' legs or 6 jumbo per serving.

Bake, broil, fry, or *braise* as in instructions for scallops.

Baked Seafood

For elegance—and speedy preparation—choose any of the following seafoods or combinations and match them with your choice of the following variations of the baking technique. Bake in a preheated moderate, 350° F., oven about 20 minutes.

1 pound fish fillets or steaks: swordfish, tuna, flounder, etc.
  and
½ pound shellfish: peeled shrimp, shucked clams, scallops, etc.
  or
1½ pounds fish
  or
1½ pounds shellfish

Au Crème

½ cup sweet or commercial sour cream
¼ teaspoon salt
½ teaspoon tarragon
Dash cayenne pepper
Dash msg
6 tablespoons grated cheese, optional

Combine all ingredients except cheese and pour over seafood that has been arranged in a single layer in a greased casserole. Sprinkle with cheese, and bake as directed above. Makes 4 servings.

Au Vin

1 cup diced vegetables (singly or in combination):
  onion, celery, green peppers, mushrooms, etc.
1 teaspoon summer savory
½ cup dry white wine
2 tablespoons butter

Mix vegetables with summer savory, and arrange over seafood that has been placed in a single layer in a greased casserole. Add wine, dot with butter, and bake as above. Makes 4 servings.

Au Sauce Piquante

1 clove garlic, diced
¼ teaspoon salt
4 peppercorns
1 teaspoon herbs and/or seeds: basil, marjoram,
  celery seed, anise seed, etc.
3 tablespoons olive oil
1 tablespoon dry white wine
1 tablespoon quick-browning aid (optional)

Crush garlic with salt, add and crush peppercorns and herbs. Add seeds, olive oil, wine, and quick-browning aid. Arrange seafood in a single layer in a baking dish and marinate about 20 minutes, turning once, then bake as above. Makes 4 servings.

Fish Au Citron

This is a delectable example of broiled fish.

>   1 fish, approximately 2 pounds
>   3 tablespoons butter, melted
>   ¼ teaspoon paprika
>   1 peeled lemon, sliced as thin as possible

Brush fish with butter, sprinkle with paprika, and broil until brown. Turn, brush with remaining butter, and cover with lemon slices. Sprinkle with paprika and broil until done. Makes 2+ servings.

Crabs Amandine

The lovely delicate soft crab shines when fried, then treated to a sauce. *Amandine* is French for "in almond sauce," and ½ to 1 pound of fish steaks or fillets may be substituted for crabs.

>   6 crabs
>   2 tablespoons flour
>   ½ teaspoon salt
>   ⅛ teaspoon pepper
>   Dash msg
>   2½ tablespoons butter, divided
>   1½ tablespoons olive oil
>   ¼ cup almonds, blanched and slivered
>   1½ tablespoons dry white wine or lemon juice

Dredge crabs in flour mixed with salt, pepper, and msg. In skillet melt 1 tablespoon butter and add olive oil. Heat *to* smoking point over medium-high flame, add crabs and fry covered about 15 minutes, or until done, turning to brown both sides. Remove crabs to a hot platter. Add remaining butter to pan, add and brown almonds, stirring occasionally for even browning. Add wine, heat, and pour almond sauce over crabs. Makes 2 servings.

Swordfish in Vermouth

Tender food braises in a hurry, as in this example, using one of the 30,000 species of fish. For menu variety, try it with the other 29,999 —or switch to shellfish.

1½ pounds swordfish steaks
Quick-browning aid (optional)
2 tablespoons butter
2 tablespoons olive oil
½ cup dry vermouth
¼ teaspoon salt
⅛ teaspoon pepper
Dash msg
Parsley, cut fine

Brush swordfish with quick-browning aid. Melt butter in a skillet. Add olive oil and, using a medium high flame, heat *to* the smoking point. Fry fish in fat until lightly browned, about 3 minutes in all, turning to brown both sides. Add vermouth, cover pan, reduce flame, and simmer about 5 minutes, or until done. Season sauce to taste with salt, pepper, and msg, and garnish with parsley. Makes 4+ servings.

Aunt Annie's Fish in Almond Sauce

Aunt Annie's cooking was regarded with awe even by a family that took fine cooking for granted. The evidence is this recipe that illustrates water-cooking.

4 pounds small whole fish, steaks, or fillets
Court Bouillon*
¾ cup cream
4 egg yolks, beaten slightly
¼ cup dry white wine (optional)
½ cup blanched almonds
Paprika (optional)
Parsley sprigs

When using whole fish, if desired, remove head and tail. Poach fish in court bouillon, and when done remove it and prepare fish Fumet* by reducing court bouillon to ¾ cup by fierce open-pan boiling. Strain, and place in a saucepan with cream. Heat *to* the boiling point and beat a small portion into egg yolks. Repeat once or twice until yolks are warmed, then stir back into main mixture. If not thick enough, cook gently, stirring constantly until thickened, about 1 minute, being careful not to let it boil. (The sauce thickens further on cooling.) Add wine and almonds and pour sauce over fish. Serve hot, at room temperature, or cold. Sprinkle with paprika if desired and garnish with parsley. Makes 4 servings.

Beacon Hill Lobster

This more unusual variation of lobster newburg is an example of water-cooking. It's an easy company dish, because all except the final heating may be done a day ahead.

    4 lobsters, about 1 pound each, poached in
        Court Bouillon*
    3 tablespoons butter
    4 large mushrooms, chopped
    1 small green pepper, chopped
    ½ cup chopped pimento
    ½ cup cream
    3 tablespoons flour
    3 tablespoons dry sherry, divided
    1 teaspoon paprika
    6 tablespoons fine dry bread crumbs
    8 tablespoons grated Parmesan cheese

Remove cooked lobsters and reduce court bouillon to ½ cup by fierce open-pan boiling. Split and clean lobsters, setting aside liver and any coral. Remove and dice meat and save shell halves. Melt butter in saucepan. Add mushrooms, pepper, and pimento and cook gently 5 minutes. Add reduced court bouillon and heat.

Place cream, then flour, in a jar and shake until lump free. Proceed as for Gravy.* Add any tomalley and coral, 2 tablespoons sherry, and paprika, and season to taste.

Add lobster meat and pile lightly into lobster shells or in a baking dish and sprinkle with bread crumbs which have been mixed with cheese. Sprinkle with remaining sherry and bake in a moderate 350° F. oven until hot and browned, about 10 minutes. Makes 4 servings.

VI

The Essence of Good Cooking–
Stocks, Soups, Sauces

SOUPS AND STOCKS

If you're fortunate, the kitchen of your childhood was filled with the wonderful smell of soup. From savory stock, your mother would produce the makings for a hearty lunch or Sunday supper. Stock added savor to sauces and also was part of the delectable gravy she served so proudly. With that kind of background you'll surely carry on the tradition in your own home.

Or if you'd like to *begin* a tradition, realize that making stock is an easy and creative operation that costs little and cannily uses food that might otherwise be wasted.

Although preparing it takes time, the waiting need not be watchful and many homemade soups can be put together in a hurry.

Soup, bouillon, consommé, broth, etc., are all made from stock. To avoid confusion, realize that *stock is a rich extract used as the base for soups as well as sauces and gravies.* But whatever it's called, however it's made, be sure it's served HOT!

Stock offers very little food value, because nutrients from the vegetables don't survive the necessary lengthy cooking period, and very few are extracted from the meat and poultry. To offer food value too, cook additional vegetables in the stock until just tender for vegetable soup.

Serve the meat or poultry with which the stock was made either in soup or separately. If served separately, season them highly to compensate for the flavor loss. The proverbial example is horseradish, constant companion to boiled beef. The meat also may be sluiced with horseradish-spiked ketchup. Chicken that has been water-cooked often appears in salad with the piquant mayonnaise compensating for the chicken's lack of flavor.

STORING STOCK

Hot liquids are cooled before storing because they might cause an elderly refrigerator to defrost. If yours can take it, refrigerate soup or stock at any temperature.

Stock cubes are a great convenience. Simply freeze strained stock in a refrigerator tray. Remove the frozen cubes and store in the freezer in a pliofilm bag. Allow about 4 cubes for 1 cup stock; 1 or 2 for sauces or gravies.

Stock keeps 3 to 4 days in the refrigerator, 2 to 3 weeks in the ice-cube section, 1 year in the freezer.

SOUP GARNISHES

Almost the entire larder may be called upon to grace a bowl of soup. As with any other food, keep in mind the principles of contrast. For *color*—slivers of green bean cooked until just tender in chicken soup. For *flavor*—chunks of ham in split pea soup. For *texture*—almonds in cream soup. For *occasions,* try some of the more complicated recipes such as Custard Cutouts.* The following simplify life:

Nuts: Toasting adds texture contrast, and almond slivers make an elegant choice.

Avocado: Cubes or wedges are particularly pretty in clear chicken soup.

Starches: Soup is a happy home for leftover cooked starches, but when noodle or rice soup is planned, opinions vary as to whether the uncooked starches should be cooked in the soup or added after they've been cooked in water. Certainly the first way is easier, but there's a disadvantage—the starches absorb a great deal of liquid, and continue to do so even after they become tender. In addition, they aren't really infused with enough flavor to offset the amount of soup they absorb. You pays your money and you takes your choice.

NOODLES. Thin fine noodles, noodle squares, long noodles, broad noodles—all may be used in soup. Because of *their* variability in size and *your* feeling about quantity, it's impossible to state exact amounts to use. For 2 quarts soup allow approximately 1 cup uncooked; 2 cups cooked.

RICE. For 2 quarts soup allow about ½ cup uncooked; 1½ cups cooked.

BARLEY (pearled). Usually an ingredient cooked with the meat and vegetable in soups such as Scotch broth. For each 1½ quarts liquid, add ½ cup uncooked barley that has been soaked in cold water 1 hour. Add to 2 quarts soup about 1½ cups cooked barley.

PASTA. Soupettes in the shape of rice, macaroni broken small, and a host of other pasta all find their way into soup. Allow about the same amount of soupettes as rice, approximately the same amount of macaroni as noodles.

Cheese: Pass grated Parmesan, Romano or Swiss to spoon into soup.

Cream.

WHIPPED. Season with salt, or spike with horseradish, and pass separately or top cups of soup. For a gorgeous glaze put under the broiler for a minute or two.

SOUR. Pass a bowl of commercial sour cream, or put about a tablespoon into each serving.

Croutons. These are an economical finale for any variety of stale bread. Crusts needn't be removed, but before the bread gets too hard, cut ½-inch cubes. Dry the cut cubes, preferably on a cooky sheet, in a preheated very slow, 250° F., oven about 20 minutes, or until brown. As an alternative sauté cubes over very low heat with just enough flavorful fat to cover the bottom of the skillet, turning to brown all sides.

CHEESE CROUTONS. Dip cubes of dry bread in melted butter, then in grated cheese, and brown as above in a preheated very slow, 250° F., oven about 20 minutes, or until brown. (Line the cooky sheet with foil to avoid a messy cleaning job.)

BREAKFAST CEREALS. Puffed wheat, bite-size shredded wheat, etc., may be substituted for croutons.

Eggs: In each soup plate, drop a raw egg. Beat it slightly, if desired, and pour boiling soup over it.

HARD-COOKED. Float slices in soup.

Herbs: Fresh or dried, these are inspiriting and pretty.

Lemon or Lime: Slice thin.

Meat: Crisp bacon bits and cooked sausage slices are delectable, as are cubes or strips of leftover meat or poultry.

Olives. Slice or cut wedges.

Onion Family: Snip chives or slice scallions into rings.

Pimento: Cut strips or cubes, or, with small fancy cutters, make stars, diamonds, etc.

Popcorn: Pass a bowl of plain or cheese popcorn as a substitute for croutons.

Spices: Powdered ginger, cloves, or other spice, sprinkled over soup before serving adds zest.

Vegetables:

COOKED. Use leftovers to garnish soup, or for delectable nutrition, heat a package of frozen mixed garden vegetables in soup.

RAW. If large, cut as indicated below, then boil until just tender in strained stock.

Asparagus, sliver	Greens, tear coarsely or shred
Beans (snap), cut julienne	Lima beans
Cabbage, shred	Mushrooms, slice
Carrots, cut julienne or dice	Okra, slice
Celery, dice	Onions, dice
Corn kernels	Peas
Cucumbers, slice	Squash (summer), dice
	Turnips, cut julienne or dice

Wine, dry. Add a spoon or two of this invisible garnish to soup before serving. The French often pass a pitcher of wine and let diners add their own to taste.

KINDS OF STOCK

An Italian phrase, *tutto fa brodo,* translates to "everything makes stock." And numerous and varied indeed are the ingredients that can go into it. Basically, however, stock is made from a combination of liquid and solid materials.

There are 2 varieties—meat and/or poultry, and vegetable. Stock made from beef is called brown stock; chicken makes white stock. Vegetable stock is usually used for water-cooking naturally tender foods.

INGREDIENTS FOR STOCK

No matter what the food—meat, poultry, vegetables—cut it small to expose as much surface as possible and thereby extract maximum flavor. Tough cuts of beef head the list of meats. To extract maximum flavor, cube or grind the meat and have the bones cracked. The bones gelatinize stock, and the marrow adds savor.

The average proportion is ⅔ meat to ⅓ bone.

Beef: Choose brisket, flank, plate, oxtail, shortribs.

Veal: Veal has less flavor than beef, but Middle European cooks often use it to extend the more expensive poultry when making chicken stock. Choose heel of round or shank.

Pork: The Chinese choose cubed pork shoulder or pigs' knuckles, and Mediterranean cooks often choose smoked ham in preference to veal for extending chicken stock. Chicken stock so augmented has wonderful rich flavor.

Lamb and Mutton: Chosen by cooks in countries such as the Balkans and Scotland, where sheep are plentiful, these make excellent, hearty soups, with intense characteristic flavor.

Poultry: Stewing chickens are used almost exclusively for stock, because young chicken has little flavor and other poultry is too expensive.

To expose maximum surface to the liquid, section poultry as follows: separate drumsticks from thighs, quarter breast, cut backbone in half. Heart, gizzard, and neck also go into the stock pot. Save the liver for broiling or frying, or poach it in the prepared stock.

When other meats are used to extend poultry the average proportion is 4 parts poultry to 1 part veal or pork.

Liquids for Stock: Most recipes direct either that meat and poultry be covered with water or give a stated amount of liquid. This is risky because the stock may then be too weak. To be sure it won't be, *use only enough liquid to almost cover the solid material.* If it's too strong, after cooking simply add cold water until stock is desired strength. To strengthen stock that's too weak, remove the cooked meat and poultry and reduce the liquid to desired strength by fierce open-pan boiling, or add a bouillon substitute, to taste.

While water is the major liquid used for stock, canned vegetable juice and liquid from cooked or canned vegetables also may be used.

Stock Vegetables: These give stock savor. Cut them coarsely to expose maximum surface to the liquid. Choose any or all of those listed below and adjust amounts to suit personal preference. Peeling is unnecessary because they're discarded after cooking.

CARROTS. Cut coarsely. Use some of their tops too.

CELERY. Cut coarsely. Remember to use the flavorful leaves as well.

CELERY ROOT. Cut coarsely.

GARLIC CLOVES. Crush. Peeling is unnecessary.

LEEK. Cut coarsely. Don't use too much of the green top, because it will discolor the stock.

ONIONS, yellow globe. Cut coarsely and don't peel, because the skin colors stock a rich yellow.

PARSLEY SPRIGS.

PARSLEY ROOT. Cut coarsely.

PARSNIP. Cut coarsely.

TOMATOES, FRESH. Cut coarsely, or use other Tomato Products.*

BUDGET MEMO: Ordinarily discarded portions of vegetables, such as woody stems of mushrooms and bruised leaves of greens, also contribute savor.

Additional Flavor Aids for Stock.

ACIDS. Dry wine, lemon juice, or vinegar helps to tenderize meat and poultry and keep seafood firm and white. Use 2 to 4 tablespoons acid, depending upon its strength, for each quart of liquid.

SEEDS. Dill, caraway, etc. Allow about 1 teaspoon to 1 quart liquid and add to the stock pot or to a finished soup.

BOUQUET GARNI. Often called for in French cookbooks, this is simply a clutch of herbs—parsley, tarragon, thyme, etc. Although tying them in cheesecloth is always suggested, this is unnecessary if the stock is to be strained. Dried herbs, about 1 teaspoon to 1 quart, may be substituted.

SALT. A necessity in stock. Your grandmother always added a dot of sugar, and you can enhance flavor with msg.

SPICES. Peppercorns add savor to the stock pot. When seasoning soup, liquid pepper is preferable to ground pepper, because the floating particles are unattractive.

Ginger, mace, cloves, etc., approximately ¼ teaspoon for 1 quart soup, lend subtle flavor, usually are added to soup rather than to stock.

BUDGET MEMO: To prove "tutto fa brodo," leftover sauces or gravies that don't contain either eggs or milk products also may be used to flavor-enrich a stock pot.

COOKING STOCK

Because tough meat and poultry are used to make stock, the water-cooking technique is a necessity. However, to extract maximum flavor, they are started half-covered with cold rather than with boiling water. To extract additional flavor, if time allows, soak meat and bones or poultry with the amount of salt called for in the recipe about an hour before cooking.

Boiling toughens meat and poultry, making it almost impossible for the juice to be extracted, so *simmer* only until the solid material is tender, and remove white meat sections of poultry as soon as they're done.

When a large proportion of bone is used, scum may rise to the surface at the beginning of cooking. Skim it off, but don't worry about the protein particles which form toward the end of cooking because the stock will be strained.

It is best to prepare stock a day ahead to give the flavors a chance to blend. In addition, the fat solidifies with refrigeration and is easy to remove. (The chefs call this "stock fat." Flavored by the meat and vegetables, it can be used when recipes call for "drippings.") However, if stock must be used immediately, skim with a spoon to remove fat. Tricks such as blotting with paper towels or straining through a linen napkin do not work.

Pattern for Meat Stock

Brown Stock
  1 large unpeeled onion, cut coarsely
  1 large carrot, cut coarsely
  4 stalks celery with leaves, cut coarsely
  6 sprigs parsley
  1 tablespoon dried herbs
  1 clove garlic, crushed
  1 tablespoon salt
  1 teaspoon peppercorns
  ⅛ teaspoon msg
  1 to 2 pounds bones, cracked
  6 tablespoons dry wine (optional)
  4 pounds beef, cut in chunks
  4 quarts cold water, approximately

Place vegetables, herbs, and seasonings in a large pot. Add bones and wine. Top with beef, and add enough water to almost cover. Cover pot and bring liquid to a boil rapidly. Reduce flame, and simmer gently until beef is tender, about 3 hours.

Remove meat and strain stock, discarding vegetables. Return

beef and marrow bones to stock and refrigerate overnight. Remove fat. Makes about 3 quarts stock.

NOTE: Many recipes direct that beef and bones be browned before cooking to darken stock. This wastes time and energy and toughens the exterior. If stock is not dark enough after cooking, use a gravy darkener.

White Stock

Proceed as for Brown Stock, above, substituting a sectioned stewing chicken for beef. Place tougher parts (gizzard, heart, neck) on vegetables, then meaty pieces and back, and end with breast, bony side down.

Clarifying Stock

If standing over a hot stove is your idea of fun, here's how to attain stock so clear that guests will be able to see the design in the bottom of the cup.

1. Strain cold stock from which all fat has been removed.
2. Measure and place it in a saucepan with 1 egg white and the crushed shell for each quart of stock.
3. Bring to a boil, stirring constantly.
4. Allow to settle 5 minutes, then strain through a sieve lined with several thicknesses of cheesecloth.

Vegetable Stock (Court Bouillon)

The French call vegetable stock *court bouillon* (*court* means "short") to differentiate it from the long, slow-cooking stock made with meat or poultry. Rarely served as soup, vegetable stock is usually prepared as a preliminary to water-cooking naturally tender foods.

Poaching in stock offers two advantages—the court bouillon adds to the flavor of the foods being water-cooked and is, in turn, infused with their savor. Then it's used as part of the sauce or served as a broth. The classic French names for some of these sauced delicacies are *Blanquette de Veau, Riz de Veau* or *Suprême de Volaille à Blanc, Homard à la Newburg, Filet de Sole Marguery.*

Foods for Poaching

Cubes of veal, veal sweetbreads (cube after cooking), calves' brains, chicken breasts (boned or not), whole fish, fish steaks or fillets, shrimp or lobster with or without shell, hard-shell crabs may be used. Any skin, bones, and shell, added with the vegetables, give the court bouillon extra flavor.

Pattern for Vegetable Stock

Water to half cover vegetables
1 teaspoon salt
2 tablespoons acid: dry wine, lemon juice, or other
¼ teaspoon peppercorns
1 small unpeeled onion, quartered
1 small carrot, cut coarsely
3 sprigs parsley
1 stalk celery and leaves
1 small clove crushed garlic, (optional)
1 teaspoon herbs: tarragon, basil, summer savory, etc.

Combine all ingredients in a large pot. Cover and boil about 20 minutes. Reduce heat, and when liquid stops bubbling add food to be poached. Cover pot and cook at a temperature below simmering until food is done.

The poached food will absorb more flavor and stay moist if allowed to cool in the court bouillon or in the following fumet. (Then shorten cooking time slightly to avoid toughening.)

Fumet

To intensify its flavor, court bouillon is usually reduced after the cooked poached foods have been removed, and is then called a *fumet*—fish, chicken, veal, etc.—and makes part of the sauce.

Remove water-cooked food and boil the court bouillon ("reduce by fierce open-pan boiling" is the French instruction). One quart court bouillon is usually reduced to 1 cup, and is enough to sauce ½ pound cooked food.

Escarole Soup

Every country has a version of vegetable soup, the soup taking the name of the predominant vegetable. The French simmer onions in fat before adding stock; the central Europeans choose cabbage and/or beets, the Italians spinach or escarole. The tenderness of the vegetable determines the cooking time and grated cheese often makes the accompaniment.

1 pound escarole, torn coarsely
4 cups Brown Stock*

Simmer escarole in stock about 15 minutes, or until wilted and tender. Makes 4 servings.

Lettuce Soup Margot

Very elegant. Substitute White Stock* for brown, and shredded lettuce for escarole. Pass toasted almond slivers.

JELLIED SOUPS

Stock made with bones usually solidifies upon refrigeration. If yours doesn't jell it's easy to rescue with commercial gelatin.

Taste the stock before chilling to be sure it's seasoned to perfection, and remember that it should be slightly saltier than normal because cold kills flavor. For piquancy, spice it with liquid pepper. Added ingredients, such as scallion rings, herbs, etc., may be stirred quickly through the jellied stock just before serving. Incidentally, jellied soup is more attractive when broken up with a fork before serving. Top garnishes also add pleasure.

Serve jellied soups COLD.

Pattern for Gelatinized Stock

1 teaspoon unflavored gelatin
1 tablespoon cold water
1 cup stock, brown or white, heated

Sprinkle gelatin on water. Add to stock and stir until dissolved. Refrigerate until firm. Increase amounts proportionately.

CREAM SOUPS

If there are objections to milk and cheese as such at your house, and you're concerned by this nutritional lack, try cream soups.

These gentle concoctions are composed basically of a sauce plus any desired puréed vegetable. Cream soups so composed are a lowest common denominator. The vegetables may be cooked in milk with which the sauce is made or, as in gourmet versions, chicken stock.

Cream soups may be as thick or as thin as you like, but the proportion for thin sauce is usual.

INGREDIENTS FOR CREAM SOUPS

Fat for Cream Soups: Choose delicate flavors, such as butter or margarine.

Milk Products for Cream Soups: Depending upon your battle with calories, choose from skim milk up to heavy cream as half the liquid. The richer the product, the more satiny the soup will be.

Liquids for Cream Soups: Use the liquid from cooked or canned vegetables, canned vegetable juice, or juice prepared by whirring fresh vegetables in an electric blender. Liquids from more than one vegetable may be combined. To intensify flavor, reduce any of these to about half by fierce open-pan boiling.

Vegetables for Cream Soups: You may use cooked or canned vegetables. Choose any you prefer and whir in a blender, purée, or use canned baby food. If starting with raw vegetables, for the following pattern, cook about 1 cup vegetables, cut small if necessary, in ½ cup any desired liquid.

Choose from asparagus, broccoli, cabbage, carrots, cauliflower, celery, corn, onions, peas, or spinach.

Flavoring Ingredients for Cream Soups.

For added savor, simmer 1 to 2 tablespoons diced vegetables—celery, onion, garlic, green pepper, or a combination—for 5 minutes in the fat called for in the sauce.

Paprika, saffron, or curry powder adds color and spice to cream soups. Herbs and seeds make a pretty garnish.

Pattern for Cream Soup

> ½ cup puréed vegetable and juice
> *or*
> ½ cup White Stock* and puréed vegetable
> ½ cup milk or cream
> 1 tablespoon butter
> 1 tablespoon flour
> ¼ teaspoon salt
> ⅛ teaspoon pepper

Combine as for Thin Sauce (see Chart for Flour-Thickened Sauces*). Makes 1 cup; may be increased, but add salt and pepper to taste.

DRIED VEGETABLE SOUPS

These hearty soups are delectable when winter winds blow cold. Split peas, whole peas, lentils, or any dried bean—black, navy, etc. —may be used. For a smooth soup, purée or whir all the dried vegetables in a blender after cooking; for a soup with texture interest, purée only half the quantity.

Binding Dried Vegetable Soups: This operation homogenizes the cooked soup because the heavy vegetable purée stays suspended in the liquid. To bind, use the proportion for Thin Sauce (see Chart for Flour-Thickened Sauces*), omitting the fat called for if the vegetables have been cooked with meat containing fat.

Liquid for Dried Vegetable Soups: Water is the usual choice, but for real savor use the liquid from water-cooked meats such as ham or tongue. Taste them beforehand and add water if they're too salty or too strong.

Dry wine also may be added—use 2 to 4 tablespoons for each quart of liquid.

Flavoring Ingredients for Dried Vegetable Soups: To augment flavor, any suggested stock vegetables may be cooked with the dried vegetables. Beef, pork, or lamb may be cooked with them too. Smoked varieties such as ham and uncooked sausage add fine flavor. Leftover meat bones, a ham skin, bits of leftover ham, tongue or corned beef scraps also make savory additions. And they will accept the usual complement of herbs, spices, or seeds.

Pattern for Dried Vegetable Soup

        1 pound (about 2 cups) any dried vegetable
        4 cups cold liquid
        2 teaspoons salt
        Stock vegetables, any variety (optional)
        1 pound meat (optional)

Soak dried vegetables in liquid overnight, or use the Quick-Soak Method.* Add enough additional liquid to make 4 cups in all and add salt. If using them, add stock vegetables and/or meat, and simmer about 3 hours, or until dried vegetables are completely tender. Purée, stock vegetables and all, or half of dried vegetables; cut meat into cubes. Bind if desired, and season to taste. Makes about 2½ quarts.

NOTE: Split peas and lentils do not require preliminary soaking. After cooking, about 1 tablespoon dry wine may be added for each cup of soup, and the soup also may be enriched with a pour of cream.

SAUCES, THE ESSENCE OF FINE DINING

As you've doubtless heard, fine cooking depends upon exquisite sauces. A great many excellent ones are quick and easy to make. Others depend upon good stock. Happily, canned beef stock, labeled "bouillon" or "consommé," makes a fine base for brown sauces. If you cook for an epicure, he'll probably take a dim view of your less than impeccable cooking efforts, but he'll also cheer when the cuisine is *oo là là*.

COOKED SAUCES

Basically, any cooked sauce contains fat, liquid, a thickening agent, and flavoring ingredients. It's considered perfect when it's flavorful and velvety smooth.

INGREDIENTS FOR SAUCES

Fats for Sauces: For delicate-flavored sauces choose butter. Meat drippings and stock fat may be used if their flavor enhances rather than overpowers the food they're to sauce. If you're a weight watcher, realize the fat may be omitted.

Liquids for Sauces: Stock, the tomato products, milk (including skim), and cream from light to heavy are most commonly used. The richer the cream, the more satiny the sauce will be. If the sauce is to be served at room temperature or cold, remember that it will be thicker too, because the butterfat will have hardened. Dry wine is rarely used alone, but a small amount adds wonderful savor to a sauce. The finished sauce will be approximately equal to the amount of liquid with which it was made.

Thickening Agents for Sauces: A variety of starches are used to thicken sauces. Egg or egg yolk is another thickening agent, 1 egg yolk being equal to 1 tablespoon flour.

FLOUR. This is most commonly used in America; cornstarch in the Orient. Other thickening agents are arrowroot, rice flour, and potato flour. Flour-thickened sauces are not as transparent and glossy as those thickened with other starches, and cornstarch and arrowroot produce a very clear sauce. To substitute, remember that flour has one-half the thickening power of any of the others.

BROWNED FLOUR. Recipes often call for browned flour as a sauce-darkening aid. Because about half the flour's thickening power is lost through this preliminary cooking, use slightly more than the usual amount.

To brown a quantity of flour, spread a fairly thin layer in a shallow pan and place it in a preheated moderate, 350° F., oven. Leave the oven door open and stir the flour occasionally to insure even browning. Store in a jar until ready for use. A small amount of flour may be browned in a skillet on top of the stove. Use a low flame and stir constantly.

EGG YOLKS. Egg-laced sauces are rich, flavorful, and a beautiful golden color. Although yolks are preferable, 1 egg may be substituted for 2 yolks.

Seasonings for Sauces: The usual trio—salt, pepper, and msg—is standard. One-quarter teaspoon salt, ⅛ teaspoon ground pepper or about 3 drops liquid pepper, and a dash of msg make a good beginning for 1 cup sauce.

Flavoring Ingredients for Sauces: For 1 cup sauce, cut fine and add to the fat called for in the sauce up to ¼ cup vegetable such as onion, garlic, celery, green pepper, mushrooms, singly or in combination, and/or any desired herb. Simmer until soft, about 5 minutes. Up to 2 tablespoons spices and/or seeds also may be simmered in the fat.

PREPARING SAUCES

Good equipment is important in the production of a smooth sauce. For best results, use a pan with a wide diameter (a shallow layer of liquid thickens more uniformly and quickly) and a wire whisk.

Stir constantly in the shape of a figure 8, being sure you reach all areas. Should the sauce lump, press it through a strainer and if necessary add more thickening.

The following chart gives proportions on which are based the majority of the sauces in the world. Because they are proportions, if one ingredient is increased or decreased, all the others must be increased or decreased proportionately.

Chart for Flour-Thickened Sauces

Sauce	Fat	Flour	Liquid
Thin	1 tablespoon	1 tablespoon	1 cup
Medium	2 tablespoons	2 tablespoons	1 cup
Thick	3 tablespoons	3 tablespoons	1 cup
Very Thick	4 tablespoons	4 tablespoons	1 cup

The normal method for preparation of sauces is unnecessarily complicated, and more time-consuming than the following Shaker-Jar Method.

1. Place the fat and most of the liquid in a saucepan and heat over a low flame until liquid warms and fat, if solid, melts.

2. In a jar with a tight cover or in a blender, place enough of the remaining liquid (it must be cold)—about 2 tablespoons for each tablespoon of flour called for—to liquefy the flour.

3. Add the flour, and shake or whir until lump free.

4. Pour flour mixture into heated mixture and stir constantly until the sauce comes to a boil.

5. Cover to prevent a skin from forming and, to keep hot, place over hot water.

Thin Sauce: This proportion is used for gravies, cream soups, and for binding dried vegetable soups. If any of these already contain fat, omit it in the above.

Medium Sauce: Use this proportion for any creamed meat or vegetable, and for bisques. Allow ½ cup sauce for 1 cup or ½ pound solid food.

Thick Sauce: Follow this proportion when a fairly heavy but not sludgy mixture is required, as in hot hors d'oeuvre, sauces for heating filled pancakes, and cooked mayonnaise.

Very Thick Sauce: Use this proportion for soufflés and croquettes.

White Sauce: Depending upon its use, follow any proportion in the sauce chart, and use milk as the liquid.

Cream Sauce: Depending upon its use, follow any proportion in the sauce chart and use cream as the liquid.

Cheese Sauce (Mornay): As soon as Medium White Sauce or Cream Sauce comes to a boil, add 1½ cups grated cheese. Remove from flame and stir until cheese melts. (If necessary, return to fire, but use a very low flame.)

EGG-LACED SAUCES

Egg yolks color, flavor enrich, and thicken sauces. Many of the classic French variety are egg-laced and finished with a fillip of wine. The liquids used can be milk or cream, stock, or a combination, depending upon whether the sauce will provide the background for meat, poultry, or seafood. For instance, sweetbreads would be sauced with half the liquid in which they were cooked and half cream; lobster in fish fumet and cream. The various names the sauces wear are *Allemande, Poulette,* and a large ETC.

The richer the cream, the more satiny the sauce, but when the stock has good flavor, if you're a weight watcher, you can combine it with skim milk. One egg yolk is the usual addition to 1 cup Medium Sauce, but up to 3 yolks may be used. With 3 yolks, omit the flour.

Preparing Egg-laced Sauce: A wire whisk will help insure success. Beat egg yolk slightly. Remove sauce from fire and, to avoid curdling, beat about ¼ cup of it into the egg yolk a tablespoon at a time. Pour warmed egg mixture back into sauce, stirring it in. If sauce is not thick enough, cook over low heat, stirring constantly, about a minute, or until it reaches desired consistency, but do not let it boil. Season to taste and stir in wine.

PRECAUTION: If an egg-laced sauce begins to curdle, remove from the heat immediately and beat vigorously until smooth with a rotary beater if you're not using a wire whisk. It probably will not need further cooking.

Egg lacing should be done just before the sauce is served, because there's a reheating problem—the additional heat can further cook the egg and cause curdling. The only way to reheat, and even this is chancy, is to stir the sauce constantly over hot, not boiling, water. One of the joys of a chafing dish is that egg lacing may be performed at table.

GLAZING SAUCES

The gorgeous brown topping that sauces in fine French restaurants wear comes from whipped cream. Add 1 tablespoon whipped cream to each cup of hot egg-laced sauce. Place prepared food in a serving dish, add sauce, and run under the broiler for a minute or two, until sauce is browned and bubbling.

Grated cheese sprinkled on before boiling, either in conjunction with the whipped cream or alone, also aids browning and adds flavor.

GRAVY

French and Italian cooks prefer natural pan juices; Americans often want their gravy thickened.

Basically gravy is made with juices left when meat, poultry, and seafood have been cooked. Usually, to increase the amount, additional liquids must be added. Choose from stock; stock and about 2 tablespoons per cup dry wine (red for beef; red, rosé, or white for poultry, veal, pork, or ham); water; or a combination. For cream gravy, use milk or cream, or commercial sour cream brought to room temperature.

Gravy from Roasts: Remove cooked meat or poultry from roasting pan and skim fat from liquid. Add up to ½ cup any of the above liquids, reserving a portion if gravy is to be thickened. In adding liquid, remember that gravy that's too strong can be diluted with water. If it's too weak, it can be strengthened with a stock substitute, but won't taste as good.

Stir to dissolve all the brown protein particles stuck to the pan. Chefs call this "deglazing." Bring to a boil, season to taste, and serve immediately.

To thicken, proceed as above, but use 1 tablespoon flour and if desired 1 tablespoon skimmed fat for each cup of liquid. Combine as directed in Chart for Flour-Thickened Sauces.*

Gravy from Skillet-Cooked Foods: Remove cooked food to a hot platter and add to the pan enough liquid to reach a depth of ¼ inch. For ease keep a pepper shaker filled with flour and shake in enough flour to achieve desired consistency, stirring constantly to prevent lumps. Bring to a boil and season to taste.

Gravy from Broiled Foods: Pour liquid from broiling pan into a skillet and proceed as for skillet-cooked foods.

Braising Liquid: Prepare as in Chart for Flour-Thickened Sauces,* using either the thin or medium proportion.

SUGGESTION: Leftover gravy makes a fine base for sauces or soup. If it's too strong, it may be diluted with vegetable juice and/or water.

Brown Sauce

> 1 clove garlic, diced fine
> ½ teaspoon salt
> ½ small onion, diced fine
> ¼ small green pepper, diced fine
> ½ small carrot, cut fine
> 4 tablespoons fat
> 2 cups Brown Stock*

Crush garlic with salt. Add vegetables and simmer in the fat until soft, about 5 minutes. Strain if desired, add beef stock, and thicken as for Medium Sauce (see Chart for Flour-Thickened Sauces*). Use Browned Flour* if desired, or color with gravy darkener.

Wine Sauce

Add ¼ cup dry red wine to Brown Sauce.

Spanish Sauce (Espagnole)

Prepare Brown Sauce, cooking 1 cup sliced mushrooms with the other vegetables, and substituting 1 cup tomato juice for 1 cup beef stock. Add ¼ cup dry red wine if desired.

Horseradish Sauce

Drain 3 tablespoons prepared horseradish and stir into strained Brown Sauce. Use with water-cooked meats, such as beef or tongue.

EASY-TO-MAKE SAUCES

Butter Sauces

These sauces are not inexpensive, but you're paying for a pleasant quartet: delectability, richness, ease, and speed.

Simple Butter Sauce

Melt ½ cup butter or ¼ cup butter and ¼ cup olive oil. When hot pour over 1½ to 2 pounds any meat or poultry that has been cooked by dry heat.

Maître d'Hôtel Butter

Depending upon acidity desired, add 2 to 3 tablespoons lemon juice or dry white wine to the above, and pour over any seafood.

Mustard Butter

Blend 1 teaspoon dry mustard with either of the above.

Garlic Butter (Sauce Provençale)

Crush a diced clove garlic to a paste with ⅛ teaspoon salt. Add ½ cup butter and simmer 5 minutes. Pour over 1½ to 2 pounds meat, poultry, or seafood cooked by dry heat, over 4 servings cooked vegetables, or toss with cooked pasta.

Herb Butter

Add 2 to 3 tablespoons finely cut herbs—parsley, tarragon, etc. —to any of the above. If using dried herbs, for complete flavor infusion warm with the melted butter for a few minutes.

Browned Butter (Beurre Noir)

In France this almost invariably sauces asparagus and artichokes. It translates to black or burned butter, and is easy to achieve. Simply cook butter to a rich nut-brown color, stirring for uniform browning. If desired after browning, add piquancy with a dash of acid such as wine vinegar. Capers add further flavor fillip. *Beurre noir* is good on vegetables and on variety meats such as brains.

Easy Steak Sauce

Remove cooked steak from skillet or broiler, and simmer a diced clove of crushed garlic in the drippings or pan liquid about 5 minutes. Season to taste and pour over steak.

Horseradish Cream

> ½ cup commercial sour cream
> 3 tablespoons horseradish, approximately
> ⅛ teaspoon salt

Combine ingredients and season to taste, adding more horseradish if necessary. Serve with cold sliced meats.

VII

International Specialties—
the Cereal World

If you're just getting acquainted with your kitchen, you may think that anything with a name as imposing as international specialties is too tough to tackle. However, a firm grasp of the fundamentals detailed in the preceding chapters will enable you to prepare any of them with the greatest of ease.

Many of these delectable specialties are based on cereals, rice, and macaroni—foods that are inexpensive thanks to their abundance. In addition, their high starch content makes them an excellent source of energy.

CEREALS

Cereals add nourishment to any meal. For instance, buttered and sugared oatmeal deep in cream makes a heart-warming supper on a winter's night. Cereals also go into baked foods such as muffins and cookies.

Cereals contain protein, and whole-grain and restored cereals boast iron and B-vitamins as well. Home-cooked breakfast cereals cost less than the ready-to-eat varieties and also offer more concentrated food value. Brands of cereal vary only slightly, so taste-test several, keeping flavor and economy in mind.

To avoid weevil infestation, store cereals in covered containers in a cool dry place. Should any become contaminated, discard and because the weevils travel, examine your remaining hoard. Then spray your cupboards with a commercial insecticide.

COOKING CEREALS

Homemakers of yore cooked cereal for hours and hours and hours in the belief that flavor would be improved. Science has proved that cooking beyond the point of "doneness" is valueless and wastes fuel. Today label directions for preparing cereal are tested by the companies and, therefore, are usually accurate.

Cooking cereal with dried apricots, prunes, and the like eliminates the need for sugar and adds flavor, food value, and variety. A pour of honey, fruit juice, maple sirup, or molasses can replace sugar *and* cream.

Cover cooked cereal to prevent a skin from forming and keep it hot over boiling water. Reheat over boiling water too.

After cooking, the amount of cereal will just about equal the amount of liquid used.

Whole-Grain Cereal: If you're a Southerner, you know and enjoy hominy. If your family background is the Balkans, you have the same rapport with whole wheat. You also know that cooking these cereals until tender takes TIME.

Presoaking cuts cooking time in half. Simply boil 2 cups water for each cup whole-grain cereal. Add cereal, return the water to a boil, turn off flame, and allow it to soak about 7 hours. Use the same water for cooking, adding more if necessary to prevent burning, then cook about 2 hours, or until tender.

Quick-Cooking Cereal: Follow label directions, but realize that stirring makes cereal gummy and is unnecessary if the water is boiling furiously when the cereal is added. Pour cereal into salted water gradually to keep it at a boil, and boil until cooked.

There's an alternate method. For a creamy consistency, place cereal in pot, add cold water and salt, and bring water to a boil. Stir once, then reduce flame and simmer until water is absorbed.

Granular Cereal: To avoid lumps in cornmeal and farina, combine the amount of cereal called for with an equal measure of cold water. Bring the remaining amount of water in the recipe to a boil and proceed as for quick-cooking cereals, above.

Fried or Baked Cereal: "Mush" is the unfortunate name for a thick cooked cereal. Fried, it is a down-on-the-farm breakfast treat.

It may be made with any granular cooked cereal—cornmeal, farina, rice, hominy grits, etc.

When preparing cereal as a preliminary to frying, reduce the cooking liquid by one-eighth. Turn the hot cooked cereal into a narrow pan, cover or brush with melted butter to prevent a crust from forming, and cool until firm.

Turn out and cut in ¼-inch to ½-inch slices. If desired, dip in dry cereal, flour, or slightly beaten egg. Heat *to* the smoking point enough fat to cover the bottom of a skillet and add the sliced cereal. Using a medium high flame brown both sides, or if speed isn't essential, fry over a low flame. (You'll reap the rewards of additional crispness and a well-dried center.) Serve fried mush with butter and sirup or with meat gravy, sorghum, or molasses.

Squares of cooked cereal may be butter-brushed and baked on a buttered pan. Allow about 30 minutes in a preheated moderate 350° F. oven.

See Potpourri of Kitchen Aids for Chart for Cooking Cereal.*

RICE

Rice is responsible for almost as many tales of cooking calamities as are baking powder biscuits. But because it combines felicitously with many foods and can grace so many courses of a menu, it seems better to have imperfectly cooked rice than to have no rice at all. Happily, some varieties present fewer difficulties than others, converted rice being the easiest to cook.

Although the converting process destroys some food value, converted white rice is more nutritious than any other except brown rice. Brown rice rates high in food value because the germ and fat haven't been removed. Because of the fat content, it may become rancid with long storage, so smell and check before use.

Regular rice varies in grain size, and packages will be marked short, medium, or long grain. Short- and medium-grain rice particles cling together after cooking—a necessity in the Orient where chopsticks are in play—so choose these varieties when rice is to be molded, as in a ring.

Wild rice is the seed of a grass, rather than a grain. It grows wild in shallow lakes and marshy lands and requires special skill in gathering. Respect should be accorded it, if only because of its astronomical price.

Store rice in a cupboard, covered to protect it from dust. Cooked rice (store covered) will keep in the refrigerator about 5 days, in the ice-cube section about 3 weeks, in the freezer about a year.

COOKING RICE

Rice is tenderized by cooking in liquid, and although it's usually boiled it also may be baked. To preserve food value and prevent gumminess, don't wash rice before cooking or rinse it after cooking.

Chopsticks are best for stirring rice, but, to prevent gumminess, avoid excessive stirring. Overcooking makes rice pasty.

To "dry" rice after cooking, lift grains gently with chopsticks or a fork so steam can escape.

To reheat rice, add enough water or flavorful liquid to cover bottom of pan, cover and heat over a low flame.

One cup raw rice yields approximately 3 cups cooked rice.

Liquid for Cooking Rice: The amount of liquid needed varies with the length of time the rice has been stored, and with the variety. Usually long-grain rice cooks more quickly than short grain; brown rice takes longer than white. If the liquid evaporates before rice is tender, add a small quantity of additional liquid.

A bit of any flavorful fat added to the liquid will help keep rice from boiling over.

The average proportion is 1 part rice to 2 parts liquid.

The more flavorful the liquid, the more delicious the rice will be. Choose from water, vegetable juice, stock, or milk, singly or in combination.

Seasonings: Choose any you like, adding them to the liquid and allowing 1 teaspoon herbs, spices, seeds for each cup of rice.

To Mold Rice: Drain cooked rice, if necessary, and rinse large or small molds with cold water. Fill with hot rice, packing it firmly, and place in a preheated slow, 325° F., oven 5 minutes. To turn out, loosen edges, place a warmed serving plate over the mold and invert quickly.

Pattern for Boiled Rice: Brown, White, or Wild

¼ cup rice
½ cup cold liquid
¼ teaspoon salt
1 teaspoon fat (optional)

Place all ingredients in a 2-quart saucepan. Cover pan and bring liquid to a boil rapidly. Stir through once, reduce heat to very low, and cook about 15 minutes, or until a grain pressed between the fingers is just tender with no hard core. (If the water boils too rapidly during cooking, tilt pan cover to slow cooking.) Makes 1 serving; may be increased.

Mary's Lemon Custard Rice

This is delectable with chicken.

2½ cups milk, divided
1 cup white rice
1 teaspoon salt
3 eggs, beaten slightly
1 tablespoon butter, melted
Juice and grated rind of 1 lemon

In top of double boiler, scald 1½ cups milk. Add rice and salt and place over boiling water in bottom of double boiler. Cook covered about 40 minutes, or until rice is tender. Combine with remaining milk, eggs, butter, lemon juice, and rind. Add salt to taste. Turn into an attractive casserole and bake in a preheated moderate, 350° F., oven about 25 minutes, or until a knife tip inserted in the center comes out clean. Makes 8 servings.
NOTE: The rice may be cooked in water, rather than milk, and obviously leftover rice may be used.

Lemon Custard Rice Pudding
Proceed as above, adding 1 cup sugar to beaten eggs. Serve for dessert, and pass a bowl of dark brown sugar and a pitcher of cream. A shaker of cinnamon probably will not be snubbed.

PASTA

"Pasta" is the Italian word for what the Encyclopaedia Britannica calls "macaroni," and nutritionists refer to as "alimentary pastes." The same dough makes all forms, and the specific names come from the shapes of the finished product. Capelli d'angelo, for instance, the most slender of the tubular variety, means "angel's hair." To confuse things, it's sometimes erroneously called vermicelli, which translates to "little worms." Noodles differ from pasta only through the addition of eggs to the dough.

Because it's bland, pasta is fine for embracing robust and forth-right sauces, and talented European cooks call upon it to extend small amounts of meat, poultry, and seafood.

STORING PASTA

Store pasta in a cupboard, covered to protect it from dust. Cooked pasta (store covered) will keep in the refrigerator about 5 days, in the ice-cube section about 3 weeks, in the freezer about a year.

COOKING PASTA

Pasta is easy to cook, and a large pot with a colander inset simplifies things further. To prevent pasta from sticking together, be sure the water is boiling vigorously before adding the pasta, and keep it at a boil throughout cooking. Stir occasionally to be sure the pasta isn't sticking to the bottom of the pot. Add large pieces of pasta, such as lasagne, to boiling water one at a time.

To avoid breaking long strands of pasta, push them gently into the boiling water as they soften. As with rice, a bit of fat added to the water will help keep it from boiling over.

Pasta should resist the teeth—*al dente* is the Italian term—so, to avoid a flabby mass, taste test it frequently toward the end of the cooking time called for. Package labels normally state the approximate amount of time required for the different varieties.

Pour pasta into a colander after cooking, and to avoid a steam burn hold the pot with both hands and pour toward you. Rinsing, sometimes called for, is unnecessary, except in the case of large pasta such as lasagne. Then it is imperative, to keep the noodles from sticking together.

To reheat pasta, first add enough water to cover bottom of pan, and heat, covered, over a low flame. Leftover pasta and its sauce also may be reheated, covered, either over a flame in a top-of-the-range casserole, or in a moderate, 350° F., oven.

Two ounces pasta make 1 serving. After cooking, ½ pound pasta makes about 4 cups.

Pattern for Pasta

    1 teaspoon salt
    2 quarts water
    ½ pound pasta: spaghetti, noodles, etc.

Use a large saucepan and bring salt and water to a vigorous boil. Add pasta slowly so water continues to boil, then stir through once. Depending upon its size, boil pasta from 4 to 15 minutes, or until just tender, stirring gently occasionally to prevent sticking. Drain and season to taste with salt, pepper, and msg.

NOTE: To avoid diluting sauces or to hold pasta until needed, suspend the colander of cooked pasta above a small amount of boiling water (for convenience use the pot in which the pasta was boiled) and cover it. Pasta will be completely drained in about 10 minutes, and may be held about 20 minutes if it's to be tossed with a buttery sauce. Combine with sauce, preferably just before serving.

GARNISHES FOR PASTA

Melted butter makes a rich but simple addition for tossing cooked pasta. Garlic Butter* or Herb Butter* add interest. Allow about 1 tablespoon per serving.

Grated cheese for spooning over pasta is an obvious and wonderful addition.

VIII

The Virtuous Vegetable

Research indicates that vegetables were snubbed even before Neolithic times—certain proof that man's tastes are tenacious. Hopefully, you and yours enjoy them because they offer so many advantages.

They come in a rainbow of colors and a medley of textures to add variety to menus. They are nutritionally valuable at small cost. When speed is a requisite, raw vegetables qualify as "instant" and many varieties cook tender in about five minutes. Finally, being fairly bland, they accept all manner of sauces and seasonings as evidenced in recipes from countries such as France and China that are noted for exquisite cuisine.

BUYING VEGETABLES

While fresh corn in January is a charming anomaly, vegetables not only taste best at peak season, but also are nutritionally superior and more economical. Depend on your newspaper or radio for peak season information.

Although it's illegal in some areas to handle vegetables at market, your best assurance of quality is a personal selection. Should this privilege be denied you, an immediate return of inferior produce will encourage the grocer to fill your basket with top quality.

If you do your own choosing, don't be destructive. To test firmness, press vegetables such as tomatoes between your palms rather than poking or pinching, replace husks on ears of corn, etc.

Because attractive appearance indicates fine flavor and top food value, look for fresh clean vegetables, and remember that size is no indication of quality.

STORING VEGETABLES

If you've ever enjoyed the flavor of sun-warmed tomatoes from your own garden, you know that vegetables begin losing savor almost immediately after picking. Even though some varieties, such as carrots, keep fairly well, they too lose flavor, color, and food value after harvesting. The refrigerator offers some protection, but most fresh vegetables taste better if stored no longer than a day after purchase. Before storing, discard any with decayed or soft areas. A vegetable crisper performs better if at least two-thirds full but is still not as effective as plastic wrap or bags. After peeling and/or cutting, store any vegetable in close wrapping.

WASHING VEGETABLES

Vegetables in markets today rarely require scrubbing. Simply rinse with lukewarm water. Some will mold if washed before storing.

CANNED VEGETABLES

Canned vegetables offer more food value than market vegetables because canners pick vegetables at peak season and process them promptly. However, they do lose food value in time, keep best in a cool place. Canned vegetables require no preliminary preparation, thereby saving time and eliminating waste.

However, the intense heat produced by pressure to which they must be subjected to kill the botulinus bacillus causes canned vegetables to lose the crisp, bright flavor of fresh vegetables cooked until just tender. Because much of the food value is in the liquid in the can, save it for sauces, soups, stews, or gravies. Canned vegetables may be added to braised dishes. Add them at the end of the cooking period because only heating is required.

A #303 can with stated weights of from 16 to 17 ounces holds approximately 2 cups of vegetable and liquid; makes about 4 servings.

Heating Canned Vegetables: To avoid further cooking, place the liquid from the can in a saucepan and boil it rapidly, uncovered, until reduced to about a third. Add the vegetable and when hot— a matter of seconds—serve with the reduced liquid and any other desired additions you fancy; basil with tomatoes, celery seeds with green beans, tarragon with carrots, etc.

FROZEN VEGETABLES

Unless you harvest your own vegetables, realize that frozen vegetables rate higher in flavor and food value than either fresh or canned.

Frozen vegetables are packed in so many different weights only an approximation of the number of servings is possible. Size of the package is some indication of the amount it contains, but your experience is the most reliable guide.

As an approximation, a 9- to 12-ounce package makes about 2 to 3 servings.

Frozen vegetables will keep in the refrigerator ice-cube section three months, in the freezer a year.

Frozen vegetables have been cooked (blanched) before freezing to halt aging. Therefore, about the only preparation necessary for most is thawing if they're to be served at room temperature, as in salads; or heating, preferably in a flavorful liquid.

A block of small vegetables such as peas—or vegetables cut small, such as asparagus tips—may be heated in their thawed liquid. Unfortunately, most package directions call for too much water and too much time.

For maximum flavor and food value, thaw frozen vegetables just before use if they're to be served cold. Otherwise heat as directed below.

If you need only part of a package, hit it with the flat side of a cleaver to separate small vegetables, such as peas. For other vegetables such as broccoli or spinach, cut with a freezer saw.

Frozen vegetables may be added to braised dishes. Thaw and add them at the end of the cooking period, because only heating is required.

Heating Frozen Vegetables:

UNTHAWED. Place in saucepan and heat over a very low flame, breaking the block with a fork as the ice melts. When they are completely thawed, cover pot, bring to a boil, and for maximum flavor and food value cook only until heated.

THAWED. Thaw in cooking vessel and proceed as above.

GARNISHES, SAUCES, AND SEASONINGS FOR VEGETABLES

Vegetables cooked until just tender have innate beauty of color and form, but, as always, compatible accompaniments add the interest of variety, and vegetable combinations also enliven your repertoire.

The following suggestions will give you an example of the color, shape, and texture contrasts that are possible: spinach with mushroom slices, lima beans with tomatoes, brussels sprouts and pecans in lemon butter, corn with green pepper and pimento, creamed cauliflower dotted with black olive wedges.

Fats: Because they contain no fat, vegetables take well to enrichment, and any flavorful fat makes them more tempting.

Choose from butter or margarine; oils such as olive, sesame, peanut, or soy; meat or poultry drippings; stock fat. Allow about 1 tablespoon fat for each cup or 4 servings of vegetable.

To vary the flavor, add to 1 tablespoon fat any of the following: a pinch of spice, such as nutmeg, dry mustard, or curry powder; a dash of liquid pepper or Worcestershire; ½ teaspoon quick-browning aid; ¼ teaspoon lemon or lime juice; ¼ teaspoon capers.

*Garlic Butter.**

Buttered Crumbs: On a French restaurant menu the word *Polonaise* means buttered bread crumbs are coming. In any language, use fine dry bread crumbs (usually white), allowing about 2 teaspoons butter and 1 tablespoon crumbs per serving. Melt the butter and remove from the flame. Add the crumbs and stir until well coated. Top any desired vegetables.

To brown the crumbs, toast in a skillet over a medium high flame, stirring for even browning, or in a very slow, 250° F., oven. Then add to the melted butter.

Cheese: Grated or crumbled cheese is a good companion for vegetables. For grating, choose Swiss, Parmesan, or Romano. Crumble semisoft cheeses such as Roquefort or blue and allow about a tablespoon per serving.

Nuts: Broken pecans, blanched almond slivers or sliced Brazil nuts offer crisp contrast. Butter-toast any beforehand if desired in a moderate, 350° F., oven about 10 minutes.

Cooked Sauces: These should swathe, rather than drown vegetables. Allow about 1 cup sauce to 2 cups cooked vegetables.

HOLLANDAISE. This enhances asparagus and members of the cabbage family.

WHITE SAUCE,* CREAM SAUCE,* CHEESE SAUCE.* These are fine on most vegetables. As much as one-third of the liquid in the sauce may be the water in which the vegetable was cooked, or reduced liquid from canned vegetables.

Herbs: Approximately 1½ teaspoons fresh herbs, cut fine, add savory bouquet to a serving of vegetables. Use ½ teaspoon dried herbs.

Lemon Juice: This tangy standby brings out a vegetable's flavor. Use the juice and/or grated rind.

Lime Juice: Choose as a change from lemon, above.

Seeds: Scattered over vegetables, these add distinctive flavor and texture contrast. Amounts vary with personal preference. Begin with ¼ teaspoon of whole seeds such as celery, caraway, poppy, toasted sesame, and work your way up to perfection.

Herb Bouquet

Choose 4 or 5 unusual raw vegetables that offer variety of color, texture, and flavor. Asparagus, wax beans, Belgian endive leaves, green pepper, and turnip sticks make an interesting collection. Make a bed of crushed ice in an attractive bowl and arrange vegetables on it.

Bouquet
    1 teaspoon salt
    4 drops Liquid Pepper,* approximately
    Dash msg
    ½ teaspoon any desired herb, such as tarragon,
        basil, or combination of herbs or seeds

Combine salt, liquid pepper, and msg. Add herbs and/or seeds and crush. Makes 1 serving.

Serve the herb bouquet in small attractive containers, such as open salt cellars, for dipping. Choose from any of the following raw vegetables:

Asparagus	Broccoli flowers
Wax beans	Brussels sprouts
Belgian endive leaves, separated	Carrot sticks

Cauliflower flowers	Mushroom slices or buttons
Celery sticks	Radishes
Cucumber	Scallions
Fennel	Tomato wedges
Green pepper	Turnip sticks

COOKING VEGETABLES

By now it should be obvious that there are a limited number of basic cooking methods. And vegetables are accorded the same treatment as meat, poultry, and shellfish. Realize, however, that even with careful cooking about a fourth of a vegetable's food value is lost. (After cooking, both food value and flavor diminish rapidly.) To offer both flavor and nourishment, when possible cook vegetables whole, peel them only when necessary, and peel thin, because most of the food value is in the area between flesh and skin. Finally, peel just before cooking and cook in the shortest possible time.

To Test Doneness: Use a cake tester or ice pick—a fork makes too many holes—and pierce to the center of the vegetable. When the vegetable is tender, the tester can be inserted easily.

SUGGESTION: Save any leftover cooking liquid to serve with the vegetable or add it to soups, sauces, gravies, etc.

Add leftover vegetables to soups, casserole dishes, sauces, fritters, soufflés. Serve mashed or in salads. Some, such as corn kernels and dried beans, may be fried.

BOILING VEGETABLES

The only difference between water-cooking vegetables and water-cooking proteins is that vegetables will not toughen with high heat, so the term used is boiling.

Bright attractive color is part of a vegetable's charm. To maintain it, realize that *green* vegetables should be cooked in very little water and uncovered for the first 3 minutes. Acid added to the water destroys color.

Red and *white* vegetables keep their color when about 1 teaspoon acid is added for each cup of water.

SUGGESTION: To be sure of amount of water, place vegetables in pan and pour over water that has been brought to a boil in a kettle.

Pattern for Boiling Vegetables

½ teaspoon salt
1 pound any desired vegetable
Boiling water

Place salt and vegetable in saucepan. Add a small amount of boiling water to small vegetables or to vegetables cut small. Half cover large vegetables with water.

Cover pan (except as noted for green vegetables, above) and boil rapidly until just tender. Drain, garnish, and serve immediately.

PARBOILING VEGETABLES

This is a preliminary tenderizing method for vegetables that require softening before stuffing or broiling. Place them in boiling water and test 5 minutes after the water has returned to a boil. The vegetables should be soft enough to scoop out for stuffing, or tender enough to require just a short broiling period. Parboiling also may be used to speed frying.

STEAMING VEGETABLES

Steaming takes longer than boiling but conserves more food value. Place prepared vegetables on a perforated rack in a pan and add boiling water to the level of the rack. Cover to keep water at a boil, and steam until vegetables are tender, allowing about 10 minutes longer than for boiling, and adding more boiling water if necessary to keep it at rack level.

BUDGET MEMO: Vegetable steamers may be purchased, but an improvised steamer (colander or sieve) is equally effective.

MASHING VEGETABLES

Potatoes boiled or baked soft are the most obvious candidates, but many vegetables may be mashed. Vegetables cooked soft enough to force through a sieve or ricer are called riced or puréed vegetables.

Pattern for Mashed Vegetables

½ cup vegetable, cooked soft
1 tablespoon flavorful fat
1 tablespoon milk or cream

½ teaspoon salt
⅛ teaspoon pepper
Dash msg

Mash vegetable until smooth. Heat the fat in the milk. Stir into
the vegetable and beat, adding more milk or part of the vegetable
liquid, if necessary, to achieve a light fluff. Season to taste with salt,
pepper, and msg. Makes 1 serving.
NOTE: An egg yolk beaten in with the liquid binds and enriches
mashed vegetables. Use one yolk for up to 4 servings.

BRAISING VEGETABLES

Any vegetable may be cooked in liquid either in the oven or on
a burner. Peel if necessary, and if desired for speed or for appearance cut in sections (halves to sixteenths), cube, slice, or dice. Cauliflower or broccoli may be separated into flowers, etc.

Fats: Choose a flavorful fat such as butter, margarine, or cream.

Liquid: Use flavorful liquids such as milk, cream, stock, or
gravy.

Flavorful Additions: From 1 teaspoon to 1 tablespoon herbs,
seeds, or spices may be added with the vegetable.

Cooking time depends upon age, size, and variety of the vegetable.

OVEN BRAISING. The temperature may vary from very slow, 250°
F., to very hot, 450° F. Place vegetable in baking dish, season with
salt, pepper, and msg. Dot with shortening or brush with liquid fat,
and add enough additional liquid to reach a depth of about ¼ inch
in pan. Add any desired herbs, seeds, etc., cover, and bake until just
tender.

BURNER BRAISING. Place vegetable in a pan, preferably in a single
layer, and add enough liquid to reach a depth of ¼ inch. Add any
desired seasonings, herbs, seeds. Cover and cook gently until vegetable is tender, up to 20 minutes, depending upon age, size, and
variety, adding more liquid if necessary to prevent burning. Season
to taste and serve the vegetable with the pan liquid.

BAKING VEGETABLES

Although baking takes longer than boiling, it saves fuel if the
oven is already in use, and also offers interesting variety. Hard vegetables such as potatoes and winter squash are the kind usually baked.

Cooking time depends upon the age, size, and variety of the vegetable.

The oven temperature may vary from very slow, 250° F., to very hot, 450° F.

Stuffed Vegetables: Seed vegetable if necessary. Parboil green peppers and eggplant; boil whole onions until tender (remove center after cooking), or scoop a portion from the inside, making a shell about 1 inch thick, and boil the shell. (Chop and use the center in the stuffing). Stuff with any desired mixture—meat, vegetables, rice, or combinations—and bake as in Oven Braising, above.

BROILING VEGETABLES

Broiled vegetables usually accompany meat, and are placed on the broiler pan with it. Peel vegetables when necessary and halve, quarter, or, if large, slice.

Brushing vegetables with fat before broiling is nice but unnecessary, as is basting them with drippings from the meat. Broiling temperatures depend upon the meat and can range from moderate to very high. Turning is unnecessary.

FRYING VEGETABLES

This cooking method is the most destructive of food value. Peel vegetables if necessary, and halve, quarter, or slice if large.

SHALLOW FAT. Use just enough flavorful fat to reach a depth of about ¼ inch in the pan. Using a medium-high flame; heat fat *to* the smoking point. Add vegetable in a single layer and fry covered, turning to brown both sides. If vegetable is not tender after browning, reduce flame and continue to cook gently to desired firmness.

DEEP FAT (FRENCH-FRIED). Dip small vegetables, or large vegetables that have been sliced or cubed, in Egg-Crumb Coating* or Fritter Batter* and fry in fat heated to 375° F. until brown, about 10 minutes, depending upon size. (Potatoes aren't normally coated.)

Although the basic principles apply to most vegetables, the following do better with special pampering.

THE ONION FAMILY

The onion family's sprightly flavor and pungency have rescued many a dish from dullness. Onions also are valuable nutritionally. Here are some of the many varieties.

BUYING AND STORING DRY ONIONS

Yellow: These multipurpose domestic onions are first choice for soups, stews, sauces, etc., and also are fine raw. Store on a kitchen shelf and check for sprouting, because if sprouts aren't removed the onion will rot. (Use the raw sprouts in salads or as a garnish.) Even diced onions keep overnight if wrapped closely in transparent plastic wrap, refrigerated, covered with foil for double insurance.

White: These are always more expensive than yellow onions, and not necessarily milder. Choose the small variety for serving whole in a stew or for creaming. White eating onions such as Bermuda and Valencia are generally too sweet to use for cooking. Store as above.

Purple: These may be called California, Italian, or Spanish onions. Diced or sliced, they add gorgeousness to a salad, but are too sweet for cooking. Store as you do yellow onions.

Shallots (Eschalots): An ingredient in great demand in French cookbook recipes, these are stored as directed for yellow onions. Yellow onions may be substituted measure for measure.

Instant Minced Onion: This is an excellent labor-saving substitute for diced onion, but at a cost, so use only when a recipe calls for a small amount of onion. Substitute in an approximate proportion of one part instant onion for four parts fresh.

BUYING AND STORING GREEN ONIONS

Scallions: There are young white onions pulled before the bulb has fully formed. Choose bunches with fresh green tops. Cut off roots and discard outer skin if torn, wilted, or dirty. Rinse and refrigerate in transparent plastic wrap or in pliofilm bags. Normally eaten raw, scallions are often sliced by the Chinese into thin rings and cooked with other foods, as in fried rice.

Leeks: Choose and prepare as you do for scallions. To be sure all soil is removed, cut in half lengthwise and examine closely between the leaves. These are fine cooked in chicken stock. Diced raw leeks also make a delicious addition to salads. The French call them "poor man's asparagus" and braise them in chicken stock. Store as for scallions.

Chives: Choose fresh green bunches and rinse. When dry, snip fine and use as a garnish. Store as for scallions.

PREPARATION

Peeling: Soak globe onions in warm water about 20 minutes for ease in peeling. To stay your tears, peel a quantity of onions under cold water. Rinse away any black dust under the onion skin. Discard any softened portions.

Slicing: Slice from root to stem and peel after slicing.

Dicing: Remove root close to base of peeled onion and cut in half from root to stem. Cover a chopping board with wax paper. Place onion on it flat side down with the root end on your left. Make ¼ inch cuts through to the board from the stem almost to the root. (If the onion is large make 1 or 2 additional cuts, parallel to the board, again almost to the root.) Slice onion perpendicular to board, making dice as large or small as desired.

Onion Juice: Cut onion in half crosswise; hold over a bowl, and scrape the flat side hard with a teaspoon.

NOTE: For milder flavor, cover pan when onions are half cooked. (Also see Vegetable Chart.*)

Rules for Special Vegetables

Basic principles are similar. (Also see Vegetable Chart.*)

GARLIC

BUYING

Actually an herb, this is such an important adjunct to cooking that it can be grouped with vegetables. Choose either white- or red-skinned garlic, being sure the bulb (the whole bud) is plump with cloves (sometimes called "teeth"). Refrigeration is unnecessary. Pungency varies with age. Odor and juiciness will tell you when to use more or less.

PREPARATION

Peeling: Smash cloves with the flat side of a broad knife or cleaver and pull loosened skin off.

Crushing: For even flavor distribution, dice garlic fine and crush to a paste in a mortar and pestle. Cheer if the recipe calls for salt too, because it acts as an abrasive, making crushing easier.

POTATOES (WHITE)

BUYING

There are many varieties, and all are least expensive from June through August. As a blanket rule, choose mealy-textured potatoes such as Idaho or Maine for baking, French frying, mashing, and boiling. Waxy-textured potatoes are better for salads, creaming, and scalloping, and incidentally take longer to cook.

Because they've lost moisture during storage, old potatoes are best for potato pancakes or dumplings. They're also superior for salads because they absorb more salad dressing.

In any variety, choose firm, smooth potatoes of fairly regular shape. Surface incisions are spade marks and detract only from appearance. Reject potatoes with perforations (worm damage) or green sunburn spots.

BUDGET MEMO: Potatoes should be reasonably clean. If immaculate and/or paper-wrapped, price but not quality will be higher.

STORING

Although a quantity of any variety of potato may be stored in a cool, dry place, early potatoes will keep only about 2 weeks. Keep potatoes in the dark too, to avoid green discoloration. Store small quantities in the kitchen and pick off and discard any sprouts. Even if sprouted potatoes have softened, they're still usable. Once you've smelled a rotten potato, advice to discard it will seem superfluous.

PREPARATION

Remove and discard sprouts and any green portions. In the interest of saving energy, remember that large potatoes will take less time to peel than their equal weight of small potatoes.

If it's imperative to peel potatoes ahead and you don't have a commercial anti-oxidant, allow them to soak in cold water to prevent darkening, but to conserve food value use the soaking water for cooking them.

COOKING

For maximum food value, boil potatoes in their jackets. Baking unpeeled is the second choice, because peeled, cut potatoes lose the majority of their nutrients.

Baking (Unpeeled): The oven temperature may range from very slow, 250° F., to very hot, 450° F. At 450° F. they'll take less time and results will be better. The longer potatoes bake, the crustier they become. For a hard, crisp crust, place potatoes on the oven floor (protect it with foil) and bake at least an hour, turning halfway through cooking. For soft-skinned baked potatoes, rub skins with fat before baking and place on a shallow tin or package in aluminum foil.

Test doneness by pressing with a towel-protected hand—they should feel soft throughout. To avoid sogginess, don't cut or prick potatoes after baking. Rather, crack them open with the heel of your hand immediately upon removal from the oven.

BUDGET MEMO: Bake one or two extra potatoes and store to use for frying, mashing, stuffing, etc.

Baking (Peeled): Coat with a flavorful fat and bake at temperatures noted above in an uncovered pan with low sides, allowing 30 minutes to 2 hours or longer.

Frying (Shallow Fat): *Raw*—fry slices in enough fat to reach a depth of a ¼ inch in a heavy covered skillet about 15 minutes, using a low flame. Uncover when potatoes are just tender, increase flame, and continue cooking until brown, about 10 minutes. (A sprinkle of paprika speeds browning.) *Cooked*—fry slices as above, but uncovered, and turn to brown both sides. Depending upon where you're from, onions fried with the potatoes earn them the title O'Brien, Lyonnaise, or German-fried.

Deep Fat (French Fry): Cut any desired shape—chips, strips, shreds. To firm softened potatoes, soak in ice water. Dry thoroughly before dropping into fat. When they are browned, remove from fat with a slotted spoon. Place in a brown paper sack to absorb grease, add salt, and shake until potatoes are coated.

POTATOES (SWEET)

There are two general types. One has fawn-colored skin, yellow flesh, and cooks dry and mealy. The Jersey is most often available in this variety.

The second type, erroneously called a yam, is white- to red-skinned, has greenish-yellow to reddish-orange flesh, is moist, and has high sugar content.

BUYING

Choose as directed for white potatoes. Small, clay-colored spots or dark blotches are not undesirable, but avoid decay, evidenced by soft spots, and discard potato even if only a small portion is spoiled.

STORING

Fresh early-fall sweet potatoes are uncured and therefore fairly perishable, so hold only about 3 days. (Even refrigeration doesn't increase storage span.) Those that come to market in late fall and winter have a longer shelf life.

COOKING

Cook as white potatoes, above.

CABBAGE-TYPE VEGETABLES

Through being cooked overlong these vegetables have become infamous for unsavory odor.

STORING

Store members of the cabbage family in tightly closed plastic bags or wrap in transparent plastic wrap to protect other refrigerated foods from absorbing their odor.

PREPARATION AND COOKING

Speedy cooking until just tender results in sweet fresh flavor and bright color. Cut them as follows:

BOK CHOY. Cut in 1½-inch lengths.
BROCCOLI. Split stalks lengthwise if they're thicker than an inch.
BRUSSELS SPROUTS. Slit an X ¼ to ½ inch deep into the root end.
CABBAGE. Cut wedges, or shred. (To retain food value, shred with knife rather than grater.)
CAULIFLOWER. The aristocrat of the cabbage family, a whole head graces a table beautifully, but uniform cooking is easier to achieve when the cauliflower is separated into flowers.
CELERY (CHINESE) CABBAGE. Slice entire stalk crosswise into ¾ inch rounds.

Boil as usual, but do not cover for 2 minutes. Then cover and boil until just tender.
SUGGESTION: Although food value is dissipated, people with delicate digestions will bless you if you boil members of the cabbage family as directed above for 5 minutes. Then drain,

rinse with cold water, place in fresh boiling water and boil covered until just tender.

DRIED VEGETABLES

Almost every country has its own dried vegetable specialty. Boston baked beans are obviously American, *cassoulet* is the French version, *cous cous* the Algerian, etc.

For flavor, food value, and economy, dried vegetables deserve bravos. Their one disadvantage if you're a weight watcher—they're generously endowed with calories. In addition, most of the dishes of which they're the backbone are delectable because of their mating with rich meats or fat poultry.

The varieties of dried vegetables are staggering. Some of the members of the family are beans—black, lima, kidney; peas—whole or split, green and yellow; lentils; plus a large ETC.

Store any in a covered container in the cupboard. *One pound dried vegetable makes about 2 cups.*

One cup dried vegetable makes about 2½ cups after cooking; 4 servings.

PREPARATION AND COOKING

Cooking time depends upon the age, size, and variety of the vegetable, plus the length of time it's been stored. With long storage, more moisture is lost, and cooking time increases. However, dried vegetables are not difficult to cook, and waiting for them to become tender need not be watchful.

Boiling: The addition of baking soda to the water softens it and shortens cooking time about one-quarter. Depending upon the hardness of the water in your area, use about ⅛ teaspoon soda for each cup of dried vegetable. Omit, however, when cooking in a flavorful liquid, because the vegetable will cook too quickly to allow for absorption.

Although cooking dried vegetables is not a spur-of-the-moment procedure, techniques developed by the United States Department of Agriculture eliminate overnight soaking. More time will be necessary if the vegetables have been stored for a lengthy period.

Quick-Soak Method

1 cup dried vegetable
2½ to 3 cups water, approximately

⅛ teaspoon baking soda
1 teaspoon salt

Place vegetable in large saucepan and add just enough water to cover. Cover pan, bring liquid to a boil rapidly, add soda, and boil 2 minutes. Remove from heat and let soak 1 hour. Add salt and simmer from 30 minutes to 2 hours or until tender, adding more water if necessary during cooking to prevent burning.

Overnight Soaking Method

1 cup dried vegetable
2½ to 3 cups water, approximately
1 teaspoon salt

Place vegetable in saucepan, add enough cold water to cover, and soak overnight. The next day add enough additional water to cover plus salt. Cover pan, bring liquid to a boil rapidly and simmer until tender, 1 to 2 hours.

NOTE: To speed cooking, add with the salt about ⅛ teaspoon soda for each cup of dried vegetable.

Baking: Prepare dried vegetables by any of the above methods, but simmer only until the skins curl back when you blow on them. Drain, reserving the cooking liquid. (Add it if the vegetables dry during baking, or use it for future reheating.)

Place dried vegetables in a heavy utensil such as a Dutch oven or beanpot. Add any rich and/or lusty meat, fresh flavoring vegetables such as onions, carrots, celery, plus a compatible sauce or seasoning.

Acid flavoring ingredients such as vinegar, tomatoes, etc., are almost always added because they increase cooking time, thereby allowing the vegetables to absorb more of the flavorful sauce.

Cover container and bake in a very slow, 250° F., oven up to 5 hours, or until tender and flavorful. (The 8-hour cooking period normally specified succeeds only in wasting fuel.)

Split Peas

4 cups water
1 cup split peas
1 teaspoon salt

Do not soak peas. Bring water to a full rolling boil. Add vegetable slowly enough so water continues to boil. Cover, reduce heat, and boil gently until peas are tender, from 20 minutes to 2 hours, adding salt to taste at end of cooking.

Lentils

Proceed as for Split Peas, above.

Parsley-Tossed Potatoes

In this example of boiling, other herbs may be substituted as may appropriate seeds or spices.

Peel 4 medium potatoes and halve or quarter, depending upon size. Boil until very soft, about 20 minutes, and drain. Melt ¼ cup butter in pan in which potatoes cooked. Return potatoes to pan with ¼ cup parsley, cut coarsely, and salt and pepper to taste. Cover pan and shake hard over a medium flame. Potatoes should be slightly broken and well mixed with other ingredients. Makes 4 servings.

Baked Potato Chips

Here the method for baking vegetables is hurried, to match the speed with which a broiled dinner is prepared. Cut unpeeled potatoes into quarters or eighths (or smaller wedges if time is very short), place in a single layer, cut side up, on a cooky sheet or on a piece of foil. Sprinkle with salt, pepper, and paprika, and bake at very hot, 450° F.

The longer these bake, the crisper and puffier they become. They're delicious served hot or at room temperature.

Twice-Baked Potatoes

Baking is a preliminary to mashing in this recipe.

Cut large baked potatoes in half lengthwise and scoop out pulp. Mash scooped-out potato until lump free and add about 1 tablespoon melted butter and 3 tablespoons milk for each. Beat, and add more milk if necessary to achieve a fluffy consistency. Season to taste with salt and pepper. Fill shells lightly and do not smooth the top. Sprinkle with paprika and bake in a preheated moderate, 350° F., oven about 30 minutes, or until browned and crusty. Allow ½ to 1 potato per serving.

Parmesan Potatoes

Follow above procedure, adding for each mashed potato about 1 tablespoon grated Parmesan cheese. Sprinkle with additional cheese.

Candied Sweet Potatoes

An example of frying, success lies in the weight of the pan.

> 2 medium sweet potatoes, cooked and peeled
> Butter
> 2 tablespoons dark brown sugar
> ⅛ teaspoon salt

Halve or quarter potatoes, depending upon size. Heat enough butter to reach a depth of about ¼ inch in a large heavy skillet. Add potatoes in a single layer. Sprinkle with brown sugar and salt, cover pan, and cook over low heat about 20 minutes, or until brown and caramelized, adding more brown sugar and butter as necessary, and turning to brown both sides. Makes 2 servings; may be increased.

> PRECAUTION: Canned sweet potatoes are too soft to prepare this way.

NOTE: If oven is in use, bake potatoes uncovered at moderate, 375° F., about 40 minutes, or until caramelized, turning them in the sirup.

Creamed Onions

The lovely onion, in unctuous sauce, well deserves its traditional place on the Thanksgiving or any other board. The recipe is an example of boiling.

> 12 small white onions
> ¼ teaspoon whole cloves
> 1 teaspoon salt, divided
> 2 tablespoons butter
> 2 tablespoons flour
> ⅓ cup reserved liquid from cooking onions
> ⅔ cup milk
> ¼ teaspoon pepper
> Dash msg
> Fresh nutmeg

Peel onions and boil with cloves and ½ teaspoon salt until just tender, about 15 minutes. Drain, reserving ⅓ cup liquid. Prepare

Medium Sauce (see Chart for Flour-Thickened Sauces*) with remaining ingredients. Season to taste, and add onions. Serve sprinkled with additional nutmeg. Makes 4 servings.

Alternate Toppings

Bacon bits, pimento, chopped parsley, bread crumbs.

Tomatoes Olga

Tomatoes are considered a fruit in every country except the United States, where the Supreme Court dubbed them a vegetable in 1893. No matter what their category, they're supremely versatile, as evidenced in this recipe that illustrates broiling.

> 4 small firm tomatoes
> 1 hard-cooked egg, chopped fine
> 1 tablespoon green pepper, chopped fine
> 1 teaspoon instant minced onion
> ¼ cup thick Mayonnaise*

Halve tomatoes crosswise. Fold egg, green pepper, and onion into mayonnaise. Season to taste. Spread cut side of tomato with mixture and broil at moderate, 350° F., about 10 minutes, or until lightly browned. If desired, bake at hot, 400° F., about 15 minutes. Makes 4 servings.

NOTE: Grated cheese is an alternate topping for these.

Artichokes Parmigiana

This recipe illustrates braising. If they are braised on top of the range the time will be shortened by about 10 minutes but results will not be as savory.

> 4 large artichokes

Filling
> 2 cloves garlic, diced
> ¼ teaspoon salt
> 4 peppercorns
> ¾ cup fine dry bread crumbs, browned if desired
> ½ cup Parmesan cheese, grated
> 2 tablespoons parsley, cut fine
> Dash msg

Braising Liquid
> 6 tablespoons olive oil
> ¾ cup water, approximately

Remove artichoke stems close to the base and with a sharp knife cut off the leaf tips about an inch down from the top. Spread the leaves open by pressing cut side of artichoke down firmly on a table.

Crush garlic to a paste with salt. Add peppercorns and crack coarsely. Mix with bread crumbs, cheese, and parsley and season to taste. Spoon between leaves, using all the filling. Place the artichokes in a baking dish in a single layer. Pour the olive oil over them and add enough water to reach a depth of ¼ inch in the pan.

Cover and bake in a hot, 400° F., oven about 30 minutes, or until an outside leaf pulls off easily. Serve hot or at room temperature, with the pan liquid. Makes 4 servings.

NOTE: Four anchovies may be mashed with the crushed garlic.

Boston Baked Beans

This is an example of baking as applied to dried vegetables. Although any variety may be used, marrow beans are particularly delicious.

>   1 pound dried marrow beans
>   2 tablespoons dark brown sugar
>   ¼ teaspoon dry mustard
>   1 cup reserved liquid from cooking beans
>   2 tablespoons ketchup
>   ¼ cup molasses
>   1 small onion, peeled
>   ¾ pound salt pork in one piece

Prepare and precook beans as for Baking Dried Vegetables.* Dissolve brown sugar and mustard in reserved cooking liquid. If desired, the juice from any pickled fruit or red wine may be used for all or part of the liquid. Mix with ketchup and molasses. Use a Dutch oven or a bean pot and pour the liquid-spice mixture over beans. Bury the onion in their midst and top with salt pork.

Cover and bake in a very slow, 250° F., oven about 5 hours, or until tender, uncovering the pot the last hour to brown the beans. Makes 8+ servings.

BUDGET MEMO: Save the skin from a baked ham to replace the salt pork. The ham bones and any leftover chunks of fat also make the beans more flavorful, and bacon rind may replace the ham skin. The water in which a ham or tongue has been cooked adds savor too.

IX

Sophisticated Fruits

Fruit has many graces. Decorative as well as delicious, a handsomely arranged bowl can go on the dining-room table and its presence in the living room is a sign of generous hospitality. Fairly low in calories, it makes a fine between-meals treat.

A glamour package of vitamins, fruit can appear at any meal—and at any course. As with vegetables, for maximum food value, peel only when necessary, peel thin, and if the fruit is to be cooked, peel just before cooking. Then cook in the shortest possible time.

BUYING FRUITS

For best buys, call upon your senses—your eyes to accept good color and refuse shriveling or decay, your nose to recognize fragrant freshness, your touch to judge ripeness.

As with vegetables, test gently for firmness: press fruit between your palms rather than poking it. Realize that size is no indication of quality. And check seasonal peak for each particular kind to bring home that happy trio—full flavor, top food value, and economy.

STORING FRUITS

To hasten ripening, keep fruit at room temperature. To maintain freshness, store it in the refrigerator. Depending upon the variety and the degree of ripeness at purchase, fruits will keep from overnight to a whole winter. All fruits must be covered after cutting, and transparent plastic wrap is most effective.

A cold fruit cellar may be used for apples and citrus fruits bought in quantity. (Because they ripen during storage, sort them often, using immediately those that have softened.) Rotten fruit must be discarded before it infects its neighbors. Except for this, handle as little as possible.

PREPARATION OF FRUITS

To conserve the juice, peel or pit juicy fruits over a bowl and serve with the fruit or save it for a beverage or aspic.

Most fruits darken when cut surfaces are exposed to air. Apples, bananas, pears, peaches, and avocados react almost immediately. (Darkening doesn't interfere with edibility; simply slice off the discolored portion.) They darken even when cooked, so serve them fairly soon.

If fruits must be sliced or peeled ahead, dip them in pineapple or citrus juice or use a commercial anti-oxidant to retard discoloration.

Extreme cold dulls aroma and therefore flavor, so serve fruit at room temperature. Hot or warm fruit requires less sugar than chilled fruit.

CANNED FRUITS

Open a can of fruit is the modern equivalent to a page of preliminary directions in a nineteenth-century cookbook. But remember that canning dissipates flavor and destroys some food value. Canned fruit is cooked fruit, and heating it before serving further diminishes food value.

A #303 can with stated weights of from 16 to 17 ounces holds approximately 2 cups of fruit and liquid; makes about 4 servings.

BUDGET MEMO: If draining canned fruit, save the juice for a beverage or aspic.

Read the labels and when available buy cans labeled with the United States Department of Agriculture grade. Graded downward from A to C, all are wholesome, the chief difference being appearance. Because Grade C is the least expensive, buy it for cobblers, pies, etc., where perfection of form is unimportant.

Some commercial canners type their fruit "Fancy," "Choice," and "Standard." These words correspond approximately to grades A, B, and C.

Fancy indicates fruit of uniform ripeness, color, and shape, canned in heavy (very sweet) sirup.

Choice indicates lower quality and moderately heavy sirup.

Standard indicates fruits less uniform in size and color, canned in medium-sweet sirup.

FROZEN FRUITS

More closely resembling fresh than canned fruit, frozen fruit is generally of excellent quality. Unfortunately, however, freezing makes most small soft fruits mushy.

Frozen fruits are packed in so many different weights, and the amount of liquid to fruit varies so greatly, experience is your only guide to quantity.

Thaw frozen fruit as the package directs. (Try it half-thawed on a hot summer day.) Thawed frozen fruits that don't darken on exposure to air keep fairly well in the refrigerator about a day. Refreezing is inadvisable.

The sirup often is excessively sweet. If you find it so, turn the frozen fruit into a sieve or colander and let the sirup drain into a bowl. (The drained juice may be used to sweeten other fruit, or added to beverages such as milk, or saved for an aspic.)

For flavor allure, marinate drained frozen fruit in citrus fruit juice, sweet or dry wine, brandy, rum, etc., or combinations of these.

ACCOMPANIMENTS FOR FRUITS

Sugar: Fruit is sweet in its own right and requires little, if any, sugar. If necessary, add very fine or confectioners' sugar to fruit to be served immediately because they dissolve instantly. For a marinade, use granulated sugar, or dark brown sugar for forthright-flavored fruits such as pineapple.

Bitters: Angostura, orange, and the like add zest to fruit. Start with a dash and taste-test.

Cream: Sweet—pour or whipped—or commercial sour cream is delectable with fruit.

Frozen Accompaniments: These add to fruit's enchantment. Choose go-together flavors and interesting color combinations.

FRUIT ICES. Made of water and flavoring; combine with fruit as a first course at a gala dinner, or as a dessert. Red raspberries are attractive with pineapple ice, blueberries complement lime ice, etc. Add a trickle of liqueur if desired—for instance, orange-flavored on strawberries with orange ice.

SHERBET. Made with milk instead of water; use as for ices.

ICE CREAM. Made with cream, for elegant occasions; stir any prepared fruit, cream whipped stiff, and brandy into ice cream and serve immediately.

Soft Custard: This is an old-fashioned delight with fruit, and the custard may make a bed or a bath for berries, sliced peaches, etc. Use fresh fruits or drain canned or frozen fruits.

Shells: Their own shells are attractive for serving melon balls, pineapple cubes, and the like. Pastry shells filled with soft custard, whipped cream, or ice cream and then topped with fruit are alluring—and add calories.

Spirits: Liqueurs, any wine, the various brandies, and rum all add fillip. Combinations such as brandy and champagne offer costly elegance. Allow about 2 tablespoons liquor, to taste, for each serving.

Flaming Fruit: Fruit becomes dramatic when flamed (flambéed). Any spirit high enough in alcoholic content to flame may be used. All except high-proof (151 proof) rum require preliminary warming.

PRECAUTION: Don't add a small quantity of spirits to a large amount of sauce and expect it to flame—it will become too diluted.

Choose brandy, rum, or a liqueur. (Test-flame a spoonful ahead of time to be sure it's high enough in alcoholic content to ignite.)

Place fruit and sauce in a skillet or chafing dish and heat. Sprinkle with sugar if desired, add your choice of spirits, and when it warms tilt pan so the flame touches the liquid. When the sauce catches fire, baste fruit (this keeps the flame alive) until the flames die. Don't worry if the flames spill on your table—they won't cause a burn if extinguished promptly.

COOKING FRUITS

As with vegetables, cooking diminishes food value. However, certain varieties such as green apples and quinces require cooking. Fruit also is cooked to retard ripening, and for variety.

With fruits, as with all other foods, a firm knowledge of the familiar cooking methods is your assurance of achieving perfect results.

Fruit may be cooked by dry heat—baked, as apples; broiled, as grapefruit; fried, as bananas. Because it lacks fat, it is not pan-broiled. Fruit also may be braised or water-cooked.

To Test Doneness: Use a cake tester or ice pick—a fork makes too many holes—and pierce to the center of the fruit. When the fruit is tender, the tester can be inserted easily.

BRAISING FRUIT

With a few exceptions, fruit must be cooked with liquid to prevent burning. Perfectly braised fruit is tender, plump, and flavorful. Braising done in a chafing dish spells glamour.

Liquids: Any fruit juice, its own or another; wine—red or white, sweet or dry, fortified or aromatized; brandy, rum, a liqueur; or water may be used.

Fat: Delicately flavored fat such as butter adds savor, but may be omitted.

Sweetening: If the fruit itself is not sweet enough, for each serving add to the liquid about 1 teaspoon sugar—granulated, brown, maple. The same amount of honey may be substituted for the liquid.

Oven Braising: Although often called baking, this is really a braising technique. Use whole or cut fruit either unpeeled or partially peeled, and add only enough of the fats and/or liquids mentioned above to cover bottom of pan. Cover and bake until tender. Temperature can range from very slow, 250° F., to extremely hot, 550° F., depending upon time, desired result, and upon whether the oven is in use for other foods. A cake tester is excellent for judging tenderness.

Burner Braising: This method saves fuel, and if you have an attractive range-top casserole, the fruit may be cooked and served in it. Burner-braise small fruit or fruit cut small. Peel if desired and place in a skillet or range-top casserole. Add only enough of the fats and/or liquids mentioned above to reach a depth of ¼ inch. Cover and simmer only until fruit is tender. After cooking, thicken and flavor sirup if desired, as directed in the Pattern for Water-Cooking Fruit.*

BAKING FRUIT

The few exceptions for cooking fruit without liquid are split or whole bananas baked in their skins, or grapefruit and orange halves. Brush split bananas with fat and/or honey, or use fat and/or a sprinkle of sugar if desired. Add sweetening and/or spirits to citrus fruits. Bake on a foil-covered pan with low sides at any of the temperatures suggested for Oven Braising, above.

BROILING FRUIT

Among other things, fruit is broiled to serve with meat. Peel if desired, slice or halve, and arrange in a broiler pan in a single layer. Brush with any delicately flavored fat and/or sprinkle with any of the sweetenings suggested in Braising Fruit.* Broil at from slow, 300° F., to very hot, 450° F., or until fruit is heated and browned.

FRYING FRUIT

Shallow Fat: To fry fruit use only enough delicately flavored fat to cover the bottom of the skillet. Heat over a medium flame, add prepared fruit in a single layer, and cook covered until tender, turning to brown both sides. If fruit is not tender after browning, reduce flame and continue to cook gently until it is of desired consistency.

Deep Fat: Fruit is cloaked in a batter before frying in deep fat (see Pattern for Fritters*).

WATER-COOKING FRUIT

Fruit cooked in a quantity of liquid is stewed—poached is the happier word—and the result is stewed fruit, or—more aesthetically —fruit compote.

Because poaching stops aging, use this method to save ripened fruit that can't be used promptly.

Soft Fruit: Most fruits are "soft," and the object in water-cooking is to retain flavor and keep the fruit from getting mushy. To achieve, peel only when necessary, cook gently in a covered container, and use sugar sparingly. One part sugar to two parts liquid is the best proportion for fruit of normal acidity.

Choose any of the liquids and sweetenings suggested for braising.

Pattern for Water-Cooking Soft Fruit

> 1 cup liquid
> ½ cup sugar
> 1 pound prepared soft fruit

Place liquid, then sugar, in a saucepan. Stir over a low flame only until sugar dissolves; then, using a medium-high flame, boil 5 minutes to make a sirup. Add fruit, cover pan, and cook gently until it is softened and plump. Makes 4 servings; may be increased or decreased proportionately.

THICKENING THE SIRUP. If you wish, after cooking remove fruit to a serving dish using a slotted spoon. Boil sirup uncovered to desired consistency, remembering that it will thicken further on cooling. Pour over cooked fruit immediately and serve hot or at room temperature.

FLAVORING THE SIRUP. Complementary flavorings—extracts such as almond and mint—added to the sirup after cooking make it tastier. Spirits make it merrier. Sample with ¼ teaspoon extract for the above; 2 tablespoons brandy, rum, etc.

Glazing Fruit: Add to ½ cup thickened sirup about 2 tablespoons jelly, marmalade, or puréed apricots (baby food is fine) and spoon carefully over fruits, adding enough to coat them.

Hard Fruit: The hard fruits—firm-fleshed pears, prunes, and quinces—must be cooked until tender before sugar is added. Bring 1 cup liquid to a boil in a wide saucepan. Add 1 pound hard fruit, peeled if necessary, cover pan, and poach gently until just tender. Add ½ cup sugar and stir only until it dissolves. Cook fruit covered, about 2 minutes longer, to saturate it with sweetened liquid.

Remove fruit and, if desired, thicken and flavor sirup as above. Makes 4 servings.

Puréed Fruit: To produce purées such as applesauce, only enough liquid is added to prevent scorching. (Later additions of sugar or honey thin purées further.)

Place in saucepan prepared fruit and only enough liquid to cover bottom of pan. Use a medium to low flame and cook covered until very soft.

Press fruit and liquid through a coarse sieve or whir in a blender. If necessary, stir in any desired sweetening to taste, choosing from those mentioned in Braising Fruit.°

Rules for Special Fruits

Basic principles are similar. (Also see Fruit Chart.°)

APPLES

BUYING

Johnny Appleseed sowed well, but he'd be hard put to recognize many of today's apple varieties. Three that are excellent both to eat out of hand and for general cooking are the Gravenstein, at peak season from July to September; the McIntosh, mature from October to January; and the Stayman, best from November to April. Recent studies indicate that Jonathan and Stayman are excellent for sauce; Jonathan and Rome Beauty are superior for baking.

Baked Apples

The following directions produce apples that hold their shape well. Allow one medium apple per serving and make a cut in the skin all around each about an inch from the stem end, or peel a quarter of the way down from the stem end. Core, being careful not to pierce bottom, and remove seeds and surrounding pith.

Pack any desired variety of sugar into the cavity. For variety, combine sugar with seeds such as anise or fennel, or chopped nuts. Dried fruits, cut small, and mincemeat are other possibilities, and then the sugar may be omitted.

Cover and bake about 25 minutes, or until almost tender. Remove from oven and let apples stand in the hot covered baking dish about 15 minutes or until completely tender. Serve hot or at room temperature with cream, whipped cream, or ice cream.

Pink Applesauce

Cut firm apples into eighths, but don't peel or core. Add ½ teaspoon "red hots" (cinnamon candy) for each apple. Prepare as for Puréed Fruit,* simmering about 15 minutes. Purée, sweeten if necessary, and serve sprinkled with cinnamon. Serve as dessert with cream. One pound apples makes about 2 cups sauce.

BERRIES

BUYING

Fresh berries are part of summer's sweetness. When buying them, beware of "top of the basket" packing. The beauties on top may be hiding inferior fruit. If the grocer won't allow you to tilt the box, be sure the basket is dry, because rotten berries often leave a telltale leak.

Buy strawberries with hulls attached. When other berries have been picked at the correct degree of ripeness, they leave their hulls behind.

Berries are best immediately after picking. Arrange them on a platter in a single layer, discarding any that are moldy. If they must be stored overnight, refrigerate uncovered.

PREPARATION AND COOKING

Purists roll berries in cheesecloth to remove any loose sand. Modern handling and packing methods make even this step unnecessary.

Washing: If you must wash berries, do so just before use. Hull strawberries after washing. To avoid bruising berries, fill a bowl with cold water. Place berries in a colander and dip the colander in and out of the water a few times.

CRANBERRIES

Formerly this fruit was trotted out only with the turkey. But its bright color and piquant flavor make it an excellent foil for other poultry and meats. Incidentally, it's a good source of vitamin C.

Cranberry Sauce

  2 cups water
  2 cups sugar
  4 cups (1 pound) cranberries

Cook water and sugar 5 minutes, as in Pattern for Water-Cooking Soft Fruits.* Add cranberries, cover, and cook about 5 minutes more, or until they stop popping. To preserve food value, don't stir until cold.

Spiced Cranberries

Tie a stick of cinnamon and 18 whole cloves in cheesecloth and add to the sugar sirup in the above as soon as sugar dissolves. Remove spices before serving.

CITRUS FRUIT

BUYING

In many countries citrus fruits are rare enough to be considered Christmas-tree treats. Americans almost automatically gulp their daily vitamin C ration.

For best buys choose firm, thin-skinned citrus fruits that feel heavy for their size. Russeting or brown surface spots don't indicate inferior fruit.

Citrus fruits aren't cheaper by the dozen, so try to find stores that sell them by the pound. They also cost more when individually wrapped, with no compensating increase in quality. Again, although the price increases with size, flavor and edible portion don't increase proportionately.

Choose *navel oranges* for slices, sections, and grated rind; *Valencias* for juice. A medium orange yields 6 tablespoons of juice.

Choose yellow-green *lemons,* because the juice will have greater acidity. A medium lemon offers about 3 tablespoons of juice.

The greenest *limes* have the most acidity. Expect about as much juice as from lemons of similar size.

Although citrus fruit rinds are nutritious, *kumquats* are the only variety commonly eaten skin and all.

In choosing *tangerines* look for loose skins and fruit heavy for its size.

PREPARATION AND COOKING

Citrus Fruit Rinds: If using fruit for both juice and rind, grate the rind first. Don't worry if a bit of the white portion grates off with it. It has no flavor and will detract from appearance only.

Graters are provided with sharp-edged holes of various sizes. The finest are specifically for grating fruit rind, but actually the second finest grates rind only a little more coarsely with far less labor.

To dry rind, spread on paper for a few hours. When dry, store in a jar with a tight cover.

Rind is measured lightly, rather than packed. It adds zest (which it is often called) to any fruit and is also delicious on ice cream, custard, pie fillings, and the like.

To achieve thin curls or "twists" of citrus rind for beverages cut with a blade peeler.

Citrus Fruit Juice: To obtain the most juice, have fruit at room temperature and roll it back and forth under your palm a few times, exerting gentle pressure.

Store fresh or reconstituted frozen juice tightly covered in the refrigerator, where it will retain a fair amount of vitamin C about 3 days. *Frozen:* It begins losing food value on thawing so shake the can at market to be sure contents are solid and keep frozen until use.

For best flavor, liquefy juice still frozen in an electric blender (to remove from can let hot water run over it briefly). Blending makes for complete aeration, and the juice doesn't require shaking before each use.

Sectioning Citrus Fruit: With a very sharp knife cut off ends to expose the flesh. Using a sawing motion, remove skin, white portion, and membrane, exposing the flesh completely. Cut between sections to the core, flip them out, and remove any seeds.

Preparing Grapefruit Halves: Halve the fruit perpendicular to the core. Slice off a thin piece of the bottom if necessary so each half will sit level, being careful not to cut through to the flesh.

A grapefruit knife simplifies the following: Remove core and seeds. Make a triangular cut around each section, loosening it *completely* from the shell.

Fill the core area with jam, wine, brandy, fruit, etc. A preserved kumquat replaces the obvious maraschino cherry nicely. If you must, sweeten the fruit with honey or sugar, or dribble over it the juice from any preserved fruit.

MELON

BUYING

Muskmelon is the general name for all in this family of many members except watermelons. Don't beat either yourself or your grocer if you've bought an inferior muskmelon. Choosing perfection is so difficult experts often err.

Your sense of smell is a fairly trustworthy, but not infallible, guide to mature goodness. The skin of a smooth melon such as honeydew should feel like a kid glove when stroked. A rough-skinned melon should have well-developed netting that stands out in bold relief. A smooth, slightly sunken stem end means the fruit has been vine-ripened and is therefore at flavor peak. Softness at the end many indicate maturity, but it also may be soft because previous customers have kneaded it.

Muskmelon odor travels, so enclose in plastic sacks before refrigerating.

There are many varieties of melon, and new ones are being developed constantly. Buy and try, if the vanguard is your favorite position and when extravagance is called for. Melons make a feast for dieters—they're calorie-low, food-value-high.

Medley with Melons

As a first course at dinner, a luncheon entrée, or a dessert, these melon rings achieve the illusion of cool freshness. Peel a muskmelon, removing all the green portion. Slice crosswise into rings 1½ inches thick, and remove seeds. Fill the center of each ring with small colorful fruits—berries, pitted cherries, etc.—and sprinkle them with confectioners' sugar. Garland with watercress or mint.

NOTE: Fruit ice or sherbet in any desired flavor, topped with small fruits if desired, may fill the seed cavity.

WATERMELON

BUYING

Your grandmother's grocer probably "plugged" a watermelon so she could taste-judge for crisp sweetness before buying, but grandma didn't have the privilege of buying miniature watermelons or wedges.

To judge a cut watermelon, look for firm, solid flesh. The melon also should have a short piece of stem attached. Don't bother knocking on a whole melon to listen for the dull plunk that indicates maturity, because an overripe melon gives off the same sound. Do check the portion of the melon that rested on the ground—it will be pale yellow when mature. Avoid melons that are soft to the touch, shrunken at the end, or have a dull, lifeless appearance.

PINEAPPLE

BUYING

Pineapples are available in several different colors, and while some varieties are wildly fragrant, others have no aroma. To test for ripeness, pull an inner leaf from the crown. It will come out readily when the fruit is ready for eating. Check carefully for bruises, decay, or mold at the base and around the eyes.

PREPARATION

A pineapple often doesn't need coring—taste to be sure.

Pineapple Rings: Using the leaves as a handle, cut crosswise slices and peel the slices.

Pineapple Cubes and Wedges: Prepare rings, as above. For cubes, peel and cut to desired size, or quarter unpeeled wedges and arrange in overlapping rows to eat out of hand.

Pineapple Cubes in the Shell

Very regal is pineapple served in the shell, with its bristly leaf crown attached. It's at home as an hors d'oeuvre or at an evening party. The fruit should appear to be intact.

Quarter the pineapple lengthwise with a sharp knife. Separate the fruit completely from the shell but don't remove it. Cut chunks of any desired size and stick each with a toothpick. Serve guests rum or brandy in stemmed glasses for dabbling the fruit.

NOTE: A combination of fruits such as strawberries, pineapple, and blueberries may be marinated in spirits or the like, then spooned into a pineapple shell.

RHUBARB

BUYING

Actually a vegetable, this gangling plant wandered into the fruit category. For obvious reasons, its colloquial American name is "pieplant." Be sure it's crisp—test by puncturing a stalk with your fingernail.

PREPARATION AND COOKING

Discard the leaves because they impart a bitter flavor.
If you like things tart, try raw young rhubarb sticks as a relish.
Rhubarb is not cooked the same way as other fruits.

Stewed Rhubarb

1 pound rhubarb stalks
⅓ cup sugar
¼ cup water

Cut stalks into 2-inch lengths and place in a saucepan. Add sugar and water. Cover and simmer about 12 minutes, or until partially broken up, watching carefully to avoid overcooking.

Baked Rhubarb

Place stalks, prepared as above, in a baking dish, and add the sugar. Cover and bake in a hot, 400° F., oven about 20 minutes, or until partially broken up.

Strawberry Rhubarb

For a pink symphony, add 1 pint hulled strawberries to either stewed or baked rhubarb a few minutes before rhubarb has finished cooking.

Pineapple Rhubarb

Add 2 cups pineapple cubes to stewed or baked rhubarb, as above, about 5 minutes before rhubarb has finished cooking.

DRIED FRUITS

BUYING

While dried fruits may not be as aesthetically stimulating as strawberries in January, they're high in food value and usually attractively low in price. Least expensive bought in bulk, they should be stored in covered tins or jars, and will keep at least a year at ordinary room temperature.

The huge specimens are succulent and attractive; the smaller cost less. Seedless raisins (the bleached variety are called "white") are small, while seeded raisins are large, costly, and worth it.

PREPARATION AND COOKING

Different kinds of dried fruit may be used interchangeably in recipes, omitted if desired, or added at whim. Amounts also may be adjusted.

Use scissors to cut dried fruits quickly, dipping blades in hot water occasionally to prevent sticking.

1 pound dried fruit—apples, apricots, currants, dates, figs, prunes, raisins—makes about 3 cups. After pitting, dates and prunes measure about ½ cup less.

Dried fruit is ready to eat, but you may prefer it softened or served with a sirup. Thanks to modern processing methods, this no longer involves tedious soaking or cooking. All you are called upon to do is "plump" the fruit. Then store in the refrigerator. Dried fruit requires little if any sweetening. Taste at the end of preparation and add about 1 tablespoon sugar or honey if desired.

Plumped in Cold Liquid: Add enough cold liquid—water, wine, fruit juice, etc.—to cover fruit. It will soften in 24 hours, and the longer it is refrigerated the richer the juice will become.

Steamed: If you want softened fruit but no sirup, place fruit in a colander or sieve and set over boiling water until plumped, about 30 minutes.

Simmered: If a recipe calls for sirup, place fruit in a saucepan. Cover with any of the liquids mentioned above and soak 2 hours or overnight. Cover pan, bring liquid to a boil rapidly and simmer about 3 minutes, or until plump. If juice is not thick enough, drain and add sugar to taste, about 2 tablespoons to ¼ cup sirup. Boil to desired consistency, stirring until sugar dissolves.

Sauced: Simmer as above until very soft. Remove any pits and force fruit and liquid through a sieve, purée in an electric blender, or beat smooth in an electric mixer.

To Cook Chestnuts: Chestnuts may be boiled, then peeled, but roasting is easier. Gash an X in each shell with a sharp knife. Place a single layer of nuts in a shallow pan and roast from moderate, 350° F., to very hot, 450° F., until they feel soft when pressed. Remove both outer shell and inner skin. They're easier to peel when hot.

X

Alluring Food Value — Salads

Way back when, spring's first furl of greens meant a happy change from root-cellar vegetables. Today, fast transportation and the refrigerator involve you with salads all year long. The dictionary defines them as one or more edible plants or other foods served with a dressing. Meaning anything goes, from a combination of assorted leftovers to a wild splurge on lobsters.

Whatever the ingredients, they shouldn't involve major work with a knife at table, nor should they be grated. When grated, they leak, look unattractive, and dilute the dressing. They also lose flavor, food value, and the crisp crunch that plays a large part in a salad's appeal.

In the interest of appearance, cut like ingredients—tomatoes, cucumbers, etc.—in wedges or cubes of the same size.

Its place in the menu determines the character of the salad. *Main-course salads* should be ample, composed of fairly filling protein foods, and richly dressed. An *accompaniment salad* should contain foods that contrast in color, flavor, and texture with the rest of the menu: for instance, a green salad with broiled chicken, or a tomato-cucumber salad with steak.

You are fortunate if you have a dining room with a table large enough to hold a salad plate and a dinner plate at the same time. A small dining room makes it more feasible to serve an accompaniment salad separately—California style as a first course, or French style as a kind of digestive bridge between main course and dessert.

Servantless service—an aspect of modern living—is eased when hors d'oeuvre kinds of food are part of the accompaniment salad. Then it can be presented in the living room on a help-yourself tray as a combination hors d'oeuvre, first course, and salad.

HORS D'OEUVRE FOODS FOR SALADS

The following foods add this kind of appetizer interest to accompaniment salads. For other suggestions, check Chapter XV.

Anchovies: Circle radishes with anchovy fillets and secure them with toothpicks. For pretty-pretty, cut a lengthwise slice from a cucumber so it will sit firmly on a plate and stick it with the belted and toothpicked radishes. Outline the cucumber with parsley.

Tuck rolled anchovies into hollowed-out cucumber slices and secure with toothpick "handles."

Artichoke Hearts: Place a block of frozen artichoke hearts in a heavy pot and, when thawed, cover pot and steam in their own liquid for about 5 minutes, or until tender. Chill and top with red caviar and a dot of sour cream, with tuna fish chunks sprinkled with capers, or with a rolled anchovy.

Stuffed Celery: Fill with creamed cream cheese and jewel with red caviar, or fill with any of the cheese spreads mentioned in Chapter XV.

Endive Leaves: Separate and stand upright in an attractive container, such as an egg cup. Serve a separate bowl of French dressing for dunking.

Mushroom Caps: Fill raw caps with cream cheese mixtures or with black caviar.

Radishes: Don't remove all the leaves and make "roses" by cutting 4 to 5 "petals" back almost to the stem. A grapefruit knife is a good tool—fit its curve on the radish curve. Serve with a plate of softened butter and use the petals to scoop it up. Dip in salt.

Scallions: Provide a dunk of French dressing.

ARRANGED SALADS

Salads may be tossed combinations of greens and other ingredients, or they may be carefully arranged. The French call the latter *salades composées* and make them symphonies of color and design. Added enhancement comes when the rim of the plate frames the salad and ingredients are in orderly array.

The principles of proportion are also important to appearance.

For example, combine tomato slices, rather than tomato wedges, with cucumber slices. Combine sections of avocado with sections of grapefruit.

Remember the principle of color contrast too—pear and persimmon as opposed to pear and apple, pink grapefruit with avocado. Garland arranged salads with greens that have definition, such as watercress or chicory.

An arranged salad on a large chop plate makes an arresting buffet table display.

Today the cute salad, even for small fry, is shunned. Happily, because food arranged with discernment is far more beautiful than that tortured to resemble bird, beast, or flower.

SALAD GARNISHES

To reward both eye and palate, keep garnishes simple and make them exciting contrasts of color, texture, and flavor. A few suggestions follow.

Carrot: Cut in sticks or rounds.

Capers: Sprinkle on salads, or, for elegant display, frost a mound of salad with mayonnaise and top with a close-together ring of about 5 hard-cooked egg slices. Fill the center of the egg ring with capers.

Celery: To fringe, remove leaves and cut stalks in 3-inch pieces, then make fairly long lengthwise gashes ⅛ inch apart at each end. Soak in ice water in the refrigerator about 3 hours.

Egg, Hard-cooked: Rice or chop whole egg, white, or yolk. Slice whole eggs or cut wedges and sprinkle with paprika and/or parsley.

Fruit Rind: Grate, or cut slivers with a blade peeler.

Herbs: Cut parsley, chives, etc., fine or decorate salad with fresh sprigs of parsley, mint, etc.

Mimosa: Mix parsley chopped fine with finely chopped hard-cooked egg.

Olives: Use whole, chop, or cut slices or wedges.

Paprika: Sprinkle on salads.

Pickles: Cut large pickles in eighths.

Pimento: Chop, cut strips, or dice.

Radishes: Make "chrysanthemums." Place radish on a chopping board, hold by the leaves and make lengthwise cuts as close together as possible almost to the leaves. Give radish a half turn and repeat. Soak in ice water in the refrigerator about 3 hours.

Watercress: Use sprigs.

RAW VEGETABLES FOR SALADS

If you're concerned about nutritional largesse, serve vegetables raw in salads. Some of the following suggested varieties may seem shocking, but taste before you veto.

Asparagus: Use tips or cut diagonal slivers.

Beans, snap: Cut on the diagonal (French).

Beans, Lima.

Beets: Cut cubes or sticks.

Broccoli: Separate into flowers.

Brussels Sprouts: Use whole, cut wedges, or shred.

Cabbage: Shred any variety.

Carrots: Cut rounds, sticks, or dice.

Cauliflower: Separate into flowers.

Celery: Dice.

Cucumbers: Slice or dice.

Fennel: Dice.

Leeks: Slice.

Mushrooms: Cut lengthwise (from cap toward stem) to make T-shaped slices.

Onions: Slice or dice any variety.

Peas.

Peppers, Sweet: Cut strips or dice.

Radishes: Slice or chop.

Tomatoes: Slice or cut wedges.

Turnips: Slice, cube, or cut sticks.

COOKED VEGETABLES FOR SALADS

"Surpluses," the intelligent French synonym for leftovers, of cooked or canned vegetables are useful in salads. Thawed, drained frozen vegetables also shine in salads. (Some—peas, corn—need no cooking; taste and see.)

Artichokes: Separate leaves and use in overlapping rings, pointed ends out, as a frame for chicken or shellfish mixtures.

Asparagus.

Beans, snap or Lima.

Broccoli.

Carrots.

Cauliflower.

Mushrooms.
Peas.
Potatoes.
Summer Squash.
Turnips.
Dried Vegetables (Lentils, Pea Beans, etc.): Toss with a quantity of diced onion, chopped parsley, and French dressing for a lusty appetizer salad.

FRUIT FOR SALADS

Perfect fresh fruits, well-drained solid varieties of frozen fruit, poached, or canned fruit all make salads appealing as an Easter bonnet. They may be served whole or halved, sectioned, sliced, or diced. Celery dice add delectable crispness, good flavor, and the charm of the unexpected to fruit salads.

Allow about ¼ cup celery to ¾ cup fruit.

MAIN-COURSE FOODS FOR SALADS

Any cooked or canned meat, poultry, fish, or seafood you like may be used for hearty salads. And they can appear at lunch, a Sunday supper, an evening party, or grace a buffet table with equal charm.

For everyday lunches, chunks of hard-cooked egg, leftover cubed ham, canned fish are obvious choices. "Company" foods are chunks of chicken or lobster, crab, or shrimp. These will be flavor-improved if marinated in French dressing 2 hours or overnight, then drained, and bound with mayonnaise or any of its variations.

The average proportion of mayonnaise for main-course salads is 1 tablespoon per serving.

The crunch of celery and the pungency of onion are almost obligatory partners to these salads.

A generous proportion for one serving is ¼ cup diced celery and approximately 1 tablespoon diced onion to ¾ cup meat, poultry, or seafood.

For verve and variety, add to any of these salads, herbs, capers, nuts, or seeds, and remember that flavorful sauces, such as Escoffier, contribute interest too. Greens, of course, make the setting. To extend salad mixtures, pile them high on tomatoes or on stoned unpeeled avocado halves. Slices or wedges of hard-cooked egg boost the protein content and add to appearance.

Tomatoes may be scooped out and filled with salad, but if you're a waste-not, want-not cook you'll simply place the tomato core end down and cut eighths or quarters almost through to the core. Spread open and pile the salad on top.

Piquant Chicken Salad

4 cups cooked chicken
1½ cups diced celery
1 tablespoon capers
¾ cup Mayonnaise,* approximately
1 teaspoon lemon juice
Salt
2 to 3 drops Liquid Pepper*

Remove chicken (water-cooked or leftover roasted) from bones and pull into chunks, discarding skin. Combine ingredients, using enough mayonnaise to coat. Season to taste, adding more lemon juice for piquancy, if necessary. Serve ringed with watercress and sprinkled, if desired, with a few capers for garnish. Makes 4+ servings.

GREENS FOR SALADS

A well-stocked refrigerator always has a quota of perky, colorful greens. Of the many varieties, remember that only the *green* greens have any food value, and that the darker their color, the more nutritious they are. Whatever the variety, remember also that good looks and high food value go hand in hand. The most readily available greens are escarole, chicory, and the many kinds of lettuce —iceberg (head), butterhead (Boston), romaine (cos), bibb, and leaf.

Less usual greens are watercress, raw spinach, and dandelion. Foreign markets, especially Italian and Chinese, provide greens in additional variety.

One kind of green tossed with French dressing or any of its variations may be used, but a combination of up to four varieties makes things more interesting.

Washing and Storing Greens: Simply remove wilted outer leaves and rinse tight-leaved heads such as iceberg lettuce. Store in plastic bags. They'll keep about 10 days.

Loose head greens often will keep up to 10 days when prepared for refrigeration as directed below. There's an additional advantage—the greens are ready to go directly into the salad bowl.

Separate leaves and wash each under lukewarm running water. Line a dish drainer with paper towels to drain leaves. Place paper towels in a plastic bag and lay the drained greens on them. Cover with more paper towels, close sack tightly, and refrigerate.

PRECAUTION: If greens are too wet they'll mold; if not damp enough, they'll dry. Let experience be your guide.

Preparing Greens for Salad: Tear loose-head greens into pieces (knife-cutting bruises them) and fill the salad bowl. If they aren't thoroughly dry, the dressing will be diluted and in addition it won't adhere, so fill the bowl about a half hour before serving. From time to time, lift and turn greens—the air will do the drying.

Tossing Salads: Fill bowl only two-thirds full. Season ingredients with salt, pepper, and msg. Add just enough dressing to coat the leaves (this takes practiced judgment), and toss gently until they have a handsome sheen. Taste, correct seasoning if necessary, and toss again. Ideally, when the bowl is empty, no dressing will be left in the bottom.

Containers for Tossing Salads: Wooden bowls are attractive, but oil collected in the pores may turn rancid. Bowls of metal, crystal, or china are multipurpose and also may be used for hot or cold soup or punch. Any bowl may double as a container for popcorn, pretzels, etc.

Tossed Salad

This is basically a green salad with added vegetables, raw or cooked, and is an ideal resting place for leftovers. Toss vegetables and greens with French Dressing* or any of its variations.

Chef's Salad

Protein foods added to a tossed salad produce the chef's salad, making it an ideal candidate for a refrigerator raid. Any variety of nuts, salted or not, and olives are delicious additions.

Simply arrange any of the following protein foods attractively on top of any greens and vegetables that have been tossed with French Dressing.*

Meat: Strips or cubes of roast beef, ham,
  salami, tongue, poultry
Cheese: Cubes or sticks
Egg, hard-cooked: Slices or wedges

GELATIN SALADS

With the exception of raw pineapple, anything up to and including a diamond tiara may be served *en gelée.* Because they must be prepared in advance, aspics save last-minute flutter. When perfect, the gelatin is firm but tender and is infused with delicate flavor. Depending upon the added ingredients, serve aspics as a first course, a meal accompaniment, a main attraction, or for dessert.

Ingredients for Gelatin Salads: Basically, gelatin molds are composed of granulated gelatin, liquid, and flavoring ingredients. Acid may be used as a tenderizing agent.

GELATIN. Unflavored gelatin is usually packaged in envelopes. Although many recipes call for a tablespoon measure, it is best to use the entire amount in the envelope (because gelatin varies in strength, the envelope may contain more or less than a tablespoon).

One envelope unflavored gelatin will jell up to 2 cups liquid.

SOFTENING GELATIN. Science has produced a modern gelatin that doesn't require soaking. Simply sprinkle one envelope gelatin on ½ cup cold liquid. It will soften in 2 or 3 minutes.

DISSOLVING GELATIN. When gelatin is softened, place it over low heat and stir until it dissolves.

TESTING GELATIN. To be sure of aspic strength, test about a tablespoon in refrigerator ice-cube compartment—it should set in about 5 minutes.

REUSING GELATIN. Melt any leftover gelatin over hot water and remold in a smaller container.

Liquid for Gelatin Salads: Your choice is fruit juice (one kind or a combination), clear well-flavored stock, court bouillon, or milk.

Flavoring Ingredients for Gelatin Salads: Surpluses not only find a home in aspics, but added ingredients also extend gelatin, improve appearance, and offer variety. Use one kind or a combination, and be sure they're uniform in shape and neither too large to sink heavily to the bottom, nor so finely minced they lose identity. Add flavoring ingredients when gelatin is the consistency of unbeaten egg white.

PRECAUTION: Ingredients added to gelatin increase the time needed for setting.

Seafood: Shrimp, lobster, crab, flaked sole, etc.

Meat: Ham, veal, tongue, poultry

Vegetables and fruits: (Raw—except pineapple—cooked, canned, or frozen): Chopped cabbage, diced carrots, pitted cherries, seedless grapes, etc.

Acid for Gelatin Salads: This may be vinegar or lemon juice. It aids in tenderizing gelatin, but an excess may prevent setting and its flavor will be apparent, so *use no more than 2 tablespoons acid for each cup of liquid.*

Centering a Mold on a Serving Plate: Dampen plate with cold water before turning the mold out, and slide the aspic into position.

Unmolding Gelatin: Hold mold in warm water to the depth of the gelatin for a few seconds. Loosen around edge of the mold with your fingers or with the tip of a paring knife. Place serving plate on top of mold, turn upside down, and shake sharply.

Praise Allah if the mold emerges after its first dip. Repeat if it doesn't.

To avoid last-minute fuss, turn the mold out about an hour before serving, garnish it, and cover with transparent plastic wrap. Refrigerate until serving time.

Garnishing Gelatin Molds: Gelatin is fragile, so tuck any greens around the mold rather than turning it out on a bed of greens.

If the elegant mold planned for your most fabulous party shows signs of refusing to set, remelt it over hot water. Meanwhile, soften a small amount of additional gelatin in cold water, dissolve in hot water and add to the melted mixture. Remold and refrigerate.

Pattern for Aspic

1 envelope unflavored gelatin
2 cups liquid, divided
or
1¾ cups liquid plus 4 tablespoons acid, divided
½ teaspoon salt
2 to 4 cups Flavoring Ingredients* (optional)

Soften gelatin in ½ cup of the cold liquid. Place over low heat and stir until gelatin dissolves. Remove from heat and add remaining liquid. Add salt and pour into molds. If using flavoring ingredients, fold them in when gelatin is consistency of egg white, then pour into molds. Refrigerate until firm. Makes 2 servings and may be increased, but increase salt to taste.

SWEET GELATIN

These are for dessert and often are called "jellies." Strong coffee is a delectable flavoring liquid (decorate with whipped cream flavored with crème de cacao), and any sweet wine is delicious too.

When creating your own recipe for a sweetened aspic, remember that more than 3 tablespoons sugar to 1 cup liquid weakens the gelatin and retards setting.

Interestingly, when sugar is used, preliminary softening of the gelatin is unnecessary. Simply combine unflavored gelatin with sugar, place over low heat and stir until it dissolves, and add remaining liquid. Because it's a sweet, reduce salt in the Pattern for Aspic* to ⅛ teaspoon.

Flavoring ingredients for sweet gelatin include your choice of any desired fruits (one or a combination) and/or nuts.

If you like things colorful, tint the liquid with food color.

Cherry-Studded Wine Jelly

        1 envelope unflavored gelatin
        2 to 4 tablespoons sugar, to taste
        ⅛ teaspoon salt
        1¾ cup wine, port, sauterne, etc., divided
        2 cups pitted black cherries, fresh or canned

Mix gelatin, sugar, and salt thoroughly. Add ½ cup wine and stir over low heat until gelatin dissolves. Add remaining liquid and chill to the consistency of unbeaten egg white. Fold in cherries.

Turn into a 3-cup mold or individual molds and chill until firm. Unmold and serve with commercial sour cream or whipped cream flavored with cherry liqueur. Makes 6 servings.

SALAD DRESSINGS

Salad dressings should complement a salad—be forthright when the salad is bland, unctuous when it's light. Too little dressing looks skimpy, but an excess is wasteful and drowns ingredients. The two basic types made with oil are mayonnaise and French dressing.

Allow about 1 tablespoon dressing for each serving.

MAYONNAISE

Preparing mayonnaise is sometimes thought of as a frantic, three-handed procedure, at the end of which the cook emerges wild-eyed and disheveled with a jar of mayonnaise and a nervous head-ache. Actually, it requires only two hands, takes about five minutes, and, although more expensive, is far superior to commercial mayon-naise or salad dressing.

Flavorful and decorative, mayonnaise has many uses. It is easier to spread than butter for sandwiches, it moistens and flavors salads, and it binds foods.

Store mayonnaise covered in the refrigerator. It keeps almost in-definitely, but taste before use to be sure the oil has not become rancid.

Ingredients for Mayonnaise: Mayonnaise is basically composed of egg, oil, and acid. Spices add piquancy, and paprika acts as a stabilizing agent.

EGG. Whole eggs may be used, but mayonnaise made with egg yolk is richer and more flavorful.

OIL. The indigenous oil of France—olive—is always specified in recipes with a French background. However, it is far more costly than corn or cottonseed oil. In addition, a delicately flavored olive oil is wasted, because the sharp spices will mask it, while a lustier olive oil may be overpowering in flavor.

ACID. Sharp vinegar is preferable for this piquant sauce, because wine vinegar is too bland and lemon juice doesn't keep.

Preparation of Mayonnaise: Mayonnaise is known technically as a stable emulsion. To help keep it together, beat ingredients in a narrow bowl with a rounded bottom and sloping sides. A rotary beater, an electric mixer, or a blender may be used.

Add the oil slowly at first and remember that throughout, addi-tions of oil should always be less in quantity than the amount of mixture already in the container.

Beat oil in completely after each addition. Intermittent beating is as effective as continuous beating.

Mayonnaise thickens slightly on standing. If made too thick, or if stored in a very cold place, it may separate.

REPAIRING BROKEN MAYONNAISE. Should separation occur during either preparation or storage, beat an egg yolk and add some oil gradually, as directed above, until the mixture begins to thicken. Then add the separated mayonnaise gradually as if it were oil. When all the broken mayonnaise has been beaten in, add more oil, if neces-sary, to achieve desired consistency. Add more vinegar and season-ings, if necessary, to taste.

The top surface of mayonnaise may discolor during storage.

Simply skim this portion off—it is usable where appearance is not important. If a few bubbles of oil are visible, again skim the surface and use as above. Stirring the oil in would make the mayonnaise separate.

Pattern for Mayonnaise

> 1 teaspoon salt
> Dash msg
> 1 teaspoon dry mustard
> 2 tablespoons acid
> 1 egg yolk
> ¼ teaspoon paprika
> ½ to 1 cup oil

Dissolve salt, msg, and mustard in acid. Using an electric mixer, whisk, or rotary beater, beat egg yolk with paprika until thick. Add a small amount of oil, beating it in thoroughly, and continue adding small amounts of oil until the sauce thickens. Beat in half the acid and continue beating in oil, adding progressively larger quantities. When half the oil is incorporated, beat in remaining acid. Gradually add additional oil until mayonnaise reaches desired consistency. Makes about 1 cup. The recipe may be increased up to 4 times the proportion given. Increase the salt to taste.

There are no hard and fast rules governing the many variations of mayonnaise. Amounts and kinds of added ingredients depend upon your palate and what the refrigerator holds. Following are some of the more eminent.

Russian Dressing

Mix about ¼ cup chili sauce with 1 cup Mayonnaise.

Thousand Island Dressing

This is so named because of the numerous flavoring ingredients.

> 1¼ cups Russian Dressing
> 1 hard-cooked egg, chopped fine
> 3 tablespoons green pepper, chopped fine
> 2 tablespoons onion, diced fine
> 4 tablespoons stuffed olives, chopped
> 1 to 2 tablespoons herb or herbs
> 3 tablespoons celery, chopped fine

Combine all ingredients.

Ravigote Sauce

Add 1 cup cream, whipped stiff, to Thousand Island Dressing. This is especially delectable with shellfish salads.

Tartare Sauce

The richness of mayonnaise plus the sharp-flavored additions make this a perfect complement for lean, bland seafood.

1 cup Mayonnaise
¼ cup sour pickle, chopped
3 tablespoons green pepper, chopped
1 tablespoon capers
1 tablespoon parsley, cut fine
5 stuffed olives, chopped

Combine all ingredients.

Horseradish Mayonnaise

Add ¼ cup horseradish, drained, to 1 cup Mayonnaise for cold meat sandwiches.

Jessica's Dressing

Mix 2 parts Mayonnaise with 1 part each chili sauce and commercial sour cream. Season sharply to taste with Liquid Pepper.*

Glazing with Mayonnaise: Mayonnaise makes an attractive glaze for a dish with no sauce of its own. Simply spread a thin even layer of Mayonnaise over the top of the heated food and bake until browned and bubbly in an extremely hot, 500° F., oven, or put under a medium broiler flame for about 5 minutes.

FRENCH DRESSING

Too much mumbo jumbo surrounds this easy-to-prepare dressing. Basically it's a proportion of 3 parts oil to 1 part acid. Amounts may be juggled at will, depending upon your palate, the strength of the oil, the sharpness of the acid, and the foods the dressing will anoint.

Unlike Mayonnaise, French Dressing is called a temporary emulsion; it separates on standing and must be blended by vigorous shaking before use. Store French Dressing covered in the refrigerator. Don't worry if the oil hardens—it will reliquefy as soon as it reaches room temperature.

Preparing a quantity of French Dressing ahead saves time, but salads must be seasoned and dressed just before serving. Lacking any made-ahead French Dressing, add about 3 parts oil and 1 part vinegar directly to the salad. Toss, season to taste, and serve.

Ingredients for French Dressing:

OIL. Olive has no peer. In the interest of economy it may be mixed with a flavorless oil such as corn or cottonseed. Be sure the olive oil you choose is not too strong for your palate.

ACID. Wine vinegar (red or white) makes the best French dressing. Lemon juice and sharp vinegar also may be used.

Pattern for French Dressing

¼ cup acid
¾ cup oil
1 teaspoon salt
¼ teaspoon crushed or ground peppercorns
Dash msg

Place ingredients in a bottle or cruet and shake until blended. Season to taste. Shake thoroughly before each use. Makes 1 cup.

Garlic French Dressing

1 clove garlic, diced fine
1 teaspoon salt
Dash msg
¼ teaspoon peppercorns
¼ cup wine vinegar
¾ cup olive oil

Crush garlic to a paste with salt and msg. Add and crush peppercorns. Add vinegar and oil and shake to blend. Continue as directed in pattern.

Herb French Dressing

Add to Garlic French Dressing ¼ teaspoon each thyme, summer savory, basil, and tarragon, adding them when the garlic is crushed. Any herb may be deleted, others may be added, and amounts may be adjusted.

Horseradish French Dressing

Add 2 tablespoons horseradish to French Dressing and use to complement seafood.

Continental Dressing

Crumble ¼ cup cheese (Roquefort, Gorgonzola, blue are all excellent) and add to French Dressing.

Cole Slaw Dressing

Another illustration of the 3-to-1 French Dressing proportion, substitute cream for the oil, and use sharp vinegar for the acid. Combine with shredded cabbage and season to taste.

XI

Success with Eggs and Cheese

Eggs are a truly multipurpose food. They can start the day, appear at lunch, tea, or dinner, and also gladden the wee small hours. And in emergencies they are indeed a cook's best friend.

Eggs are valuable nutritionally, too, and a good diet includes four a week. In protein content they are almost the equivalent of meat, poultry, or seafood.

BUYING EGGS

Because eggs play such an important role in cooking, it's wise to know how to choose them. Except in areas where eggs are broken out of the shell and sold in transparent plastic containers, they are a pig in a poke. Lacking a look-see, your only exterior guides to quality are a dull, rather than shiny, shell and government grading. Grade labels give you the quality, size, date of inspection, and shell color. Incidentally, the only difference between brown and white eggs is the color of the shell.

All government grades are wholesome; grade AA is the most expensive; grade B, the lowest, is therefore the least expensive.

Grade AA or A: Their impeccable freshness is indicated by well-centered, firm, upstanding yolks and thick whites. Delicate flavor makes them delectable for soft-cooking, and the thick white means they'll hold shape perfectly when poached.

Grade B: Grade B eggs are excellent in any dish where they're an adjunct rather than the star of the recipe. Older than Grade A, the yolk is flatter, and the white thin.

The size of the egg, not quality, dictates price. So for economy choose large eggs in late winter and spring, small or medium eggs from August through November. Eggs are least expensive in spring.

Most recipes are based on medium eggs. Two egg yolks may be substituted for 1 whole egg and vice versa.

Depending upon size, 4 to 6 whole eggs make 1 cup; 7 to 9 egg whites make 1 cup; 14 to 19 egg yolks make 1 cup.

Using Half an Egg: If dividing a recipe that calls for one egg, beat it slightly and use half the amount. A medium egg equals about 3 tablespoons.

BUDGET MEMO: When a recipe calls for a measured amount of egg white, and you're short by a whisper, make up the difference with cold water.

STORING EGGS

Eggs require refrigeration, so no matter how loudly your grocer protests freshness refuse to buy them from a counter display. Because freshness is fleeting, buy eggs in small quantities and be sure to use the older ones first. (Pencil an X on the shells to distinguish them.)

Whole Eggs: Refrigerate in the grocery carton or a covered container because the shells are porous and let odor as well as air in. Store large end up to keep the air pocket in the large end and the yolk in the center. If shells are dirty, rinse them, but just before use, to avoid removing their natural protective coating. Carefully stored eggs age fairly gracefully. If perfectly fresh when purchased, eggs often may be used even after five weeks. No one will have to *tell* you when an egg is rotten.

Yolks: Refrigerate about a week by adding cold water to cover, and covering the container. Drain the water before use. Because oil —the fat in the yolk—and water don't mix, the water will pour off readily even if the yolk has broken.

Whites: Refrigerate about a week covered. Egg whites may be frozen; will keep about 6 months in a freezer.

Cooked: Unshelled—store in the refrigerator about 10 days. Shelled—refrigerate about 3 days.

HANDLING EGGS

Breaking: Crack shells *sharply* on the edge of your bowl. When using more than one egg, check freshness by breaking each into a separate container before adding it to the others. Remove any bits of shell with a shell half.

Separating: Eggs separate best when cold because the yolk, which contains fat, is firm. (With age, egg whites become thin and watery, and therefore the egg becomes increasingly difficult to separate.) Egg separators are available but the chef's trick is to break egg into a small container. Pour the whole egg into your cupped palm, and allow the white to slip through your fingers into a second container.

LEFTOVER EGGS

Yolks: Toss with salad greens before adding French dressing. Make cakes (sponge, gold), custards or cream fillings, egg-laced sauces, Hollandaise sauce, ice cream, mayonnaise, noodles. Glaze bread, rolls, etc. Coat fried foods. Add to whole eggs for scrambling or to omelets.

COOKING EGG YOLKS: Drop into simmering water and poach gently about 8 minutes, or until firm. Use riced for garnish.

Whites: Add to salad greens before tossing with French dressing. Make cakes (angel food, silver), boiled frostings, fruit whips, meringues, custard. Glaze bread, rolls, cookies, etc. Coat fried foods. Add to whole eggs for scrambling, or to omelets. Add one additional white to soufflés when a recipe calls for from 1 to 4 eggs; 2 whites for a 5- to 8-egg recipe.

BEATING EGGS

One of the important roles eggs play in cooking is to make foods—soufflés, cakes, and the like—rise. The air beaten into them acts as a leavening agent.

Eggs incorporate more air at room temperature because they are more elastic and will beat to greater volume. In addition, less time is required for beating.

Choose a bowl with a small rounded bottom and sloping sides

because the beater will work more efficiently, and be sure the bowl is neither too large nor too small.

PRECAUTION: It's almost impossible to beat a scanty portion of yolk thoroughly except in a small narrow bowl with a small beater.

After beating, to avoid breaking the air bubbles, remove clinging egg by slapping the beater across your palm, rather than hitting it on the side of the bowl.

Whole Eggs and Egg Yolks:

SLIGHTLY BEATEN. Beat with a fork or chopsticks only until white and yolk are blended.

WELL-BEATEN. Use an electric mixer or rotary beater. Beat until lemon-colored, about 100 strokes with a rotary beater. With longer beating eggs become thick—a stage specified for many cakes and tortes. Worry here about a tired arm, rather than about overbeating.

Egg whites:

Thick fresh whites hold air best, so choose them to ensure a high, wide, and handsome angel-food or sponge cake.

Even a dot of fat cuts volume, so be sure utensils aren't greasy. And because the yolk contains fat, remove even a spilled trace from the whites with a shell half.

Cream of tartar, a stabilizing agent, helps keep egg whites firm. There are two additional advantages. First, it's impossible to beat egg whites uniformly, so although the entire mass won't be beaten stiff, none of it will be overbeaten to the "dry" stage. And second, because folding is easier with a soft mass, there will be less danger of breaking the air bubbles.

Add ⅛ teaspoon cream of tartar for each egg white.

Salt helps egg whites foam, but too much cuts volume. Allow a few grains for each white; ¼ teaspoon salt for 1 cup of egg whites.

If using a rotary beater, to speed beating add salt and cream of tartar when whites begin to foam. With an electric beater add them at the beginning.

Egg whites may be beaten to four *useful* stages:

1. FOAMING. At this stage the bubbles are large and the mass flows easily and is transparent. Use to clarify, as stock; to coat, as in breadings; and to thicken, as in tapioca.

2. SOFT FOAM. The mass has smaller bubbles and is white, glossy, and moist. It flows but won't peak. At this stage, begin adding sugar for meringues.

3. STIFF FOAM. The mass is only slightly foamy; air bubbles are

smaller and all about the same size. The egg whites are glossy and moist, and soft rounded peaks form when the beater is withdrawn *gently*. Use cream of tartar and beat to this stage when egg whites are to be folded into foods.

4. STIFF BUT NOT DRY. The mass is glossy, moist, and smooth, with barely discernible air bubbles. Firm, upstanding peaks are formed when the beater is withdrawn *gently*, and the mass may be cut with a knife. Beat to this stage if omitting cream of tartar.

Egg whites beaten beyond this stage are called "dry." (Owing to overbeating the air bubbles have broken just as a balloon bursts when filled with too much air.) The mass will be lumpy and gray and scatter from the beater. Throw them away or try to interest a dog or cat.

*Folding** is the method used to combine beaten egg whites with other mixtures to avoid breaking the air bubbles.

COOKING EGGS

Because eggs are proteins, they toughen with excess heat and over-cooking. Even hot water comfortable to the hand "cooks" egg onto a plate.

SUGGESTION: For ease in washing, rinse egg dishes with cold water immediately after use. Then wash in hot water.

To indicate gentle cooking, the terms "hard-" and "soft-cooked" are currently preferred to "hard-" and "soft-boiled."

Cooking time varies with the size and number of eggs being cooked, the fuel used, the weight of the pan, etc. The times given below are guides you'll no longer need when you've gained experience.

IN THE SHELL

Place eggs in as small a pan as possible and add cold water to cover. Cover pan and bring water to a boil rapidly.

Soft-Cooked Eggs: Turn off flame as soon as boiling point is reached. Depending upon degree of doneness desired, remove eggs immediately or allow them to remain in the covered pan up to 4 minutes.

Coddled Eggs: Cook as above, allowing 4 to 8 minutes from the time flame is turned off.

Hard-Cooked Eggs: As soon as boiling point is reached, turn off heat and allow eggs to remain in pot about 20 minutes. Plunge into cold water immediately: (1) to stop the cooking; (2) to avoid the green discoloration on the surface of the yolk (harmless but unattractive); and (3) to make handling and shelling easier.

TO SHELL. Eggs are easiest to shell on removal from the cold water. Crack all over, roll between your palms, and beginning at the large end slip shell off with the side of your thumb.

Eggs slice best when chilled.

PRECAUTION: Eggs tarnish silver almost on contact, so use a doily between them and your heirloom platter.

OUT OF THE SHELL

Poached Eggs: To achieve a perfectly shaped poached egg, remove it from the nest as soon as it's laid. Vinegar added to the water may help keep the whites of elderly eggs from scattering, but it also will flavor and may toughen the eggs.

LIQUIDS FOR POACHING EGGS. Milk, cream, soup, vegetable juice, or sauces, as well as water, may be used.

Fill a pan, preferably straight-sided, with enough liquid to cover eggs generously. Bring liquid to a boil. Make a whirlpool with chopsticks, fork, or spoon by stirring liquid vigorously, beginning at the outer edge and stirring into the center. When the stirring has created a deep funnel, add all at once one or more eggs broken out of the shell. Cover, remove from flame, and allow to stand until whites are firm, about 10 minutes; or, if time is short, simmer about 5 minutes.

Remove eggs with a slotted spoon and, if desired, put on a paper towel to absorb excess liquid before placing them on toast or any other base.

Fried Eggs: Add just enough flavorful fat (butter, bacon or sausage drippings, olive oil, etc.) to cover bottom of skillet. Use a medium-high flame and heat *to* the smoking point (eggs stick only if the pan is too hot or too cold). When all the eggs have been added, reduce flame to very low, cover skillet, and cook to desired firmness, allowing about 4 minutes.

For crisp, lacy edges, uncover pan and increase heat for a few seconds at the end of the cooking period.

If you like your eggs once over, turn with a wide spatula when whites are partially set.

Scrambled Eggs and Omelets: The French technique for scrambled eggs and omelets is almost identical. The result is cloud-soft perfection.

A medium-high flame and fork-mixing at the beginning of cooking to expose all the mixture to the heat quickly are the "secrets." A heavy 8-inch pan, preferably aluminum and with no seams, gives best results. Use it only for eggs or Thin Pancakes.* Washing isn't necessary—just wipe with a paper towel after use and store in a pliofilm bag to keep it dust free. If you are making more than one omelet at a time and the egg sticks, remove as much as possible with a fork. Then sprinkle the pan heavily with salt and "scour" hard with wax paper until the surface is silky-smooth. Wipe out excess salt. Should sticking continue, scour pan with a metal pad.

French Omelet

> 1 medium egg
> 1 tablespoon water
> ⅛ teaspoon salt
> Few grains pepper (optional)
> 1 teaspoon butter

With a fork, beat all ingredients except butter only until egg is well mixed. Heat skillet over a medium-high flame, getting it so hot that when butter is added it will foam high almost immediately without browning. When butter melts, pour in egg mixture. As soon as egg starts to cook (which should be almost instantly), mix quickly with a fork until mixture is almost dry. Cook until omelet is just dry but not brown—about a minute more—being careful not to overcook.

With a fork, begin folding (rolling) omelet toward you, starting at back of pan, and make 3 folds parallel to the handle. The first fold encloses about one-third of the omelet; the second encloses about two-thirds, and with the final roll the omelet is flopped out onto the plate. Makes 1 serving.

NOTE: For a 3-egg omelet, increase butter to about a tablespoon, but do not increase water.

Scrambled Eggs: Although directions usually call for stirring the eggs in a greased skillet over low heat, try cooking them as for French Omelet,* above. When cooked to desired consistency, push eggs out onto plate, rather than rolling them into shape.

Baked (Shirred) Eggs: These are a lovely excuse for lighting the oven on a cold day, and take to all kinds of fancifying. When baked and served in *cocottes*, they have French cuisine airs.

Butter a small baking dish and break in an egg, being careful not to break the yolk. Sprinkle with salt, pepper, and, if desired, paprika. Dot with about a teaspoon of butter and bake in a pre-heated moderate, 350° F., oven about 15 minutes, or until white is set.

NOTE: About a teaspoon of cream may replace or be used with the butter, and a sprinkle of grated cheese also may be added. Cooked vegetables or fairly heavy gravies and sauces left over from braised dishes provide delectable bases for baked eggs.

SOUFFLÉS

Soufflés add delicious allure to your culinary repertoire. They're also a delectable ending for leftovers such as poultry, seafood, and vegetables. Basically a soufflé is composed only of a simple-to-make sauce plus eggs.

A well-made soufflé can wait a short while for guests. Although it will shrink upon removal from the oven (the contraction when heat meets cold), it will never disgrace you by collapsing.

Flavoring ingredients provide the descriptive adjectives—"chicken" as in chicken soufflé, "mushroom" as in mushroom soufflé, etc.

The air beaten into the egg whites acts as an insulating agent, and prevents heat from reaching flavoring ingredients, so precook them. Cut them small, too, or they'll sink to the bottom.

Depending upon the kind of soufflé, the liquid may be half milk and half compatible stock—chicken for chicken soufflé; fish fumet for fish soufflé.

For sweet soufflés, very fine sugar is preferable to granulated because it dissolves more readily and is less likely to break the air bubbles.

Baking Soufflés: Don't grease baking dishes, because slippery sides won't allow the mixture to cling and rise. To avoid the un-pleasant aftermath—scrubbing—line containers with foil.

Although any utensil that withstands oven heat may be used, designed-for-the-purpose porcelain soufflé dishes produce best re-sults. In addition, they look pretty on the table. Fill the baking dish seven-eighths full for a towering, well-browned soufflé.

Moderate, 350° F., is the best temperature. But if guests are tardy, the heat may be reduced to very slow, 250° F. It also may be increased to very hot, 450° F., when necessary. Soufflés baked at lower temperatures will not be as high, but will be firmer; those baked at higher temperatures will have more crust and be fluffier.

With overbaking, a soufflé will be dry. The French prefer theirs underdone with a runny center, but a watery soufflé indicates too much heat.

Unbaked soufflés may be frozen and will keep about 3 months. Don't attempt to freeze more than a 4-egg recipe because, during baking, the outside will burn before the inside thaws. Bake a frozen soufflé at moderate, 350° F., and allow about 15 minutes more time.

Pattern for Soufflé

Sauce

> ¼ cup liquid, divided
> 1 tablespoon butter
> 1 tablespoon flour
> 1 egg yolk
> ⅓ cup flavoring ingredient
> ⅛ teaspoon salt
> Few drops Liquid Pepper*

Place most of the liquid in saucepan with butter. Heat gently until butter melts. Place remaining liquid (it must be cold) and flour in a jar with a tight cover or in a blender. Shake or blend until lump free. Pour into hot mixture all at once and stir constantly until sauce comes to a boil.

Beat egg yolk slightly. Beat in a small amount of the sauce, and repeat once or twice until egg yolk is warmed. Then stir into main mixture. Add flavoring ingredient of your choice, and season to taste. Cover container to prevent skin formation.

Leavening

> 1 egg white
> Pinch of salt
> ⅛ teaspoon cream of tartar

Beat egg white, salt, and cream of tartar to a stiff foam.* Fold sauce into egg whites as soon as they're beaten, but the unbaked soufflé mixture may be allowed to stand about 30 minutes. Bake in a preheated moderate, 350° F., oven about 20 minutes for a 1- to 4-egg soufflé; about 45 minutes for a 4- to 8-egg soufflé. A soufflé has finished baking when it is well-browned and firm when the dish is shaken. When soft-centered it will be slightly shaky. Makes 1 serving; may be increased.

Chicken Soufflé

Follow the Pattern for Soufflé,* using half milk and half chicken stock for the liquid. Add to the sauce ⅓ cup cooked chicken, cut small.

Seafood Soufflé

Follow the Pattern for Soufflé,* using half Fish Fumet* or White Stock* and half milk, and add to the sauce ⅓ cup cooked seafood, cut small.

CUSTARDS

"Fitten for an angel" (or an invalid), custards can be exciting, sophisticated, and picture pretty. There are two kinds—soft and baked—and in both the main ingredients are egg and liquid, the egg being the thickening agent.

Soft Custard: Delectable alone, soft custard also makes a wonderful filling for tarts, cream puffs, and éclairs, and may be used as a dessert sauce, too.

A wire whisk is best for making soft custards. Overcooking and/or too much heat makes custards curdle. Should a soft custard curdle slightly, it often may be rescued but will not be as thick. Remove from the heat immediately, place pot in a saucepan of cold water, and beat custard vigorously—if not using a whisk, with a rotary beater.

Using yolks, rather than whole eggs, lessens the danger of curdling and will reward you with a richer, more attractive custard. Custards made of egg whites alone won't be as rich or as tender.

After cooking, cool a soft custard quickly by pouring it into a bowl. Allow air to circulate around the bowl by slipping a knife under it. Stir briskly a few times to further speed cooling. Before refrigerating, cover the surface with wax paper to keep a skin from forming.

If a soft custard is too thick when cold, it may be thinned to desired consistency with cream, rum, brandy, etc.

Pattern for Soft Custard

2 egg yolks
1 cup milk, divided
2 tablespoons sugar
Pinch salt
¼ teaspoon flavoring extract

To keep yolks from sticking, pour a small amount of cold milk into the top of a double boiler. Add yolks, sugar, and salt, and with a wire whisk or fork beat only enough to blend. Scald remaining milk and add gradually. Whisk or spoon-stir constantly over hot, not boiling, water until mixture will cling to (coat) whisk or spoon. It will take about 15 minutes. Stir in flavoring extract. Makes 1 cup.

NOTE: Homogenized milk increases cooking time by about 10 minutes.

SUGGESTION: With experienced care, a custard may be prepared over very low direct heat.

Coffee Custard

Follow the Pattern for Soft Custard, using ½ cup strong coffee and ½ cup milk for the liquid.

Brown Sugar Custard

Follow the Pattern for Soft Custard, substituting dark brown sugar for granulated.

Baked Custard: A much-admired dessert in Spanish countries, where it's called a *flan,* this can be a thing of joy. For smoothness, if desired, strain the mixture through cheesecloth before baking.

Remove a custard from the oven when barely solid, rather than firm in the center, because it continues to cook, therefore thicken, during cooling.

Pattern for Baked Custard

Pinch salt
⅛ teaspoon flavoring extract
⅓ cup milk, scalded
1 egg yolk
2 teaspoons sugar

Add salt and extract to milk. In a bowl beat egg yolk with sugar lightly to avoid forming a froth, and gradually whisk in milk. Pour at once into custard cups placed in a baking pan. Pour boiling water into the pan to within one inch of the top of the cups.

Bake in a preheated hot, 400° F., oven about 12 minutes, or until custard doesn't feel excessively sticky when touched lightly, and when a knife blade (silver is best for testing) inserted halfway between the center and the outside rim comes out shiny, rather than milky. Remove custard cups from hot water immediately. Makes 1 serving; may be increased.

NOTE: Custard may be baked in a single large dish, rather than in individual cups. Increase baking time about 20 minutes for a 4-egg custard.

Homogenized milk increases cooking time by about 15 minutes.

Fresh nutmeg may be grated over custard before baking, or it may be sprinkled with shredded coconut.

If custard is to be turned out, a tablespoon of maple sirup, honey, dark brown sugar, or maple sugar may be placed in cups before the custard is added. These then make a sauce.

Custard Cutouts

To float in clear chicken stock and earn it the title "Royale," omit sugar and bake a ½-inch layer of custard. Use small fancy cutters to make stars, diamonds, etc.

MERINGUES

Just as there are firm and soft custards, so are there hard and soft meringues. The ways hard meringue is shaped make kisses (small cookies), meringue shells, and tortes. Soft meringues top pies, puddings, produce baked Alaska, and the like. Both types of meringue are made basically of egg white and sugar, and very fine sugar gives best results. The difference is due to baking time and temperature.

Hard Meringue: For best results, choose a cool dry day for making it. When perfect, it will be crisp, tender, and delicately browned.

Baking: Cover cooky sheets or pans with a film of flour or with unglazed paper. Test with a cake tester to be sure centers are dry, and be sure kisses or shells are cool before removing them. If they stick, gently pry them off with a spatula dipped in cold water.

Hard meringues keep extremely well stored in tins.

Pattern for Hard Meringue

1 egg white
Pinch salt
⅛ teaspoon cream of tartar
¼ cup sugar
⅛ teaspoon vanilla or almond extract

Beat egg white with salt and cream of tartar to a Soft Foam.* Sprinkle no more than 2 tablespoons sugar over the surface and beat until completely incorporated. Repeat this procedure until all sugar is added. Beat in flavoring extract and continue beating until the mass holds its shape. Form with spoon or pastry bag, allowing about ½ inch between each.

Bake in a preheated slow, 300° F., oven until delicately browned, allowing 20 to 60 minutes, depending upon size and shape of meringues. The recipe may be increased.

Meringue Kisses

Fold into the above ¼ cup of any of the following: broken nuts, shredded coconut, candied fruit (drained if necessary) and drop from a teaspoon. Makes twelve 1-inch kisses.

Chocolate Kisses

For chocolate meringue, fold into the above pattern one ounce bitter chocolate, shaved, and any of the ingredients added above. Makes twelve 1-inch kisses.

Soft Meringue: Fine-grained, soft, delicately browned meringues that cut easily without tearing and don't shrink or "weep" are the mark of perfection. The air beaten into the egg whites acts as an insulating agent and prevents fillings from overcooking or, as in Baked Alaska, ice cream from melting. Adjust sugar to personal taste and/or the sweetness of the filling and the crust.

Soft meringues are made exactly the same way as hard meringues. When possible, pile them on warm filling and bake immediately.

Soft meringues will hold about an hour in the refrigerator before baking. After baking, refrigerate only if left over.

Pattern for Soft Meringue

1 egg white
⅛ teaspoon cream of tartar
Pinch salt
2 tablespoons sugar
⅛ teaspoon flavoring extract (optional)

Prepare as for Hard Meringue.* Spread over pies, puddings, etc., being sure to cover filling completely. Swirl attractively with bowl of a spoon, or make peaks. Bake in a preheated hot, 425° F., oven about 5 minutes, or until delicately browned. This amount covers a surface 3 inches in diameter. Increase proportions at will.

CHEESE

Unlike eggs, cheese is a man-made miracle. There are over 400 varieties, all using milk as a base. Further proof of man's marvelous ingenuity is that new varieties keep being invented. Some American innovations are Liederkranz, Cream, Monterey, or Monterey Jack. They're superb, but our imitations of imported cheeses leave a great deal to be desired.

So many varieties of cheese mean you're sure to find several that please you. There are other benefits of cheese: it is high in protein and fat (a pound equals approximately a gallon of milk); it makes a simple-to-serve lunch or dessert; and it is an ingredient in many distinctive dishes.

The more than 400 kinds of cheese break down into about 18 distinct groups, which in turn fall into three classes, generally interchangeable in cooking. The classes, called "soft," "semisoft," and "hard," are grouped according to consistency, type, and extent of ripening. Being able to identify the varieties by name and type will enable you to substitute in recipes readily available cheeses for hard-to-finds. Just be sure they're of the same class—soft, semisoft, or hard.

STORING CHEESE

The keeping quality of cheese is determined by the variety. Soft cheese, with its high liquid content, dries and spoils rather rapidly; hard cheese keeps well. Should hard cheese mold, remove and discard the molded portion.

It is frequently suggested that hard cheese be wrapped in a vinegar-soaked cloth for storage. However, the acid in the vinegar will change the flavor of the cheese. Simply store cheese tightly covered, preferably in transparent plastic wrap or in a pliofilm bag.

Except for grated cheese, which is an on-hand convenience, freezing seems an unlikely need. Body and texture of most soft cheeses and a great many of the semisoft variety are damaged by freezing. If you must, be sure pieces are no less than an inch thick and a pound in weight. Wrap tightly and freeze up to 6 months.

Serve cheese at room temperature because flavor and consistency are better then.

Soft: Refrigerate about 2 weeks.

Semisoft, Hard: Refrigerate up to 9 weeks.

Grated: Keeps about 1 year in the freezer.

Prepared Dishes Containing Cheese: Refrigerate about 2 days; keep in the ice-cube section about 1 month; in the freezer about 1 year.

VARIETIES OF NATURAL CHEESE

For practical differentiation, the soft cheeses, such as cottage or cream, make spreads and dips. The semisoft, such as Cheddar or Muenster, make sandwiches, wedges, or cubes for hors d'oeuvre, and find their way into salads and hot dishes.

Some of the semisoft cheeses, such as Roquefort, when thinned with milk or cream, are fine for spreads or dips.

The hard cheeses, such as Parmesan (and some of the semisoft —such as Cheddar and Swiss—that harden with age), are excellent for breading mixtures, hot dishes, and seasonings.

Soft Cheese: Because of the large proportion of moisture, this has less food value than hard cheese. Brie, Liederkranz, Camembert are a few examples. The two following are used most commonly in cooking.

COTTAGE CHEESE. Made from skim milk to which a culture has been added, it is then treated in a variety of ways. That, and the many names it has gathered, can lead to confusion, so read package labels. "Creamed" cottage cheese has been enriched with cream.

For cooking, choose small curd because it holds shape well. For salads and the like, the large curd is better because it mixes readily with other foods.

When recipes call for cream cheese, dry cottage cheese pressed through a fine sieve, or drained creamed cottage cheese may be substituted. The creamed variety may be drained and substituted for dry cottage cheese. (Ricotta, made with goat's milk, is the Italian version of cottage cheese.)

One pound of cottage cheese equals approximately 2 cups.

CREAM CHEESE: Although less expensive bought in bulk, unfortunately it's often available only in packages.

Semisoft Cheese: The Englishman helping himself to marbled Stilton, the Frenchman dining on blue-veined Roquefort, and the Italian enjoying green-threaded Gorgonzola are all eating semisoft cheeses. Many cheeses such as Cheddar, Provolone, and Emmentaler, which begin as semisoft cheese, become hard with age.

Hard Cheese: The most prevalent hard cheeses are Parmesan and Romano. Hard cheese is used for grating, and cubes whirred in an electric blender make this an almost effortless operation. (Purchased grated cheese is likely to be inferior in quality and stale, as well as extremely expensive.)

Six ounces hard cheese make about 1 cup grated.

BUDGET MEMO: Hard ends of bulk cheese are often sold at bargain prices.

Process Cheeses: Not natural cheese, packages must be labeled "process." They have been heated, which halts ripening, so flavor and texture remain constant. Their advantages over natural cheese are convenience of use, good keeping quality, and smooth melting. But the flavor of a process cheese is rarely, if ever, the equal of the cheese it imitates; it often costs more; and, because it's usually uniform and soft, the interesting texture of the original is likely to be lost.

Cheese Foods or Spreads: These are made by adding cream, nonfat dry milk solids, and mineral salts to process cheese so it will spread readily. Various flavoring ingredients—crushed pineapple, pimento, chives, etc.—are often added.

COOKING CHEESE

The rules that apply to all proteins—use heat as low as possible and do not overcook—apply to cheese too. Therefore, grate, grind, or cube cheese so it will melt to smooth perfection.

In the interest of flavor, choose cheese strong enough not to be overpowered by other foods in recipes.

SPREADS, DIPS, AND DRESSINGS

Cream cheese is an accommodating base for a variety of recipes. The cheese may be thinned with cream—sweet or commercial sour—milk, fruit juice, rum, brandy, etc. The amount of liquid added makes a spread, a dip, or a dressing.

Tangy Dip

A dip shouldn't be so thin it sloshes down shirt fronts, nor so thick it breaks potato chips or pretzel sticks used for dunking.

½ pound cream cheese
½ pint commercial sour cream, approximately
½ teaspoon salt
3 tablespoons horseradish, approximately

Cream the cheese and add enough sour cream for dunking consistency. Season to taste with salt and horseradish. Pile lightly in a bowl and garnish with paprika or chopped parsley.

Serve surrounded with raw vegetable sticks for dipping: celery, scallions, carrots, turnips, etc. Makes 10+ servings.

Delectable Salad Dressing

Cream ½ pound cream cheese and beat in ¾ pint commercial sour cream. Add salt to taste. Serve over fruit or vegetable salads, and color-dapple with paprika or minced herbs.

XII

Blaze of Glory—
Popovers to Crêpes Suzette

Batters can sashay through your menus from breakfast to bed-time. Containing essentially eggs, flour, and liquid, they produce an amazing variety of products—golden muffins, proud, puffy pop-overs, and waffles—those eminently edible checkerboards.

Because batters contain so few ingredients, they must be put together cannily. But the cooking methods are the familiar ones, and knowing how the ingredients behave will enable you to turn out products that make you proud.

INGREDIENTS OF BATTERS

Flour: Except for the delicate waffle, strong all-purpose flour is best. Flour contains gluten, and although, as in bread, gluten de-velopment is sometimes encouraged by kneading, stirring or beating batters too much toughens them.

As a child you probably enjoyed the paste you made with flour and water. In producing successful batters, your aim is to avoid this kind of pasty mass. Fat comes to your aid—because it in-terferes with the formation of gluten. But some batters contain little or no fat, and therefore must be stirred only slightly. Rich batters can take more vigorous beating.

The recipes in this chapter are written for flour measured after sifting. To avoid this operation, review the material on flour in Chapter II. It is unnecessary to resift other dry ingredients with the flour—simply spoon-stir them together.

Liquids: Milk produces a richer, better-tasting product than water, and adds the dividend of food value. For flavor variation, fruit juice may be substituted.

BUDGET MEMO: Dry skim milk powder may be substituted for milk—mix it with the flour and substitute water for milk.

Fats: In addition to making batters tender, fat also adds savor. Any good-flavored fat may be used—butter, margarine, bacon drippings, etc.

Sugar: Adds flavor and aids browning.

Leavening Agents: Some batters are required to rise to great heights. Their ascent can depend upon baking powder or baking soda, or the air beaten into eggs.

Flavoring Ingredients: Ingredients such as flavoring extracts, spices, fruit, etc., lend variety and interest to batters and may be added to, or omitted from, recipes at will. Amounts also may be adjusted. Follow the directions for Flavoring Ingredients for Cookies.*

MIXING METHODS FOR BATTERS

Batters are divided into two types, *pour* and *drop*. The procedure for putting batters together is almost unvarying. Combine all the liquids. Mix the dry ingredients. Then combine by stirring or beating, depending upon the type of batter.

DROP BATTERS

Batters made with a large proportion of flour to liquid produce griddle cakes, waffles, and muffins. Because they contain little or no fat, the liquid and dry ingredients are combined by spoon-stirring, rather than beating.

GRIDDLE CAKES

Call them flapjacks, pancakes, or griddle cakes, but be sure the batter isn't so thin it overspreads on your griddle, or so thick it heaps up solidly. Test-fry a few drops and stir in more flour if the batter is too thin; more liquid if too thick.

Storing Griddle Cakes: Leftover griddle cake batter, covered, keeps in the refrigerator several days (taste to be sure it hasn't soured); 1 month in the ice-cube section; about 5 months in the freezer. When the fried cakes are cold, they may be frozen. For ease in removing the number you need, place wax paper between each and tuck into a pliofilm bag.

Serve cakes hot off the griddle by frying when needed. Serve them hot out of the *oven* by reheating a single layer of frozen cakes on a jelly roll pan in an extremely hot, 500° F., oven about 10 minutes.

Frying Griddle Cakes: A griddle holds more cakes than a skillet, and because it has no sides, turning them is easier. For even heat distribution, use a griddle that is neither too large nor too small for your burner. Aluminum griddles distribute heat uniformly, become well seasoned through use, and then require little, if any, greasing—especially when the batter contains at least 2 tablespoons fat.

Cakes stick when the griddle is too hot or too cold. In addition, a griddle that is too cold cooks cakes so slowly the leavening escapes. A griddle that's too hot burns cakes before they've finished cooking throughout. Within these two extremes, realize that the hotter the griddle, the more tender the cakes will be.

Heat a greased griddle *to* the smoking point; an ungreased griddle until a few drops of cold water sprinkled on it bounce violently and disappear almost immediately. Then test-fry a few drops of batter.

Turn griddle cakes when the edges are slightly dry and, because handling toughens them, turn only once. They've finished baking when they settle to a practically level surface.

Pattern for Griddle Cakes

> 3 teaspoons baking powder
> ¾ teaspoon salt
> 2 tablespoons sugar
> 1½ cups flour, measured after sifting
> 1 egg
> 1 cup milk
> 2 tablespoons fat, melted or liquid

Stir baking powder, salt, and sugar into flour. Beat egg slightly and beat in milk and fat. Add liquid ingredients to dry ingredients all at once and stir only until dry ingredients are moistened. Bake cakes on a preheated griddle. Makes 12+ medium griddle cakes.

Sour Milk Griddle Cakes

These have two advantages—they are lighter and you get a medal for not wasting milk. Substitute sour milk for sweet in the above. Reduce baking powder to 1 teaspoon and add with ½ teaspoon baking soda to the dry ingredients.

Buckwheat Cakes

Substitute buckwheat flour for half the amount of regular flour in either of the above.

Cornmeal Cakes

Substitute cornmeal, stirred before measuring, for half the amount of flour in the Pattern for Griddle Cakes or in Sour Milk Griddle Cakes.

Pancake Pie

A leisurely Sunday breakfast is a joy only if you are at table, too. You can be when griddle cakes are on the menu by simply stacking large cooked cakes on a plate and dabbing each with butter. Keep in a warm oven or on an electric heating surface, and don't call, "Come and get it," until all the cakes have been fried. Then cut the stack into pie-shaped wedges.

WAFFLES

Waffles are griddle cakes' rich relations. They always contain egg and fat, usually in quantity, and recipes sometimes call for cake flour to further insure light tenderness.

Follow the manufacturer's directions for seasoning a waffle iron. After that, greasing won't be required.

Because the thermostat may not be completely accurate, test it by using the rules and temperature tests noted for griddles. The normal waffle iron takes about 8 minutes to preheat, and a waffle is baked when the iron almost stops steaming—about 4 minutes.

Although some recipes direct that egg whites and yolks be beaten separately, this additional chore doesn't make waffles *that* much lighter. Simply add the whole egg as you would the yolk. When recipes call for cocoa or molasses, to avoid scorching waffles, use a slightly cooler iron.

For a waffle that's filled out to the edges, pour the batter into the center of the iron and fill it to about 1 inch from the outside edge. The less batter you use, the thinner, crisper, and drier the waffle will be.

SUGGESTION: To butter waffles painlessly, add melted butter to the sirup. To keep them crisp to the end, pour sirup under rather than over them.

Storing Waffles: Store waffle batter and baked waffles as directed for Storing Griddle Cakes.*

Pattern for Waffles

2 cups flour, measured after sifting
3 teaspoons baking powder
½ teaspoon salt
2 tablespoons sugar
2 eggs
2 cups milk
6 tablespoons fat, melted or liquid

Combine batter as directed in Pattern for Griddle Cakes* and bake in a preheated waffle iron. Makes 6+ servings.

Wagon Waffles

Substitute sour milk for sweet in the Pattern for Waffles. Reduce baking powder to 2 teaspoons and add with 1 teaspoon baking soda to the dry ingredients. Sprinkle waffles copiously with confectioners' sugar and eat out of hand.

Cheese Waffles

Mix ¾ cup grated cheese with the dry ingredients.

Ham or Bacon Waffles

Strew 1 to 2 tablespoons cooked ham bits on top of batter before closing the iron, or omit fat and place ½ strip of uncooked bacon on batter.

Gilded Lily Waffles

To prevent scorching, use a slightly cooler iron and mix ½ cup of your choice of the following with the dry ingredients: dried fruit, cut small; chopped nuts; chocolate chips; blueberries.

MUFFINS

Although muffins couldn't be easier to make, they always evoke admiring "aahs" of pleasure. They're welcomed at breakfast, brunch, lunch, or tea. And on nights when economy is imperative, you can serve hot-out-of-the-oven muffins for dessert, to butter and spread with your choice of preserves or jam.

Consider yourself an accomplished muffin maker when you turn out tall, tender muffins with straight sides and slightly rounded tops. They should have no peaks, no cracks, a golden brown, slightly glazed crust, and rough, pebbly texture. The crumb should be moist, but the grain will be fairly coarse.

Mixing Method for Muffins: Stir the liquid and dry ingredients together with as few strokes as possible, and stop as soon as the dry flour lumps are moistened. The batter should be lumpy and drop sharply from the spoon.

Baking Muffins: To avoid losing leavening, speed batter from bowl to oven by greasing muffin pans before mixing. Grease the bottom of each cup lightly and fill cups only two-thirds full. (A soup ladle makes even distribution easy.) If there isn't enough batter to fill all the cups, to prevent burning, add water to the empties.

Shallow muffin pans will give you crusty muffins, and there are some available with raised centers that insure tall muffins too. Paper baking cups, either placed on cooky sheets or tucked into muffin pans, eliminate greasing and pan washing and help keep muffins fresh. Muffin batter also may be baked in layer cake or loaf pans. It is then called quick loaf bread and, because of pan depth, is likely to develop a crack in the top crust. Quick loaf bread stays fresher if left in the pan, and its flavor is improved after 24 hours. If you want to remove it, wait 5 minutes after baking and allow it to cool on a cake rack.

Before baking any muffin batter, for delectable kitchen aroma and palate pleasure, sprinkle with a mixture of 2 parts sugar to 1 part cinnamon.

In an emergency, store tightly covered pans of muffin batter in the refrigerator, but don't expect high rising if they're held longer than a half hour.

To reheat leftover or frozen muffins, sprinkle with cold water and place in an extremely hot, 500° F., oven about 10 minutes.

Pattern for Muffins

> 3 teaspoons baking powder
> ½ teaspoon salt
> 2 tablespoons sugar
> 2 cups flour, measured after sifting
> 1 egg
> 1 cup milk
> 2 to 4 tablespoons fat, melted or liquid (The more fat, the more tender the muffin.)

Combine dry and liquid ingredients as directed in the Pattern for Griddle Cakes,* and fill greased muffin pans two-thirds full. Bake in a preheated hot, 400° F., oven about 20 minutes. The muffins have finished baking when a cake tester inserted in the center comes out clean. Makes approximately 12 muffins.

NOTE: Muffin ingredients may be combined as directed in Mixing Method for Butter Cakes.* (Then don't melt the fat.) The extra work will reward you with a tender, cakelike product.

Cornmeal Muffins

Substitute 1 cup cornmeal, stirred before measuring, for 1 cup of the flour in the Pattern for Muffins.

Whole-Wheat Muffins

Substitute 1 cup whole-wheat flour, stirred before measuring, for 1 cup of the flour in the Pattern for Muffins.

Soybean Muffins

Substitute 1 cup soybean flour, measured after sifting, for 1 cup of the flour in the Pattern for Muffins. Soybean meal may be substituted for soybean flour.

Gilded Lily Muffins

Into any of the above, mix ½ cup of your choice of the following with the dry ingredients: dried fruit, cut small; chopped nuts; chocolate chips; grated cheese; blueberries.

QUICK COFFEE CAKES

The word "quick" in the title means no yeast is used. The word "coffee" means it's a fine accompaniment for that lovely brew. *Blitz kuchen* ("lightning cake") is German for this easy-to-do batter, and the only drawback is that quick coffee cakes stale within a day or two. A versatile confection, they may be served at breakfast, as a substitute for bread at dinner, or as a dessert.

Of the many variations, the following will please cinnamon addicts.

Cinnamon Coffee Cake

2 cups flour, measured after sifting
3 teaspoons baking powder
¼ teaspoon salt
1 tablespoon cinnamon
1 cup sugar
2 eggs

Milk
½ cup shortening
½ cup nuts, chopped

Mix dry ingredients. Break eggs into a measuring cup, beat slightly, and fill cup to the 1-cup mark with milk. Cut shortening into dry ingredients as in Mixing Method for Pie Dough* and reserve 3 tablespoons of mixture. Combine liquid and dry ingredients and stir only until dry flour lumps are moistened.

Turn into a 9 × 13 × 2-inch pan and sprinkle reserved shortening mixture over the batter. Sprinkle with nuts and, if desired, additional cinnamon. Bake in a preheated moderate, 375° F., oven about 25 minutes, or until a cake tester inserted in the center comes out clean. If not brown enough, place under broiler for a few minutes, watching carefully to prevent burning. Serve hot or at room temperature.

NOTE: Fruit juice may replace the milk. The cinnamon may be omitted, or another spice or spices may be substituted. For other variations, choose any of the ingredients listed in Gilded Lily Muffins,* increasing the amount to 1 cup.

POUR BATTERS

Pour or thin batters are responsible for thin pancakes (crêpes), fritters, and popovers. As with all batters, they're easy to put together, and the acclaim they win is far out of proportion to the energy involved in preparing them.

THIN PANCAKES (CRÊPES)

Thin pancakes are part of every country's repertoire—and fabulous in any language. They literally should be *crêpes*—thin as veils.

The pancakes will be more tender if the batter is allowed to "rest" about 20 minutes after beating. (The elastic gluten strands that make batters tough will, like pulled rubber bands, relax.) The batter will thicken on standing, so before frying add enough additional milk to achieve the consistency of light cream, because the thinner the batter the thinner the cakes.

If the crêpes are a spur-of-the-moment operation, use a tablespoon less flour and increase the liquid, if necessary, to achieve the consistency of light cream.

Store thin pancakes as described for Storing Griddle Cakes.*

The best kind of pan to use and its care are described under Scrambled Eggs and Omelets.* Heat as directed for a griddle.

If you're sure the skillet is the correct temperature and the cakes are sticking, the batter may be too thin. Correct by adding a small amount of additional flour and beating the batter smooth.

For ease, pour the batter from a pitcher. If you've poured in too much, quickly pour the excess back into the pitcher. If you haven't poured in enough, quickly pour in a bit more.

Turning Thin Pancakes: A crêpe takes only about 1½ minutes to cook. When it begins to brown, with a table knife loosen the edge farthest away from you. Bend it so it will stand upright. When cool enough to handle, grasp the standing edge with fingertips of both hands, pull the cake toward you (not up), and flip it over.

The second side doesn't really need further cooking, but browning will enhance its appearance. This will take only about a half minute. When it is browned, flop the cake from the pan to a plate. To avoid breaking the brittle edges, don't straighten the stack of cakes until all have been fried.

Pattern for Thin Pancakes

> 2 tablespoons butter, melted
> 1 egg
> ¼ cup milk
> ¼ cup flour
> ¼ teaspoon salt
> 1½ tablespoons sugar

Melt butter in skillet to be used for frying cakes; skillet should require no further greasing during frying. Beat egg well, combine with milk, and add butter that has been melted in skillet. Mix dry ingredients, add to liquid, and beat with a rotary beater until lump free. Using a medium-high flame, heat skillet *to* the smoking point. Pour in only enough batter to film the bottom, and roll quickly for even distribution. Turn to brown both sides. Makes about 6 cakes. NOTE: If increasing the recipe, do not increase salt.

If the cakes are to enclose meat, poultry, or seafood, reduce the sugar to ¼ teaspoon. One-quarter teaspoon herbs may be added to the batter.

Crêpes Suzette

The beauty of thin pancakes served in a sauce is that both crêpes and sauce may be made ahead. An added attraction—there's nothing like a show of blue flame to impress your guests. In this French classic, the pancakes are heated in an orange-flavored sauce, then flamed.

The following sauce recipe is a lowest common denominator, and it will keep at least 2 weeks in the refrigerator. Flaming is optional.

    3 thin pancakes
    1 tablespoon butter
    1 tablespoon orange juice
    1 tablespoon sugar
    1 tablespoon spirits—cognac, white rum, etc. (optional)

Fold each pancake in half twice to make a tricorn. Melt butter in a heavy skillet or the blazer of your chafing dish. Add orange juice and sugar and stir only until sugar dissolves. Cook until slightly thickened. Add folded pancakes and cook until they've absorbed almost all the sauce, turning them over for even saturation. Pour spirits into skillet, and when it warms light it as directed for Flaming Fruit.* Makes 1 serving; may be increased.

NOTE: If desired, add to the orange juice 1 tablespoon grated orange rind, 2 to 3 drops orange or other bitters, 1 to 2 tablespoons liqueur —Triple Sec, Chartreuse, Grand Marnier, etc.

Cover Batter

Chicken, shrimp, and the like—actually any tender raw foods —are delectable dipped in batter before frying in deep fat. They're succulent too, because the coating seals the juices in. For success, keep in mind the directions for Deep-Fat Frying.*

    ½ teaspoon salt
    1 cup flour, measured after sifting
    1 egg
    1 cup liquid: milk, beer, water, etc.
    2 to 2½ pounds raw food, cut or sectioned if necessary

Prepare batter as directed in Pattern for Griddle Cakes,* stirring only until smooth. Dip raw food in batter and fry in deep fat heated to 375° F., turning to brown both sides.

Food as small as shrimp takes about 5 minutes in all; a chicken thigh about 20 minutes. Drain on absorbent paper. Makes 6 servings. NOTE: If increasing the recipe, don't increase the salt.

Should batter fail to cling, dip food in flour before dipping it in the batter.

If frying sliced fruit (apple rings, pineapple rings, etc.), depending upon tartness, add about 2 tablespoons sugar to the dry ingredients.

FRITTERS

Cooked foods such as corn, clams, codfish and rather soft uncooked fruits need binding before frying, so the batter is made thicker than Cover Batter.

Frying in deep fat produces wonderful golden puffs, but any fritter may be fried as for griddle cakes, and will then resemble a pancake. Because success depends primarily upon the temperature of the fat, keep in mind the rules for Deep-Fat Frying.*

Pattern for Fritters

3 teaspoons baking powder
½ teaspoon salt
1¾ cups flour, measured after sifting
1 egg
1 cup milk
2 cups cooked food, cut small if necessary

Prepare batter as directed in Pattern for Griddle Cakes,* stirring only until smooth. Combine with vegetables or fruit and drop spoonfuls into deep fat heated to 375° F. Allow about 10 minutes, turning to brown both sides. Makes 6 servings.
NOTE: For hors d'oeuvre, use a teaspoon to make very small puffs. If increasing the recipe, don't increase the salt.

If fruit is tart, add about 2 tablespoons sugar to the dry ingredients.

POPOVERS

Universally admired, by new rules these crusty puffs are simpler than ever to prepare. Consider yours a triumph if they rise high, are irregular in shape, have rich brown tops, thick crusty walls, and are moist and hollow inside.

Grease deep muffin pans, custard cups, or iron pans. (Iron pans heat slowly so may be prewarmed about 15 minutes to speed baking.)

Popovers are partially leavened by heat, so resist the temptation to open the oven door during baking. Because browning does not indicate doneness, remove one popover as a test. If it falls, bake the remainder a few minutes more. If browning is too rapid, reduce the heat to moderate, 375° F. Popover batter may be prepared in the morning and baked before dinner.

Pauline's Popovers

Pauline upholds the banner of good cooking in a family dedicated to that art.

> 1 cup milk
> 1 cup flour, measured after sifting
> ½ teaspoon salt
> 1 tablespoon melted fat
> 3 eggs

Place all ingredients in bowl and mix only until eggs are well blended and there are no large flour clumps. Grease muffin tins or custard cups all over and fill at least ¾ full. Place in cold oven, set thermostat at very hot, 450° F., and bake ½ hour. Puncture four sides of neck to let out steam. Turn oven off and allow popovers to dry 10 minutes longer. (If necessary, they may be turned on their sides and kept there an additional 15 minutes.) Makes about 6 popovers in custard cups or muffin tins.

Toad in the Hole

In France and in England this is served as a luncheon entrée. It's a good one.

In an 8-inch skillet, fry 1 pound Pork Sausage* and pour off all but ¼ inch of the fat. Add popover batter and bake as for popovers, puncturing the neck at several places. Serve wedges. Makes 4 servings.

Yorkshire Pudding

This is a typical British partner to prime ribs of beef ("joint" is what the roast is called there). Pour ¼ cup roast beef drippings into an 8 X 8 X 2-inch pan, add popover batter and bake as above, cutting into squares. Makes 6+ servings.

Manhattan Pudding

The batter makes a wonderful bread to serve even in a house bare of roast beef drippings. Simply substitute melted butter and proceed as for Yorkshire Pudding.

XIII

Terrible Temptations—
Cookies, Cakes, Pies, etc.

If desserts weren't so tempting, everybody wouldn't be fighting them. Negligible nutritionally, bad for the teeth, bursting with calories, usually eaten at the end of a large dinner (meaning no time to work them off), they contribute nothing to a meal—but pleasure.

COOKIES

To offer your share, if you have never baked anything, begin with cookies, because whether they are outsize "dunkers" or pretties in party trim, all of them are easy to make. And preparing them is excellent basic training for cake baking. Although the mixing method is similar, as you will see if you compare it to butter cakes, it's less tricky, and perfection is easier to attain.

If you own an electric mixer, follow the manufacturer's directions for mixing cooky dough. You can consider the cookies you bake blue ribbon when they're tender, regular in shape, uniform in color, and have even cells. Thin cookies should be crisp. Drop cookies, containing more moisture, should be soft.

STORING COOKIES

If you keep more than one variety of cooky on hand, avoid storing soft and crisp cookies together, because crisp cookies will absorb moisture from soft cookies and wilt. If cookies have become limp, simply crisp in a slow, 300° F., oven about 10 minutes.

You can store an orange, a lemon, or an apple with soft cookies to help keep them soft. The dividend—the cookies will absorb delicate flavor from the fruit. A metal box is convenient for storing a large quantity of cookies. To save space, overlap cooled cookies in circles, building up as many layers as the box will hold.

Cooky Dough: Store in the refrigerator about 3 weeks, in the ice-cube section about 3 months, and in a freezer about 6 months.

Baked Cookies: Cookies made with butter will keep about a week; those made with shortening that doesn't require refrigeration at least 3 months; in the freezer 6 months.

Cookies with fruit and/or nuts will keep about 3 weeks in the refrigerator, 2 months in the ice-cube section, and up to a year in the freezer. Freeze cookies undecorated, then decorate and/or frost, when they have thawed.

INGREDIENTS FOR COOKIES

All the variations make cooky baking an exercise in creative pleasure, because ingredients as shocking as pepper can go into them (the German *pfefferneusse*), and a myriad of fillings and adornments increase the galaxy.

The suggestions for substitutions that follow will allow you to tailor any cooky recipe to your preference, whim, or cupboard provisions. For best results, be sure all ingredients are at room temperature.

Shortening: Solid shortenings such as butter, margarine, and lard (see how to substitute it in Chapter II) may be used for cookies. Hydrogenated vegetable shortening contains a chemical emulsifying agent and is excellent because it incorporates more air during creaming, resulting in cookies with superior texture.

Hydrogenated vegetable shortening and lard contain no liquid. If up to 2 tablespoons of the liquid called for in the recipe is added to them beforehand, it will be easier to blend them with the sugar. If the recipe doesn't call for liquid, cream the shortening with the flavoring extract.

When recipes direct that sugar be added to creamed shortening, add it gradually, if by hand, and beat the mixture until light and fluffy.

Eggs: Choose medium eggs of respectable quality.

Flour: Most cooky recipes call for all-purpose flour, because delicacy of texture isn't required. Variables such as egg size and humidity affect the amount of flour required.

Too much flour makes cookies tough; too little means they'll overspread. With the following simple test, yours will always be just right, and it won't be necessary to sift the flour. In time, your eye will recognize the "sandy" texture.

Flour Test for Cookies: For drop cookies, rolled cookies, refrigerator cookies, or cookies made in a shooter or press.

1. Beat in almost all the flour called for in the recipe.

2. Touch the dough lightly with an unfloured finger and add more flour only if your finger comes away sticky. (To avoid an excess, add in small amounts.)

3. Bake one cooky on a piece of aluminum foil to test.

Flour is always beaten into cooky dough. To avoid toughness, use as few strokes as possible and beat only until it's completely incorporated.

Liquid: Milk is the liquid most commonly called for in cookies, but water plus dry milk powder (mix with the flour or use reconstituted), evaporated milk (after dilution as directed on labels), strong coffee, fruit juices, spirits (wine, bourbon, etc.) may be substituted. Milk contains fat, so batters and doughs made with it stay fresh longer.

Flavoring Ingredients: Any of these is interchangeable, may be omitted or increased, and amounts may be adjusted at will.

FLAVORING EXTRACTS. Those such as lemon, vanilla, almond, and orange add fillip, and they may be substituted measure for measure. Add extracts to the shortening so their aroma will permeate.

Grated orange or lemon rind may replace extracts. Substitute 1½ tablespoons freshly grated rind or 1 tablespoon dried rind for each teaspoon extract called for. Add with the flour.

NUTS, BROKEN OR CUT SMALL. These may be added to any except a cooky dough that is to be rolled or put through a shooter or press. Crunch is your object, so choose a non-waxy variety such as pecans, Brazil nuts, or filberts. One-quarter to ½ cup nuts is a good proportion for a recipe that calls for 1 cup flour. Add nuts at the end of the mixing, using as few strokes as possible.

FRUITS. Dried, candied or glacé fruits, or coconut are also optional additions. Use as for (or combine with) nuts.

SPICES. One or a combination of your favorite spices may be added to any cooky recipe or omitted at will. If adding spices, omit flavoring extracts. Amounts of spices called for also may be adjusted. Use about ½ teaspoon spices for each cup of flour called for and mix with the dry ingredients.

For variety, part of a recipe may be mixed with spices, part with fruit and/or nuts.

CHOCOLATE. Unsweetened chocolate, melted, may be added to cooky dough at will. Use 1 ounce for each cup of flour and beat it in after the eggs are added. In any except cookies to be rolled or put through a shooter or press, if desired, add ½ cup semisweet chocolate pieces to each cup of flour called for in the recipe. Fold them in after the flour has been added.

COCOA. Sift with the dry ingredients, allowing about 3 tablespoons cocoa for each cup of flour.

BAKING COOKIES

Cooky sheets are easier to use than pans with sides, because the cookies can be slid off. Also, no sides mean better browning. (In an emergency, turn a cake pan upside down.) Two or more sheets allow you to operate like a production line expert, filling one pan while the other bakes.

When cookies contain shortening, pans usually do not require greasing. Test yours by baking a row of cookies on an ungreased area.

If cookies bake too slowly, they'll dry out, so place the oven rack where browning is fastest (usually the top rung because heat rises). Also, preheat the oven.

Moderate, 365° F., is the best temperature. Allow a little less time for baking cookies containing chocolate, molasses, or fruit, and if necessary to avoid burning, reduce the oven heat by about 25°. The baking times given can be only guides because of variations in oven insulation, the heaviness of cooky sheets used, etc., so watch the first batch carefully and allow the same amount of time thereafter.

Cookies have finished baking when they're nicely browned. To avoid breaking them, wait a minute or two, then remove with a wide spatula. If you wait too long they may stick. Should this happen, run the sheet quickly over a top burner or return the pan to the oven for a minute or two.

It's often unnecessarily suggested that cookies be cooled on wire cake racks, but any flat surface will do. Avoid stacking them while warm, because they'll stick together.

Washing cooky sheets between batches is not necessary. Just scrape off any clinging crumbs with a spatula.

KINDS OF COOKIES

Kisses, brownies, lace cookies, snickerdoodles, and cinnamon stars are just a few of the delightful names for cookies, and a staggering number of variations can be made from the basic patterns. However, no matter what they're called, all cookies are made either from a soft or a stiff dough. Soft cookies are dropped from a spoon to make drop cookies. On days when speed is imperative, bake the dough in cake pans and cut into squares or bars, or in pie pans and cut into wedges.

Cookies made from a stiff dough can be shaped as your fancy dictates—from a Halloween witch to a fat Santa. If you begrudge time spent with a rolling pin and cooky cutter, realize that any recipe for a stiff-dough cooky may be sliced as for refrigerator cookies, shaped into balls, or pressed from a pastry shooter or cooky press.

It's possible to increase or decrease cooky recipes (don't increase the salt). The number of cookies a recipe makes is calculated by the amount of flour called for.

One cup flour will yield approximately twenty 2-inch cookies.

DROP COOKIES

If you're a novice, you'll probably want to begin your baking career with the simplest kind—drop cookies. Ease doesn't detract from their deliciousness. Depending upon the ingredients, the drop cooky repertoire ranges from a rather solid heaped-up cooky like hermits, to a quite soft, flat butter cooky. The dough should be stiff enough to require pushing from a teaspoon.

Normally a teaspoon of dough makes 1 cooky, but cookies can be midget-size for fancy occasions. Make cookies as near the same size as possible so they'll finish baking at the same time and look attractive on your serving plate. Allow about 2 inches between drop cookies because they spread during baking. You're likely to get more cookies on a sheet when you line them up in rows.

Pattern for Drop Cookies

2 cups flour
½ teaspoon salt
1 cup shortening

1½ teaspoons flavoring extract
¼ cup liquid, divided
1 cup sugar
1 egg

Mix flour with salt. Cream shortening with extract and half the liquid, beating until light and fluffy. Add sugar gradually, if by hand, and beat it in well. Add egg and beat well. Beat in remaining liquid. Add enough flour so when dough is touched lightly with an unfloured finger it comes away clean. Push from a teaspoon onto cooky sheets. Bake on the top rung of a preheated moderate, 365° F., oven until browned, about 15 minutes.

NOTE: If baking dough in cake or pie pans, use the center rung of the oven and allow about 25 minutes. They have finished baking when a cake tester inserted in the center comes out clean.

For variations, see Flavoring Ingredients for Cookies.*

BAR COOKIES

Brownies are sometimes called Chocolate Indians and delight diners no matter what their name. Cooks cheer, too, because any dough baked in a cake pan, then cut into bars or squares, is quick and easy to do.

Brownies

The size of the pan helps make brownies either cakelike or chewy. In the following recipe, choose a 9 × 9 × 2-inch pan for cakelike brownies, a 9 × 13 × 2-inch pan if you like them chewy. Brownies are easier to cut when warm (it's not necessary to remove them from the tin) and keep best in the refrigerator.

2 ounces unsweetened chocolate
¼ cup milk
2 eggs
¾ cup + 2 tablespoons sugar
1 teaspoon vanilla
½ cup cake flour, measured after sifting
½ teaspoon salt
¼ cup shortening, melted
½ cup pecans, broken coarsely

Using a low flame, melt chocolate with milk. Stir to make a paste. Beat eggs well, add sugar, and beat until well mixed. Beat in cooled chocolate mixture and vanilla. Mix flour with salt and combine with chocolate mixture. Beat in shortening and nuts. Bake in a preheated moderate, 350° F., oven about 20 minutes, or until a cake tester inserted in the center comes out clean.

NOTE: About ½ cup candied fruit, particularly orange peel, added with the nuts makes for delicious variety.

ROLLED COOKIES

Rolling dough for cookies is excellent preliminary practice for pie baking, and wood, porcelain, or marble are good surfaces. For your first attempt, a pastry canvas and a stockinette-covered rolling pin offer surefire success. Choose a good hardwood rolling pin with loose handles and ball-bearing construction. Although a fair amount of skill is required, a dough of the correct consistency won't prove troublesome, and a recipe containing only a small amount of fat will be easiest to roll.

To ease rolling, refrigerate dough until firm, about 2 hours, or freeze about 15 minutes. For ease in handling, remove and roll only the amount of dough your surface can accommodate.

Use only enough flour (the same variety used in the recipe) on both pin and rolling surface to prevent sticking, because dough absorbs flour during rolling and the excess will toughen cookies. First flour the pin—directly over the rolling surface—then brush the surface with the flour that has fallen off.

Round the dough into a ball and with the pin pound surface and sides lightly to keep the edges from cracking. Stroke, rather than press, dough, and use as few strokes as possible. Roll from the center of the dough to the outside edges, lifting the pin at the end of each stroke to avoid making outside edges too thin. Press any cracks together.

Pick up the dough occasionally and rotate it a quarter turn (but do not turn it over). This increases flakiness and makes the dough easier to roll into a round or oblong. When picking up the dough, scrape free with a spatula any that has stuck, and add a small amount of flour to that area of the rolling surface.

It's easy to repair dough. If ends separate, pinch them together. Repair holes by rolling a piece of extra dough over them.

Roll cooky dough anywhere from $\frac{3}{16}$ to ¼ inch thick, remembering that the thinner the dough, the crisper the cooky. For easy handling of cutouts such as gingerbread men, roll dough ¼ inch thick.

Dip cooky cutters in flour only as necessary and shake off any excess. Cut cookies close together and use a wide spatula to transfer them from board to cooky sheet, scooping them up with the edge because the tip may pull them out of shape. Place rolled cookies ½ inch apart because they spread very little during baking.

Collect and refrigerate scraps separately, and, when all the dough has been rolled, knead the scraps together lightly, roll, and cut them. Because they've picked up extra flour and have been handled more, cookies made from the scraps will be tougher. Leave those at home if you're entering a baking contest, and remember also that prize-winning rolled cookies should stack as evenly as a deck of cards.

Pattern for Rolled Cookies

2 cups flour, measured after sifting, approximately
½ teaspoon salt
½ cup shortening
½ teaspoon flavoring extract
¾ cup sugar
1 egg
2 tablespoons liquid

Mix flour with salt. Cream shortening with extract until light and fluffy. Add sugar gradually, if by hand, and beat it in well. Add egg and beat well. Beat in liquid. Add enough flour so when dough is touched lightly with an unfloured finger it comes away clean. Roll and cut as directed, and bake in a preheated moderate, 365° F., oven about 15 minutes, or until browned.

NOTE: For variations, see Flavoring Ingredients for Cookies.*

Gingerbread Men

1 cup shortening
1 teaspoon vinegar
¾ cup sugar
1 egg yolk
1 cup molasses
½ cup sour milk
4 cups flour, approximately, divided
1 teaspoon baking soda
½ teaspoon salt
1 teaspoon cloves

½ teaspoon allspice
1 teaspoon ginger
Seeded raisins

Cream shortening with vinegar. Add sugar gradually, if by hand, and beat until light and fluffy. Add egg yolk and beat well. Add molasses and sour milk and mix well. Mix 1 cup of flour with baking soda, salt, cloves, allspice, and ginger. Beat it into the sugar mixture gradually. Add enough more flour, about 3 cups, so when dough is touched lightly with an unfloured finger it comes away clean.

Roll on a floured surface and use a cutter to make gingerbread men. Cut the raisins in half to make eyes, nose, and mouth, and give the gentlemen 3 whole-raisin waistcoat buttons. Bake in a moderate, 365° F., oven about 10 minutes, or until browned.

REFRIGERATOR (SLICE) COOKIES

Choose any stiff-dough cooky recipe—rolled, shooter, press, as well as refrigerator—and shape on wax paper into a long roll or bar. Then refrigerate or freeze until firm. It's easier to shape half the dough at a time if a 2-cup flour recipe has been prepared. Slice dough ⅛ to ¼ inch thick, using a thin sharp knife and a gentle sawing motion. (If the dough is too cold it will crumble. Then simply wait a few minutes until it softens slightly.) Place slices about 1 inch apart on cooky sheets and decorate as desired.

PRESS OR SHOOTER COOKIES

At wedding receptions the bride and groom are often honored with cookies pressed from a pastry shooter in the shape of their initials. To make them, simply refrigerate or freeze until firm any dough suggested for refrigerator cookies. Fill a cooky shooter and press your p's and q's onto a cooky sheet about ½ inch apart. Cooky presses come with various inserts that shape bird, beast, or flower.

BALL COOKIES

Choose any of the doughs mentioned for refrigerator cookies and chill until firm. Pinch off pieces of the dough and roll gently between your palms to form balls about ¾ inch in diameter. Place each about 2 inches apart on the cooky sheet. The balls will flatten slightly during baking. To insure this and gain a design as well, press each ball down with the tines of a fork before baking.

The balls of dough may enclose fruit—candied or dried, nuts, chocolate chips, etc.

For *thumbprint cookies,* dent the dough to make a cavity. Fill with a dot of thick jam or marmalade. A sprinkle of nuts, chopped fine, adds irresistibility.

Binnie's Butter Cookies

A button of pink icing topped with a pistachio nut makes these delectable cookies picture pretty.

> ½ cup shortening
> 1 teaspoon vanilla
> ¼ cup sugar
> 2 egg yolks
> 1¼ cups flour
> ¼ teaspoon salt

Cream shortening with vanilla. Add sugar gradually if by hand, and beat until light and fluffy. Add egg yolks one at a time and beat well after each. Mix flour with salt and add only enough so when dough is touched lightly your finger comes away clean. Roll and cut dough into shapes, shape into a roll and slice, make balls, or fill a cooky press or shooter. Bake cookies in a preheated moderate, 365° F., oven about 15 minutes, or until browned.

DECORATING COOKIES

Decorations are a large part of a cooky's charm. For variety, choose two or three from the following for each batch of cookies. Any of these may be put on before the cookies are baked.

Cinnamon Candies ("Red Hots").

Chocolate Sprinkles.

Coconut Flakes or Shreds.

Dragées (Silver Shot).

Egg: For a glossy varnish, beat yolk, white, or whole egg slightly and paint on cookies with a pastry brush.

Fancies: Plain or varicolored sugar dots are available at the fancy grocery store.

Fruit: Crystallized, dried, or candied, cut small. Place on cookies cut side down.

Nuts: Chop, or use perfect whole nuts of any variety.

Seeds: Anise, fennel, caraway, poppy, or sesame.

PRECAUTION: Store anise-seed cookies separately because they're so pungent any cooky stored with them will absorb their flavor.

Sugar: Granulated, plain or colored. For a crinkled effect, sprinkle cookies with plain granulated sugar and dot with a drop or two of water.

Icing Cookies: After baking, brush on any Sugar Frosting* with a pastry brush before cookies have cooled. The icing may be tinted with vegetable color if desired, but keep it on the pastel side. Any of the decorations listed above may be pressed into the icing before it hardens.

SERVING COOKIES

Cookies that haven't been iced look demure when sprinkled with confectioners' sugar before serving.

Arrange cookies of the same size or with similar trim in rows. For attractive appearance, overlap all except bar cookies. Avoid using doilies on the serving plate because they become unattractively fat-stained.

CAKES

Benighted indeed is the American who has never had a birthday cake—a dish even more typically ours than apple pie. With good cakes to buy from bakery or box, making one from scratch might seem fruitless—except for two things: pride of achievement and the joy of well-earned compliments.

Perfection in cakes is judged by a thin tender crust with a moderately rounded top surface, either smooth or slightly pebbly. The texture will be moist and velvety, the cells fine-grained and uniform in size. The crumb should be elastic—test by rubbing a bit in your fingers—the cake itself high, light, and handsome with fragrant aroma and flavor.

When you've mastered cookies you won't find the few additional directions for turning out successful butter cakes any great challenge. The information listed under Beating Eggs* will guide you in making a perfect sponge-type cake.

Despite the fact that butter and sponge cakes are quite different, certain rules apply to both: be sure all ingredients are at room temperature; use standard measuring cups and spoons for accurate measure; and handle the batters lightly so the air bubbles won't break.

STORING CAKES

Cakes keep well tightly covered in tins, in pliofilm bags, or covered with transparent plastic wrap. Cakes may be refrigerated, and will keep in the freezer six months.

Preferably freeze before icing, then frost when the cake has thawed, or unwrap immediately, so icing will not stick.

SUGGESTION: When wrapping cakes, a few toothpick "props" inserted in the top will help keep icing from being smeared.

INGREDIENTS FOR BUTTER CAKES

Essentially, butter cakes contain fat, sugar, eggs, flour, and liquid. For full information on these, see Ingredients for Cookies.* Except as indicated below, do not substitute, add, or delete any ingredient in a recipe.

Fat (Shortening): Solid fat makes a better-textured and more flavorful cake than liquid shortening, for which special recipe procedures are required.

Eggs: Judge a cake for richness by the number of eggs called for. Recipes often suggest separating eggs for butter cakes. However, if they're added one at a time and the batter is beaten well after each, this is unnecessary. Less muscle is involved if you beat the eggs in a separate bowl with a rotary beater until they're thick and lemon-colored, then beat them into the batter. If using an electric mixer, follow manufacturer's directions.

Flour: Softer than all-purpose flour, cake flour produces a light cake with delicate texture.

Although some recipes specify two siftings of the measured amount of flour with the other dry ingredients, only one is necessary.

Leavening Agents: Butter cakes rise partially because of the air beaten into them and partially because of heat, but baking powder is the chief leavening agent. Its action begins as soon as liquid touches it, so sift it with the flour rather than, as some recipes direct, dissolving it in the liquid.

THE CONVENTIONAL CAKE METHOD

This is the best method for putting butter cakes together, and memorizing it will speed mixing.

    PRECAUTION: When a friend offers you a cake recipe, follow her method if it differs from the conventional.

    The following supposes you're mixing the cake by hand, and a rubber spatula is the best tool.

    There's no danger of overbeating cakes until the flour and liquid ingredients are added. Then proceed speedily to avoid loss of leavening, and gently—use as few strokes as possible to avoid breaking air bubbles.

Mixing Method for Butter Cakes

    1. Cream shortening with the extract and about 2 tablespoons of the liquid called for in the recipe.

    2. Add sugar gradually. Beat well after each addition, and continue beating until mixture is light and fluffy.

    3. Add eggs one at a time and beat well after each addition.

    4. Sift flour with other dry ingredients. Add about ¼ of the amount to shortening mixture and *beat* only until incorporated.

    5. Add about ⅓ of the liquid and *stir* only until incorporated. (To prevent lumps, be sure there's no flour on the sides of the bowl before adding liquid.)

    6. Continue to add dry and liquid ingredients alternately as directed above, ending with dry ingredients.

    7. Stir in any added ingredients: nuts, candied fruit, etc.

    Cake Pans: The following guide will help you choose a pan of the correct size. (If pan is too small, the batter will overflow; if too large, the cake will spread out, rather than up. As a general rule, fill pans ⅔ full. Incidentally, because of pan depth, the top crust of a loaf cake always cracks.

    Although normally an aluminum pan doesn't require greasing, if you're concerned about sticking, lightly grease the bottom preferably with vegetable shortening or oil because the milk substance in butter can cause sticking. Silicone parchment makes a good substitute for greasing and makes the pan easier to wash, too. Cut it to fit the bottom of the pan and dampen it slightly, if necessary to make it adhere.

If your pans are an inheritance from great-grandmamma and you can't bear to throw them away, grease the pan, cover the bottom with wax paper cut to fit, and grease the paper. Peel and discard the paper as soon as the cake is turned out.

SUGGESTION: For cupcakes, fill muffin pans or paper cups, placing paper cups about 1 inch apart on cooky sheets.

Guide to Baking Butter Cakes

Amount of Flour in Recipe	Pan Size	Baking Temp. (Preheated Oven)	Minutes, Approx.
2–3 cups	One 13 × 9 × 2-inch sheet	Moderate, 365° F.	35
	One 9 × 5 × 3-inch loaf	Slow, 325° F.	60
	Two 8- or 9-inch layers	Moderate, 365° F.	25
	One 9 × 9 × 2-inch square	Moderate, 365° F.	40
	About 2 dozen medium cupcakes	Moderate, 365° F.	20

BAKING BUTTER CAKES

Because heat helps make cakes rise, be sure the oven is preheated to the correct temperature. To maintain that temperature throughout, don't open the oven until time to check doneness. Because cake cell walls are fragile, try to keep the kitchen tranquil during the first quarter of the baking period.

Cakes rise more in the center, so for an even cake gently push the batter up to the sides of the pan, leaving a slight depression in the center, and be sure the oven rack is level. Place the pan in the center of the oven for even heat circulation. If baking layers, allow air space between pans and sides of the oven. If space is limited, use two oven racks and stagger layers. Don't bake other foods with cakes, because odors and moisture will be absorbed.

To avoid a dry cake, test about 5 minutes before the time called for in the recipe. Butter cakes have finished baking when they shrink slightly from the sides of the pan, when a cake tester inserted in the center comes out clean, and when the cake, touched lightly in the center, springs back.

A new-baked cake is fragile, so allow it to "repose" 5 to 10 minutes before turning it out of the pan or it may fall apart. To avoid sogginess, turn out on a wire cake rack. (If cake sticks, hit rack and cake sharply on the table rather than trying to pry it out with a knife.) Sheet or loaf cakes can stay in the pan and will stay fresh longer when cut as served.

PRECAUTION: It's usually not wise to increase or decrease cake recipes. If you do, don't increase the salt proportionately.

Pattern for Butter Cake

> ½ cup shortening
> 1 teaspoon flavoring extract
> 1 cup liquid, divided
> 1 cup sugar
> 3 eggs
> 2½ cups cake flour, measured after sifting
> 4 teaspoons baking powder
> ½ teaspoon salt

Follow Mixing Method for Butter Cakes* and bake in layers, muffin pans, etc., as directed in Guide to Baking Butter Cakes.*

White (Silver) Cake

Use milk as the liquid, almond as the flavoring extract. Substitute 6 egg whites for whole eggs. Add ⅛ teaspoon cream of tartar for each white and beat to a Stiff Foam.* Gently fold beaten whites into batter after last addition of dry ingredients.

Yellow (Gold) Cake

Use milk as the liquid, orange or almond as the flavoring extract. Substitute 6 egg yolks for whole eggs, adding them as for whole eggs.

Orange Cake

Use orange juice as the liquid in either White or Yellow Cake, and substitute 1½ tablespoons grated orange rind for the flavoring extract. If desired, fold in 1 cup chopped candied orange peel.

Spice Cake

Prepare either Butter or Yellow Cake, sifting about 1 tablespoon mixed spices with the dry ingredients. Omit extract. For darker color, substitute dark brown sugar, packed firmly, for granulated.

Fruit and/or Nut Cakes

After the dry ingredients have been added, stir in 1½ cups of fruit and/or nuts (see Flavoring Ingredients for Cookies*) in any of the above variations.

Chocolate Cake

This is the kind of feather-light chocolate cake that people keep asking for again, and again, and again.

> ½ cup shortening
> ½ teaspoon vanilla
> ¾ cup sour milk, divided
> 1⅓ cups sugar
> 3 eggs
> 3 ounces unsweetened chocolate, melted
> 2 cups cake flour, measured after sifting
> ¾ teaspoon baking soda
> ½ teaspoon salt

Follow Pattern for Butter Cakes,* beating chocolate in after eggs are added.

SPONGE-TYPE CAKES

If your cooking is at all inspired it won't be long before you're surrounded by egg whites, so when you make an angel-food cake, you add the virtue of thrift to pride. Although rather characterless of itself, sponge cake is an admirable base for many attractive desserts. Sponge-type cakes improve with aging, so if convenient bake them 2 days before serving.

Sponge cake is made with whole eggs; angel-food with egg whites. The air beaten into the eggs is what makes the cakes tower tall. Easier to produce than butter cakes, when perfect, they're tender, moist, and light as a summer breeze. Recipes may be divided or increased. Do not increase the salt proportionately.

BAKING SPONGE AND ANGEL-FOOD CAKES

These are composed primarily of egg, which, being a protein, toughens with overcooking, so a tube pan is best for baking large sponge-type cakes. The center tube speeds baking and prevents the cake from overcooking on the outside before the center finishes baking.

Don't grease tube pans for sponge-type cakes (the principle is the same as for soufflés). However, a wax paper or silicone parchment cutout in the bottom of the pan will insure easy removal. Peel the paper off as soon as the cake is removed.

As with butter cakes, place pans in the center of the oven and make the same tests for doneness. To avoid shrinkage, don't expose sponge-type cakes to drafts until cold.

When warm, cakes baked in tube pans are too delicate to support their weight, so invert the pan and allow them to hang, but only until cool. Some tube pans also have "feet" which allow air to circulate around the cooling cake, preventing sogginess. If your pan lacks feet, invert it on a cake rack. When cake is cool, turn the pan right side up and gently loosen around sides and tube with a narrow spatula. Invert the cake onto your serving plate, and if cake sticks hit the plate sharply on the table once or twice.

Cutting Sponge-Type Cakes: Because a knife will crush these cakes, pull into slices with a cake breaker or 2 forks. Hold forks back to back, insert tines into the cake close together, and gently pull apart.

Cake Pans Other than Tube: For variety, sponge-type cakes may be baked in thin layers or sheets. Use silicone parchment, or grease the pan bottom and add an ungreased wax paper cutout to fit. Remove from pan and cool as directed in Baking Butter Cakes.*

Guide to Baking Sponge-Type Cakes

Number of Eggs in Recipe	Pan Sizes	Baking Temp. (Preheated Oven)	Minutes, Approx.
5–6-egg sponge	One 9-inch tube	Moderate, 350° F.	35
8–12-egg white angel-food	One 9-inch tube	Moderate, 350° F.	40
6-egg sponge *or* 4–6-egg white angel-food	One 13 × 9 × 2-inch pan *or* Two 8 × 8 × 2-inch layers *or* Three 8-inch round layers	Moderate, 350° F.	25

Pattern for Angel-Food Cake

> 1 cup egg whites
> ¼ teaspoon salt
> 1 teaspoon cream of tartar
> 1 teaspoon almond extract
> 1¼ cups sugar (preferably very fine), sifted
> 1 cup cake flour, measured after sifting

Using an electric mixer or rotary beater, whip the whites with the salt and cream of tartar to a Stiff Foam.* Beat in extract.

With a rubber spatula, fold in sugar, sprinkling only a heaping tablespoon of it over the surface at a time, and being sure it's incorporated after each addition. Add flour as for sugar, in about 4 parts.

Turn into a prepared pan, making sure batter touches the sides, and cut through it 5 or 6 times with the spatula to break any large air bubbles. Level the top, and bake as directed in the Guide to Baking Sponge-Type Cakes.*

Fruit and/or Nut Angel-Food Cake

When all the flour has been added, fold in 1 cup fruit and/or nuts (see Flavoring Ingredients for Cookies*).

SPONGE CAKE

A few of the justly famous desserts based on sponge-cake batter are jelly roll, charlotte russe, dobos torte, and icebox pudding. Although recipes may vary from the basic procedure, none will present a problem once you've learned the sponge cake technique.

Pattern for Sponge Cake

> 1 tablespoon lemon juice
> 2 tablespoons water
> 1 tablespoon grated lemon rind
> 6 eggs, separated
> 1 cup sugar (preferably very fine), sifted
> ¼ teaspoon salt
> ½ teaspoon cream of tartar
> 1 cup cake flour, measured after sifting

Combine lemon juice, water, and lemon rind. Using an electric mixer or rotary beater, beat egg yolks until homogeneous. Add sugar, salt, and lemon juice mixture and beat until thick and lemon-colored.

Beat egg whites with cream of tartar to a Stiff Foam,* and using a rubber spatula fold them into the yolk mixture. Fold in flour gradually, incorporating it completely after each addition. Turn into a pan, making sure batter touches the sides, and cut through it 5 or 6 times to break any large air bubbles. Level the top. Bake as directed in Guide to Baking Sponge-Type Cakes.* Invert, and as soon as cool remove from pan.

Fruit and/or Nut Sponge Cake

When all the flour has been added, fold in 1 cup fruit and/or nuts (see Flavoring Ingredients for Cookies*).

Jelly Torte

Prepare half the Pattern for Sponge Cake recipe, and bake in a 9 × 13 × 2 inch pan prepared as directed for Cake Pans Other Than Tube.* When cold, remove cake and make 3 crosswise cuts so you'll have 4 even layers. Thin orange (or other) jelly to spreading consistency with sherry and spread 3 of the layers. Stack layers and sprinkle the top heavily with confectioners' sugar.

FROSTINGS

Besides being decorative, frostings add flavor to cakes and, by protecting them from air, help keep them fresh. Frostings are also useful as fillings for cake layers and cookies.

Frosting Cakes: For a level cake, stack layers before frosting to determine best placement. Arrange all layers flat surface up. If necessary gently brush off any crumbs with a pastry brush.

A long, narrow, flexible spatula will speed your work. Spread part of the frosting evenly between layers to within ¼ inch of the edges. Pile remaining frosting on top of cake and spread top and sides. (If layers slip, secure with a cake tester.) Smooth sides by running spatula around them. Swirl or peak soft frostings with the bowl of a tablespoon to further improve their appearance.

When frosting a sheet cake, spread evenly, covering cake to the outside edges. A sheet cake looks attractive cut into a variety of shapes after icing hardens. Make *triangles* by cutting squares in half diagonally. For *bars* cut narrow 1 × 2-inch strips. For *circles* or *diamonds,* use a cooky cutter. Serve on a large handsome plate.

BUDGET MEMO: Save the crumbs for topping ice cream, puddings, or desserts (see Decorating Cookies* for hints on how to add glamour to frostings).

SUGGESTION: Iced cakes are easiest to slice with a knife dipped in cold water.

UNCOOKED FROSTINGS

Uncooked frostings are simple to make, and the spreading consistency is easy to adjust—additional liquid for thinning; additional sugar for stiffening. There's no waiting either—cakes may be frosted

5 minutes after they come out of the oven because these icings spread better on a warm cake.

SUGGESTION: If the icing hardens before you've had a chance to smooth it, heat spatula by holding it in very hot water a few minutes. Shake off the water before smoothing the icing.

For a simple and attractive design, just before the icing hardens, draw the tines of a fork gently over the frosting in straight vertical rows, then in horizontal rows, being careful not to cut through to the cake.

Ingredients for Sugar Frostings: Only three ingredients make a confectioners' sugar frosting as easy as ABC.

CONFECTIONERS' SUGAR. This must be sifted after measuring to remove lumps. To keep confectioners' sugar from scattering over your counter top, sift it onto wax paper placed in a bowl. Remove the wax paper with the sugar and funnel out or spoon-scoop it. With increased beating, an icing made with confectioners' sugar loses the raw sugar taste.

LIQUIDS. Cream, strong coffee, fruit juice, maple sirup, spirits, or even water may be used alone or in combination.

FLAVORINGS. Choose any extract or replace with double their amount of grated citrus fruit rind.

Pattern for Sugar Frosting

⅛ teaspoon salt
2 tablespoons liquid, approximately
2 cups confectioners' sugar, sifted
1 teaspoon flavoring extract
or
2 teaspoons grated citrus fruit rind

Dissolve salt in liquid and add to confectioners' sugar, beating it in gradually to avoid lumps. Add only enough liquid for spreading consistency, and beat in flavoring extract. The recipe may be increased or decreased. Yield: Enough for tops and sides of two 8-inch round layers or 12 cupcakes. Half the recipe will cover the top of a 13 × 9 × 2-inch sheet cake.

Fruit

Substitute ¼ cup crushed fruit—berries, peaches, pineapple, etc.—for liquid. If necessary, thin with lemon juice.

Chocolate

Beat in 1 ounce unsweetened chocolate, melted, after liquid has been added.

Cocoa

Mix 3 tablespoons cocoa with the confectioners' sugar.

The further complication of shortening in a Sugar Frosting produces a creamy-rich icing. This added enrichment makes it a luscious complement for sponge or angel-food cakes.

Pattern for Butter Frosting

> ½ cup butter
> ⅛ teaspoon salt
> 1 pound confectioners' sugar, sifted
> ¼ cup liquid, approximately
> 1½ teaspoons flavoring extract
> > *or*
> 1 tablespoon grated citrus fruit rind

Cream butter. Add salt to sugar and beat in gradually. Add enough liquid for spreading consistency. Add any flavoring extract and beat until fluffy. The recipe may be increased or decreased. Yield: Enough for top and sides of two 9-inch layers, three 8-inch layers, a 9-inch tube cake, or 24 cupcakes.

Fruit Butter Frosting

Substitute ⅓ cup crushed fruit—berries, peaches, pineapple, etc. —for liquid. If necessary, thin with lemon juice.

Chocolate Butter Frosting

Add 3 ounces unsweetened chocolate, melted, to butter-sugar mixture.

Cocoa Butter Frosting

Add ⅔ cup cocoa to the confectioners' sugar.

Snow Peak Frosting

Cheers for this fluffy frosting that needs no cooking. Though, unless you own an electric mixer, it involves muscle.

> 1 egg white
> ¾ cup sugar, preferably very fine
> ¼ teaspoon cream of tartar
> 1 teaspoon flavoring extract: almond, vanilla, etc.
> ¼ cup boiling water

In a small deep bowl, combine egg white, sugar, cream of tartar, and extract. Add boiling water and beat at high speed in an electric mixer or with a rotary beater until mixture holds stiff peaks. The frosting will keep about 4 hours in the refrigerator, uncovered;

overnight, covered; and may be frozen. Yield: Enough for tops and sides of two 8-inch layers.

NOTE: If desired sprinkle with fresh or prepared coconut flakes or shreds.

Creole Frosting

Substitute ¾ cup dark brown sugar, packed firmly, for very fine sugar.

FILLINGS

If baking a layer cake and then making a frosting strike you as child's play, you may want to add the complication of preparing a filling as well. It should be saluted as a labor of love!

Custard-type fillings add the adjective "cream" to cakes. Preserves, jams, jellies, marmalade, or fruit butters are easy and delectable fillings for cakes or cookies.

PIES

Very few men don't think a perfect pie is one of the world's loveliest sights and although making your first crust may take courage with your second you'll realize it's "easy as pie."

Set your sights for a light, crisp crust that has a blistered, golden brown surface and is tender enough to break easily, but not so tender it crumbles when cut. The filling, of course, should be of admirable consistency and flavor.

SUGGESTION: Handsome silver containers with oven pie pan inserts add aesthetic pleasure to pie for dessert. Lacking one, place the pie in its pan on an attractive serving plate but for ease in cutting and serving do not remove the pie.

STORING PIES

Pie dough keeps about 10 days in the refrigerator, 1 month in the ice-cube section, 8 months in the freezer. Baked pastry shells keep about a week in the refrigerator, but don't freeze well. Fruit pies keep about 1 month in the ice-cube section, about 7 months in the freezer.

Leftover cream or custard pie, with or without fruit, and fruit pie will keep about 2 days in the refrigerator without spoiling.

Soft meringue doesn't keep well in the refrigerator or freezer.

PIE DOUGH

The best way to learn how to make a pie crust is to watch an expert in action. No need to get the recipe, however, because the proportions are standard.

INGREDIENTS FOR PIE DOUGH

Flour: Although some recipes specify cake flour, strong all-purpose flour is more elastic and therefore produces a flakier dough that's easier to handle.

Shortening: Good-flavored solid shortenings are usual for pastry. (Liquid shortening requires special procedures.) Lard (see how to substitute it in Chapter II) makes superior pastry—rich, short, and tender. Hydrogenated vegetable shortening also may be used. Both butter and margarine contain liquid and produce a rather hard, brittle crust.

Too much shortening makes a delicate but difficult-to-handle crust, but a miserly approach results in a thick, doughy crust.

Liquid: Water is the liquid normally used, and chilling is unnecessary. Juices such as orange or pineapple may replace water. They contribute no flavor, but their acidity helps make crust tender.

Too much liquid makes tough, sticky pastry that's hard to roll. With too little, the dough will be crumbly and impossible to roll.

Salt: Although recipes usually suggest mixing the salt with the flour, dissolving it in the liquid insures even distribution and makes for a more tender crust.

MIXING METHOD FOR PIE DOUGH

As noted in the discussion of batters, flour mixed with water makes paste. To avoid a pasty mass, the fat is cut into the flour. This procedure protects the flour from the liquid and insures a short crust.

Cutting Fat into Flour: For ease, choose a large bowl with a narrow, rounded bottom. Place flour in the bowl, add fat, and coat your fingertips with the flour. Pinch fat and flour together, being careful not to allow your palms to come in contact with the mixture because their warmth might melt the fat. A pastry blender or two knives also may be used, but the personal touch is more effective.

Cutting fat and flour until the particles are the size of peas makes for a mealy crust. For a flaky crust, continue until the particles resemble coarse cornmeal. For uniform tenderness, cut until all the particles are approximately the same size, but realize that too much cutting makes the mixture pasty, and then it's almost impossible to incorporate the liquid.

Adding Liquid: Flour varies in thirstiness, so it's impossible to specify an exact amount of liquid. Toss the dough with a fork, simultaneously pouring in only as much liquid as necessary to dampen the fat-flour clumps so they hold together. Add liquid gradually, and only to the dry portions, because the moistened clumps will continue to absorb liquid.

If you're a novice, you may find it easier to sprinkle the liquid from your fingertips or to use a perforated sprinkler-top bottle.

Turn the moistened clumps onto a piece of wax paper and enclose them in the paper. Then open the top so no dough will be caught in the folds and gently press the dough into a ball.

Firm dough is easier to roll and will be more tender (the gluten strands will "relax"), so chill it if there's time, allowing about 2 hours in the refrigerator, 25 minutes in the ice-cube section, 20 minutes in the freezer.

SUGGESTION: Should the dough crumble excessively during rolling, pull the pastry into bits in a bowl and toss with enough additional liquid to make it hold together.

The principles for rolling any dough are identical, so review the instructions for Rolled Cookies.*

Pie Pans: Any shape pan may be used for pastry. Standard pans for pie are 8 or 9 inches in diameter and about 1¼ inches in depth. For a crisp, nicely-browned bottom crust, choose oven glass or a dull metal pan. (Shiny metal reflects heat and prevents the undercrust from baking well.) Pie pans do not need greasing.

Pattern for Pie Dough

¾ cup shortening
2½ cups flour, measured after sifting
1 teaspoon salt
5 tablespoons water, approximately

Cut shortening into flour. Dissolve salt in water and add it gradually. For a mealy crust, use only enough liquid to hold particles together; for a flaky crust, use slightly more. Makes one 9-inch double-crust pie or about nine 4-inch tart shells. Recipe may be increased or decreased.

SUGGESTION: Practice making dough with half the pattern for pie dough.

DOUBLE-CRUST PIES

Bottom Crust: Divide dough, allowing slightly more for the bottom crust. Roll it into a circle ⅛ to ¼ inch thick. A thinner crust may break, a thicker crust is gross.

Invert the pie pan and place it gently on the rolled dough. Cut around it with a knife, making a circle of dough 1 inch larger than the pan. To transfer dough from board to pan, roll it around your pin or fold it in half or in a tricorn before picking it up.

Fitting dough into the pan requires a finicking touch. Without stretching the dough, press it gently but firmly against bottom and sides to exclude air bubbles. Slash excess dough from the rim with a table knife.

PROTECTING THE BOTTOM CRUST. You'll hear of methods ranging from witchcraft to nonsense that supposedly will prevent a soggy bottom crust. The only ones that work are brushing it with melted butter (this adds flavor too) and, when feasible, thickening the filling.

Top Crust: Roll remaining dough about an inch larger than the pan. Fold it in half and, to allow the steam to escape during baking, gash a small opening near the center, being sure to cut through both thicknesses of dough.

Just before putting the top crust on, pat the rim of the lower crust lightly with water so the top will adhere. Place the top crust on the filling, being careful not to stretch it, and again slash off excess dough from the rim.

Sealing the Crust: For a simple and attractive seal, press the rim of the crust together all around the edges with the back of the fork tines.

Fluting Pie Crust: A standing edge acts as a dike, so is especially useful when the filling is juicy. To flute, push the rim of dough in from the outer edge of the pan with the index finger of one hand, while pressing toward it with the thumb and index finger of the other hand.

To help prevent shrinkage, hook and press outside edges of the flutes firmly under the rim of the pan.

THICK FLUTING. Roll the dough for the top crust 1 inch larger than usual and turn the excess under the edge of the lower crust.

SUGGESTION: If your fingertips can take heat, the flutes may be reshaped after about 3 minutes of baking.

Glazing Pie Crusts: Because a pale pie is unattractive, brush the surface of the dough with melted butter and allow it to harden before baking the pie. A brush of milk, cream, or slightly beaten egg yolk may be used instead, but butter adds more flavor and, because it won't puddle, makes a uniform glaze.

SINGLE-CRUST PIES

A single-crust pie may be allowed to display its allure openly. Simply follow directions for a Bottom Crust, finish the edge as desired— flute, fork-stamp, etc.—and add filling.

Pastry Lattice: If you'd like the filling to wink through a lattice, roll dough into an oblong approximately equal to the diameter of the pan and cut ½-inch strips. Moisten the rim of the bottom crust with water and place the strips across it, allowing ½ inch between each. If desired, top with additional strips placed at right angles, or for fancy-fancy, weave them through those already in place. The strips may be cut with a pastry jagger (the wheel pinks them), and artful cooks also twist the strips gently several times before putting them in place.

Fasten the strips by pressing them firmly to the edge of the bottom crust. Trim off excess dough, and flute the rim or stamp it with fork tines.

PASTRY SHELLS

These make delectable containers for custard, fruit, ice cream, and the like. More water may be used in the dough for a pastry shell. Roll and fit it into the pan as directed for a Bottom Crust.*

To prevent buckling, prick bottom and sides of the dough every two or three inches with a fork. Opening the oven door doesn't harm pie dough, so check the shell after about 3 minutes of baking and prick it again if it's not lying flat.

Bake a pastry shell on the top rung of a preheated very hot, 450° F., oven about 12 minutes, or until delicately browned. (Shells allowed to brown too much will soak up the filling.) Cool and, if desired, remove to an attractive serving dish. Fill the shell when cold.

Tart Shells: These miniatures spell work! Invert a muffin pan (or custard cup) and measure up one side of the cup, across the bottom and down the other side. Use this measurement as your diameter for the dough and cut circles of the required size. Fit the circles of dough around the outside of the cups, being careful not to stretch them. Pleat the edges in 3 or 4 places, pressing the pleats together to make wings.

Place muffin pans or custard cups on a cooky sheet pastry side up. Bake as directed for a pastry shell, allowing only about 10 minutes.

LEFTOVER PIE DOUGH

If you munched on baked scraps of leftover pie dough at your mother's knee, no sales talk will be needed. The following suggestions can be a treat for the neighborhood small fry, or the scraps may be used for hors d'oeuvre.

Cinnamon Snails: Roll dough into an oblong about ⅛ inch thick. Sprinkle with a mixture of 3 parts sugar and 1 part cinnamon. Roll tightly like a jelly roll and cut 1-inch slices. Place snails on a cooky sheet, cut side up, and bake in a preheated hot, 425° F., oven about 10 minutes, or until browned.

Hors d'Oeuvre Snails: Spread pastry with softened butter and cover with sharply seasoned spreads such as anchovy, shellfish, tongue, ham. Bake as above.

Cheese Straws: Roll pastry into an oblong about ¼ inch thick. Sprinkle with grated cheese, pressing it into the dough. Fold the dough into thirds and press it down firmly. Roll into an oblong again and, if desired, sprinkle with cayenne pepper.

With a knife or pastry wheel, cut strips measuring about 5 × 1 inch. Twist the strips gently two or three times and place on a cooky sheet, pressing the ends down firmly to secure them. Bake as specified for Cinnamon Snails above.

PIE FILLINGS

FRUIT FILLINGS

The filling of a perfect fruit pie is touched with sweetness and not quite thick. It's composed simply of prepared fruit (pitted, peeled, hulled, etc.), sweetening, a thickening agent, and spices. The tartness of the fruit determines the amount of sweetening, and honey or sugar—granulated, maple, or brown—may be used.

Choose any desired spice—cloves, cinnamon, nutmeg, etc.—or combinations, but be sure they don't overwhelm the flavor of the fruit.

Thickening Agents. Flour is the usual thickening agent, and the amount depends upon the juiciness of the fruit. Mix it with the sugar and spices and spread half the mixture over the bottom crust. Add the fruit and sprinkle it with the remaining flour mixture.

Other thickeners are quick-cooking tapioca, crumbs—bread, cake, cooky—or almonds chopped fine. Scatter them over the bottom crust, and, depending upon the juiciness of the fruit, allow 1 to 2 tablespoons for a 9-inch pie. Mix sweetening and spices with the fruit.

Baking Fruit Pies. To avoid an overflow of fruit juice, center a "chimney" of uncooked macaroni upright in the gash in the top crust. To be sure you won't have to scrape spills from the oven, place the pie pan on a piece of aluminum foil about 3 inches larger than the pan.

Bake fruit pies on the lowest rack of a preheated hot, 425° F., oven until the fruit is tender (test by piercing it with a cake tester as soon as the juice bubbles through the gash in the top crust), and the pastry is brown. Allow about 35 minutes for a double-crust pie, about 30 minutes for a single-crust pie.

SUGGESTION: When baking a single-crust pie of firm fruits (apple, peach), cover the fruit filling with foil for the first 20 minutes.

Should the crust get too brown before the fruit is tender, invert a pan over the pie.

Fruit Fillings for a 9-Inch Pie

Fruit	Amount	Sugar	Flour	Spice
Apples, peeled and sliced	5–6 cups	¾–1 cup	1–2 tbs.	1 tsp.
Berries	3½ cups	½–¾ cup	4 tbs.	—
Cherries, sour, pitted	3–3½ cups	1–1¼ cups	4 tbs.	½ tsp.
Peaches, sliced or halved	3–3½ cups	½–¾ cup	2–4 tbs.	½ tsp.
Rhubarb, diced	3½–4 cups	1¼ cups	5 tbs.	½ tsp.

CUSTARD FILLINGS

You can consider your custard pie impeccable when the filling has delicate flavor and velvety texture. To help prevent a soggy bottom crust, use as little water as possible in the pastry dough and be sure the crust has no cracks or holes. Chill the shell about an hour before baking the pie, and use an egg-rich custard.

Custard Filling

> ½ cup sugar
> 4 eggs, beaten slightly
> 3 cups milk, scalded
> Nutmeg (optional)

Combine sugar with eggs and stir milk in gradually. Pour into a 9-inch chilled unbaked pastry shell and sprinkle with nutmeg, if desired. Bake on the lowest rung of a preheated hot, 425° F., oven about 25 minutes, or until it doesn't feel excessively sticky when touched lightly, and a knife (preferably silver) inserted halfway between the center and the outside rim comes out shiny, rather than milky. Cool on a rack at room temperature.

Variations

One half teaspoon extract—vanilla, almond, etc.—may be added to milk, and ⅓ cup coconut grated fine, or 1 cup pecans chopped fine, may be added to custard mixture before pouring it into the shell.

SUGGESTION: A browned top will entice the eye. To achieve it, melt 2 tablespoons butter in the pan before adding milk for scalding.

Any extra custard may be baked separately as directed for Baked Custard.*

Olive's Lemon Meringue Pie

Olive has a bewitching hand with pies, and lemon is her specialty.

> 2 cups water, divided
> 1½ cups sugar
> ¼ teaspoon salt
> 1 tablespoon grated lemon rind
> 7 tablespoons cornstarch
> 6 eggs, separated
> 1 tablespoon butter
> ¼ cup lemon juice
> 6 to 8 drops yellow vegetable color, optional
> 1 8-inch pastry shell, baked

Place in a saucepan 1½ cups water, sugar, salt, and lemon rind and bring to a boil, stirring only until the sugar dissolves. Dissolve cornstarch in remaining water and add to sugar mixture gradually, stirring constantly. Cook gently until clear and thick. (If sauce tastes starchy at this point, cook covered over boiling water 15 minutes longer, stirring occasionally.) Remove from heat.

Beat egg yolks well and beat a small amount of sauce into them. When warmed, stir back into sauce, and add butter. When butter melts, stir in lemon juice and vegetable color. Turn into pastry shell.

Prepare Soft Meringue* with the egg whites and spread it on the warm filling. Bake in a very hot, 450° F., oven about 5 minutes. Makes 6+ servings.

BAKING POWDER DOUGH

Shortcakes, dumplings, meat pies, cobblers and the like are all made from baking powder dough, which differs so little from pastry you'll find making it even easier than pie!

BISCUITS

The basic ingredients are the same as for pastry and so is the method of combining them. For flaky biscuits, when cutting the fat into the flour, keep the particles fairly large. Too little liquid makes tough, compact biscuits; too much means they won't be shapely.

Any of the following seasoning ingredients may be mixed with the flour: ¼ teaspoon dry mustard or curry powder; ½ teaspoon herbs; 1¼ teaspoons seeds—caraway, celery, cardamom, etc.; 1 tablespoon grated orange rind.

Shaping Biscuits: Biscuits may be made any desired size and thickness. Simply remember that they rise about double during baking, and that while sliver-thin biscuits may be dainty, they also are likely to be dry.

Roll the dough ½ inch thick and cut with a lightly floured biscuit cutter or a drinking glass. Or, for ease, pat the dough into an oblong and cut squares, rectangles, or diamonds with a knife, lightly floured if necessary.

Baking Biscuits: Use a cooky sheet for uniform browning. With aluminum pans, greasing is unnecessary. Place biscuits about 1 inch apart if you like them crusty; allow them to touch if you prefer them soft. (Also know that if they touch they'll rise higher because each little brother has a brother to lean against.)

Texture will be better and biscuits will rise to greater heights if the dough is kneaded. Eighteen light strokes, about ½ minute, of kneading are sufficient. Biscuits that have not been kneaded will be smaller but more tender and crisp-crusted. To avoid sogginess, after baking break biscuits rather than cutting them.

Pattern for Baking Powder Dough

> 2 cups flour, measured after sifting
> 3 teaspoons baking powder
> 1 teaspoon salt
> 4 tablespoons shortening, preferably lard
> ¾ cup milk, approximately

Mix flour with baking powder and salt. Cut in shortening. Make a well in the center of the mixture and add the milk slowly, stirring with a fork until dough is soft and fairly moist. Knead if desired. Pat or roll about ½ inch thick, shape as desired, and bake in a preheated very hot, 450° F., oven about 15 minutes, or until browned. Yield: About sixteen 2-inch biscuits or top crust for a 4-quart casserole.

Drop Biscuits

Increase the milk in the above pattern to 1 cup and push the dough from a spoon, as for drop cookies.

Waffle Biscuits

Pat baking powder dough ¼ inch thick and bake in a waffle iron until browned.

Cheese Biscuits

Depending upon the sharpness of the cheese, combine about ½ cup grated cheese with the flour.

SHORTCAKE

Shortcake dough is sweeter and richer than biscuit dough. Simply increase the shortening in the Pattern for Baking Powder Dough* by 1 tablespoon and mix the flour with 1 tablespoon sugar. Top milk or cream may be substituted for milk. Shape individual biscuits or make two large rounds.

Break in half crosswise after baking and butter the bottom half lavishly. Flood with slightly crushed fruit, sweetened if necessary. Put the top half on inverted so the soft inside makes a cup, and cover with additional fruit. Serve with cream, whipped if desired.

XIV

Beautiful Beverages

Up to now, ways to judge food, beginning "It is perfect when" have been offered. There are as many ways to judge a host or hostess. Certainly giving is part of hospitality and even for unexpected guests the welcome should be followed promptly by the offer of food or drink. Bare indeed is the cupboard that can't offer at least a cup of cheer, and whether the cheer is coffee, tea, milk, or spirits, the offer alone will make guests feel welcome.

MILK PRODUCTS

Milk contributes much to good health, so it's wise to drink the recommended 2 cups (16 ounces) a day. Children require a quart. Cheese, custard, cream soups, etc., may be substituted.

STORING MILK PRODUCTS

All milk products spoil rapidly, so keep them in the coldest part of your refrigerator. Because they absorb odors they must be covered. If soiled, wipe bottle or carton tops before storage.

Although more expensive than bottles, milk cartons have formidable advantages—light in weight, with protected, nondrip spouts, they also take less space in the refrigerator. Their opacity protects the milk's riboflavin content. Finally, they don't break and needn't be returned. If you find you've carried a leaking carton home from market, simply refrigerate it upside down. A good-looking covered refrigerator pitcher for milk means speedy and attractive table service.

Whole and *skim milk, flavored milk drinks,* and *cream* keep about a week in the refrigerator.

Buttermilk, commercial sour cream, and *cultured milk,* such as yoghurt, keep about 10 days in the refrigerator.

Condensed and *evaporated milk* keep a year in a cupboard, but cans should be inverted after 6 months. Opened cans keep 10 days in the refrigerator.

Homogenized milk, cream, and *whipped cream* keep in the freezer at least 3 months.

Store *powdered milk* covered in a dry place. It doesn't sour with age, but does lose flavor after a year.

If milk or cream sours but hasn't molded, and its flavor is still good, use for cooking.

For ease in washing, rinse pans used for heating milk products in cold water both before filling and after use. Watch milk products closely during heating because they scorch readily—and to retain food value don't let them boil.

TYPES OF MILK PRODUCTS

Pasteurized Milk: Heated to destroy bacteria, this is available as is or, at slightly higher cost, homogenized.

Homogenization distributes the fat globules, keeping them in suspension. The milk then tastes richer and is slightly more digestible. However, the cream cannot be poured off for separate use. (To distribute the cream in nonhomogenized milk, shake the container just before pouring.) There is danger of curdling when homogenized milk is used in soups, sauces, gravies, scalloped potatoes, cooked cereals, custards. It also tends to make cornstarch puddings granular.

Skim Milk: Fat-free milk.

Buttermilk: Slightly richer than skim milk, this is produced with the liquid remaining after making butter.

Certified Milk: This milk, from certified herds, doesn't require pasteurization, but it is expensive and difficult to find.

Evaporated Milk: Homogenized whole milk with half the water removed. To substitute for regular milk, dilute with an equal amount of water.

Yoghurt: Whole or partly skimmed milk with a culture added that thickens it and acidifies the flavor.

Condensed Milk: Similar to evaporated milk, with sweetening added.

Powdered Milk (whole or nonfat dry milk solids): An inexpensive substitute for natural milk, this is obtainable whole or skimmed. To reconstitute, follow package directions.

SUGGESTION: Add extra food value to any batter or dough by combining up to 2 tablespoons dry milk powder with each cup of flour called for in recipes.

Chocolate Milk: Whole milk with chocolate sirup added. Chocolate milk drink is partially skimmed milk flavored with cocoa powder.

Cream: When a recipe calls for cream, light cream is implied. Undiluted evaporated milk may replace cream. Choose heavy cream for whipping and for ice cream. Homogenized cream may be medium or light, has been treated like homogenized milk, and won't whip.

Certified Cream: See Certified Milk.

Commercial Sour Cream: Sometimes called dairy sour cream, this has the same calorie content as light cream. Rich and thick, it is a manufactured product. To prevent curdling when adding it to hot mixtures, let it stand out until it is room temperature.

Souring Milk or Cream: Milk or cream may be soured with about a tablespoon of vinegar or lemon juice per cup. If souring is not apparent (aroma and clabbered appearance), increase the acid, but always use only the amount of milk or cream called for in the recipe.

NOTE: Sour milk and buttermilk are interchangeable in recipes.

Whipping Cream: All cream whips better and stays firm longer when it's a day or two old. The cream will not whip unless the fat is firm, which is why chilling is necessary.

For best results, whip only a pint of heavy cream at a time and don't add sugar until whipping is almost complete or after cream is stiff.

Although it's normally unnecessary, bowl and beater (rotary or electric) also may be chilled. Watch carefully during beating, because overbeaten cream separates. (Should this occur, see Making Butter.*)

NOTE: To avoid a buttery texture, whip cream for frozen desserts only to the consistency of soft custard.

1 cup (½ pint) heavy cream makes 2 cups whipped.

Whipping Light Cream: In an emergency, it is sometimes possible to whip light cream: Add 2 tablespoons confectioners' sugar for each cup cream and beat frothy. Add 3 to 4 teaspoons lemon juice and beat stiff. Prepare just before use because it deflates rapidly.

COCOA

Although we think of cocoa or chocolate primarily as a drink for children, in France, in Vienna, and in South America a pot of chocolate is a much-admired adult beverage. As is so often the case with simple foods, achieving perfection requires care. The problem—to cook the starch in the cocoa completely so the drink will be homogeneous. Unfortunately, shortcuts won't work.

Pattern for Cocoa

> 1 tablespoon cocoa
> 1 tablespoon sugar
> Few grains salt
> ¼ cup water
> ¾ cup milk

Place all ingredients except milk in saucepan and bring to a boil, stirring until sugar dissolves. Boil 3 minutes, add milk, and heat to scalding. Makes 1 cup, may be increased.

NOTE: It is almost impossible to avoid a skin formation. Heating the milk in a covered double boiler may help, and rotary beating before serving discourages it for a short period. If the milk skin offends you, serve the cocoa in a covered pitcher.

Hot Chocolate

Substitute ⅛ ounce unsweetened chocolate, shaved fine, for cocoa.

Mexican Chocolate

Beat about 1 teaspoon cinnamon into prepared Cocoa or Hot Chocolate.

COCOA SIRUP

If you enjoy cocoa, speed things by preparing a made-ahead sirup of all ingredients except the milk in Pattern for Cocoa,* and store in the refrigerator.

COFFEE

Perfect coffee has rich flavor and sparkling transparency. Although there's nothing more enticing than its smell in the making, the more aromatic it is then, the worse it's likely to taste, because excessive heat is driving the flavor out of the pot and into the room.

A pound of coffee contains less than a half teaspoon of the flavor-imparting volatile oil, and the trick is to keep it from evaporating. Because it is partially released through grinding, a cup of coffee made from an only adequate, but freshly ground brand will taste better than coffee made from a magnificent variety that has become stale. For impeccable freshness, beans should be snatched from the roaster, ground, and prepared immediately. To come close to paradise, buy and grind (or have ground) small quantities.

STORING COFFEE

Unopened vacuum cans stay fresh about a year, but there's a gradual flavor loss. Store opened ground coffee in the refrigerator, preferably tightly rolled in a pliofilm sack. For convenience, keep your coffee measuring spoon in the sack too.

BREWING COFFEE

Just as in making stock, the more coffee surface is exposed to the water, the more flavorful the coffee will be. Therefore, for maximum extraction choose a fine grind, and for good flavor use fresh cold water.

Again as with stock, coffee that's too strong can be diluted with cold water, so err in that direction, because there's no remedy for weak coffee.

Although differences of grade and grind are partially responsible for strength or weakness, the only way to insure really strong coffee is to be unstinting in the amount you use. A pound of coffee makes about 40 cups.

Allow 2 tablespoons coffee (1 coffee measuring spoon) for 1 measuring cup water, plus 2 tablespoons coffee for the pot.

Coffee Makers: No matter what type you buy, follow manufacturer's directions, and for best results use at no less than three-fourths capacity.

Cleanliness affects flavor, but washing pots with soap or a detergent may leave a film. Simply rinse them with cold water after use. When coffee stains are visible, fill the pot with water, add about ½ teaspoon baking soda and boil a few minutes. Or soak coffee makers with hot water and about ¼ teaspoon trisodium phosphate, generally available at hardware stores.

After use, rinse cloth filters in cold water and baking soda, and allow to stand in clean water.

Dripolators or *Vacuum-type* makers retain maximum flavor with minimum extraction of bitterness, and fine grinds may be used. Special filter papers successfully keep grounds and oil out of the brew.

Percolators drive off flavor and aroma, and there's danger of boiling. A well-constructed pot and controlled percolation time help. But the time varies both with the amount of coffee made and the speed of percolation.

Pot coffee requires a coarse grind. There is a choice of methods. Either place the required amount of coffee in a pot, pour boiling water over, stir and brew at heat lower than simmering for about 10 minutes. Or pour cold water over the coffee, place over low heat, bring to a boil, and stir. With either method, add a dash of cold water to settle the grounds and allow the coffee to stand a few minutes before straining.

Iced Coffee: This tastes best made double strength and poured over ice immediately.

Flaming Coffee: Brandy-burning spoons simplify this procedure, and either brandy or rum (high-proof rum—151 proof—will flame immediately) may be used. Fill cups with coffee and lay the brandy-burning spoon on it or hold a teaspoon over the edge of the cup. Fill with the spirit of your choice and when it warms—in about a minute—light the alcohol. Don't let it burn too long, or the alcohol will evaporate. Stir the flaming spirit into the coffee.

TEA

Next to water, tea is the least expensive beverage—1 pound makes about 200 cups, so buying an exquisite variety is not an extravagance. Small tea-taster packages allow you to sample the many kinds and to have a variety for different occasions.

Teas differ in method of manufacture, rather than in leaf, and the smaller and more broken leaves release maximum flavor. The word "pekoe" (pronounced *peck-o*) refers to leaf size and tenderness, rather than to a particular variety. The following list covers a few of the more distinctive teas.

VARIETIES OF TEA

Green: Unprocessed and unfermented, this is almost colorless and has a delicate flavor.

Darjeeling: A heavy-bodied tea of deep amber color, often called the tea of connoisseurs.

Keemun: Black tea, often called English breakfast tea.

Lapsang Souchong: A rare tea with wonderful smoky flavor.

Earl Grey's: Several companies mix this blend of teas. It has great elegance and subtle bouquet.

Scented Teas: Tea leaves combined with petals of various exotic flowers—jasmine, gardenia, or yulan (a flower of the magnolia family)—make these a bouquet of fragrance.

STORING TEA

Keep leaves or tea bags in tightly covered tins on the kitchen shelf. Tea begins to lose flavor after 6 months.

BREWING TEA

A perfect cup of tea is clear, sparkling, fragrant, and flavorful without being bitter. Begin with fresh cold water and add the tea just as soon as the water comes to a boil. (As water boils, it loses oxygen and tea made with it will taste flat.) Color is no indication of strength —tea steeped less than 3 minutes will not have yielded all its flavor— and in most varieties after 5 minutes' release of tannin, the element that makes tea bitter, begins. Most varieties have steeped sufficiently in about 5 minutes.

Scalding the pot beforehand helps keep the water hot enough to extract maximum flavor. Pour the boiling water over the tea and cover the pot.

After steeping, decant into a fresh pot (preferably of glass or pottery) and have a pot of freshly boiled water at hand for those who prefer their tea weak. If all the leaves have been removed, the tea may be reheated.

Allow 1 teaspoon tea to 1 measuring cup water, plus 1 teaspoon tea for the pot.

Tea Concentrate

This comes to your rescue when there's a crowd.

>1½ quarts fresh water
>¼ pound loose tea

As soon as the water reaches a full rolling boil, remove from heat and immediately pour over tea. Stir to immerse leaves. Cover and let stand 5 minutes. Strain into a teapot until ready to use. To serve, pour about a tablespoon of concentrate into a cup and fill the cup with piping hot water. Makes about 45 cups.

The concentrate keeps in the refrigerator about 3 weeks, 3 months in the ice-cube section, and a year in the freezer.

Iced Tea: Although iced tea often clouds upon refrigeration, the cloudiness detracts only from appearance. If it offends you, add a small amount of boiling water to clear it.

Easy Iced Tea

The Tea Council of America is responsible for this simple new method for making iced tea.

>1 quart fresh water
>6 tablespoons tea

As soon as the water reaches a full rolling boil, remove from heat and immediately pour over tea. Brew about 5 minutes, depending upon desired strength.

Stir, then strain tea into a pitcher containing 1 quart fresh cold water. Refrigeration is not required. Just before serving place ice cubes in a tall glass and fill glass with tea. Makes 2 quarts; may be increased or decreased.

Flaming Tea: See Flaming Coffee.*

FRUIT BEVERAGES

Fruit beverages are variously labeled. To know what you are buying, check the following list.

Fruit Juices: Fruit juice or juice and very finely divided pulp.

Sugar, but not water, may be added. Prune juice, the exception, is a water extract of dried prunes.

Fruit Nectars: Usually made from fruits without much natural juice, such as apricots or peaches; these are combinations of fruit juice and pulp with water, and sometimes sugar and fruit acid.

Fruit Juice Drinks or Ades: A combination of fruit juice with water, sweetened and fortified with fruit acids or citrus oils.

Imitation Fruit Juice Drinks: These are made of water, sweetened and flavored with fruit acids, citrus oils, and artificial flavors and colors and contain no fruit juice.

ALCOHOLIC BEVERAGES

Much has been said—often to the point of purple-faced argument—about the ONLY WAY to prepare various mixed drinks. Making and serving them is the gentleman's prerogative, but if you're doing the buying the following chart will help you judge the amounts needed.

The average drink—highball or on the rocks—contains 2 ounces alcohol, and at a come-and-go cocktail party 3 drinks per person is average. At a dinner party, figure 2 drinks before dinner, about 3 after dinner.

WINE

Wine, endlessly fascinating, is almost as encyclopedic a subject as food itself. But you can proceed through a lifetime of meals equipped only with the following information: Dry wine is sometimes called "table wine." Dry red wines are full-bodied, and therefore usually best with characterful red meats and lusty-flavored poultry such as goose. Because chilling kills flavor, dry red wines are normally served at room temperature.

Dry white wines are usually served with light meats—veal, pork, ham, poultry, and shellfish. These are at their best when slightly cooler than room temperature.

As with any rules, break these at will and, if you like sweet wines with other than desserts, offer them, but better give guests a choice.

Many American wines are excellent, but often the labels are not very helpful. One guarantee of superiority is a wine labeled with the variety of the grape from which it's made. This is called a "varietal" name as opposed to a "generic" name. For example, a varietal label that reads "Pinot Noir" means that at least 51 percent of the wine was made from the grapes that produce a Burgundy in France.

A generic label, such as Burgundy, on an American wine is meaningless, because Burgundy is the name of the region in France where the Pinot Noir grapes that make the wine were grown.

Champagne labels asserting the wine is produced by the "champagne," rather than "bulk," process, insure superiority. On American champagne labels, the words *brut, sec, extra dry*, etc., have been misused to the point of meaninglessness.

The French say a wineglass should never be full and never be empty. In a filled glass, the bouquet is lost, while an empty glass indicates a less than hawk-eyed host. Open a bottle of red wine and fill glasses about an hour before dinner to allow the tannic acid, which makes wine taste bitter, to evaporate. "Let it breathe" is the expert's phrase.

COOKING WITH WINE

By now you realize that cooking with wine is as simple as cooking with water, and that when just enough wine is used all the other foods are enhanced. Because the whole can never be better than the sum of its parts, know also that an excellent wine ennobles a recipe, a good wine is fine for daily use, and a poor one will produce the results to be expected from any inferior ingredient. Avoid bottles labeled "cooking wine."

Incidentally, as far as teetotalers are concerned, assure them that heating carries off the alcohol.

XV

Tempting Hors D'Oeuvre

"Come by for a drink" is an invitation rarely refused. And it's the kind of casual hospitality that allows you to invite friends more frequently. Included here is a collection of speedy-to-assemble foods to make this kind of entertaining easy. For "Dinner is served" occasions, you'll find a repertoire of more elegant hors d'oeuvre that have the virtue of advance preparation.

Whether spur-of-the-moment or complicated, hors d'oeuvre should have character, but not be rich and filling, because they're intended as thirst whetters, not appetite satisfiers. They should be salty, sharp, and spicy. You'll notice that when they are, people will dip in less frequently—a distinct advantage if you've taken time and trouble with the meal to follow.

Foods that double as hors d'oeuvre or appetizers have been noted in previous chapters. The following additional suggestions will make yours a sought-after table, and most of them are equally at home as entrées at lunch, on a buffet table, or at an evening party.

Hors d'oeuvre, a French idiom, translates to "outside the work." The word *oeuvre,* therefore, is correctly spelled without a final "s." *Antipasto,* the Italian word for appetite-whetting foods, means "before the pasta."

It's almost impossible to gauge with exactitude the amount of hors d'oeuvre foods to prepare. But don't worry about running short if they precede dinner, and for other occasions choose from those that keep well. If you're blessed with a freezer, you can be more than generous without a worry in the world.

GARNISHES FOR HORS D'OEUVRE

Tortured platter decorations such as beets cut to resemble roses are becoming as extinct as the blade can opener. Happily, because they're time consuming to make, and, unless you have the artist's touch, look silly and messy, rather than elegant.

The trimmings described in Salad Garnishes* simplify life. Wreaths of parsley or watercress add to the attractiveness of platters, and of the two, parsley wilts less rapidly.

ARRANGING HORS D'OEUVRE PLATTERS

Whether casual or formal in character, and whether served in bowls or on a tray, keep in mind the contrasts of color, texture, and flavor. Lusty hors d'oeuvre like *guacamole* best precede an informal dinner; the elegance of caviar should preface a splendid menu.

Neat arrangement is an important part of allure, so serve orderly arrays, placing together foods that are alike in color and shape. And be sure platters are neither sparsely filled nor heaped. To keep from being kitchen-tied and to insure a table that always looks fresh, prepare several small platters. Then when one is almost depleted, you can replace it promptly.

INGREDIENTS FOR HORS D'OEUVRE

Bread and Crackers: Unusual foods (but not the kind that make guests' hair stand on end) pique appetites, and an interesting variety of bread and crackers adds to the pleasure of hors d'oeuvre. Try the new ones as they appear, and don't neglect the following.

BREAD. Pumpernickel, French, or Italian whole wheat. For crispness, if desired, dry slices of the two latter in a preheated slow, 250° F., oven about 20 minutes.

MELBA TOAST. Slice stale bread very thin, arrange slices on a cooky sheet and dry in a preheated slow, 250° F., oven about 30 minutes.

CRACKERS. Choose from delectables such as Poppers, Euphrates Wafers, Bath Oliver Biscuits, beaten biscuits, Hard Water Crackers, pilot wafers, Swedish crisp bread.

Antipasto Foods: Markets in Italian neighborhoods offer a marvelous selection. Some examples are cold cuts such as *prosciutto, pepperoni, capocollo, mortadella. Caponata,* an eggplant spread, is available in cans; olive *condite*, sometimes called *jardinière*, may be purchased in bulk as well as in jars.

PÂTÉS

Pâté, French for "paste," is the generic term for smooth blends of selected foods. The virtues of pâtés are many—they may be prepared in advance, and often from leftovers. Guests come to *them*, relieving you of the job of passing a platter. Some not only keep well, but improve with age, especially when touched with spirits such as brandy or light rum.

Binding Agents for Pâtés: Mayonnaise, creamed butter, French dressing, cream—sweet or commercial sour—or creamed cream cheese thinned, if necessary, with milk or sweet or commercial sour cream may be used. Add enough "thinner" so mixture spreads easily with a knife. If pâté is to be used for scooping up with fragile foods such as potato chips, thin further.

Seasoning Pâtés: Keep piquancy in mind and season authoritatively to taste with such sauces as Brown-Quick, Worcestershire, Escoffier. Other additions to make palates sit up and take notice are Liquid Pepper,* horseradish, capers, dry mustard, garlic, onion, green olives, pickles.

Foods for Pâtés:

AVOCADO, MASHED. This is called *guacamole* in Mexico. Season with enough Liquid Pepper,* lime juice, chopped garlic, onion, for robust flavor. Use corn chips and the like to dip.

HAM OR TONGUE, GROUND. Mix with celery and onion that have been chopped fine or ground, and bind with mayonnaise, commercial sour cream, or creamed cream cheese. Season sharply and add a sauce such as Escoffier.

LIVER—PÂTÉ DE FOIE GRAS. The most *luxe* of the liver spreads is made from specially fed geese. Any other poultry liver may be used, and although the flavor is harsher often beef or calves' liver makes pâté. After the livers have been cooked gently in a flavorful fat in which onions have been fried, the mixture is chopped or puréed (the sometime addition of chopped hard-cooked egg extends the pâté), and seasoned to taste.

CHICKEN OR TURKEY, GROUND. Prepare as for ham, and add, or garnish with, capers if desired.

SHELLFISH. Prepare as for ham.

SARDINES. Drain sardines, mash, and blend with about 1 tablespoon creamed butter for each 4-ounce can. Season sharply with lemon juice. If desired, add stuffed olives chopped fine.

SPREADS

Creamed cheese mixtures are called spreads, rather than pâtés. Cream cheese, beaten with equal parts of Roquefort or blue cheese is delectable, rich, and sharp. If necessary, thin any cheese spread with sweet or commercial sour cream or milk. Shape into a ball if you like, and roll in broken pecans or coarsely crushed pretzels. Refrigerate until firm. The spreads will keep at least 3 days.

These mixtures are, of course, fine for stuffing celery, too.

Anchovy Cream Cheese Spread

If you're feeling languid, you can substitute anchovy paste for anchovies, but the result won't be as delectable. In either case, an electric mixer does a magnificent job.

    1 two-ounce can anchovy fillets
    ½ pound cream cheese
    2 tablespoons onion juice, approximately
        or
    1 tablespoon instant minced onion

Crush anchovies. Add oil from the can and cheese, and beat until fluffy. Add onion juice and, if necessary, thin to spreading consistency. Makes about 1 cup.

BUTTERS

One part *vegetables*, such as chopped pimento; *herbs*, such as minced chives; *greens*, such as watercress cut fine; cooked *shellfish*, chopped fine or ground; or *anchovies*, mashed or paste, blended with 2 parts creamed butter make delectable spreads.

One cup butter will spread a 1-pound loaf of bread. These butters will keep in the refrigerator about 3 days, and may be frozen.

VEGETABLES

In Chapter X on salads you'll find many foods that make fine hors d'oeuvre. Actually, any vegetable, raw or cooked, is delicious marinated 2 hours or overnight in French dressing, or in the liquid drained from vinegar pickles.

For hurry-up service, simply dust raw vegetable sticks with salt, msg, and your choice of herbs or seeds. Some examples are carrot sticks with tarragon, celery with celery seeds, tomato wedges with basil, etc.

Raw vegetables add interest to an *antipasto* platter or may join the pickles and preserves in a relish dish. They're also attractive stuck porcupine-fashion into a bowl of crushed ice and may be used as a scoop for dips, as in the following example.

Caviar Dip

    1 four-ounce jar red caviar
    ½ bunch chives, cut fine
       or
    1 tablespoon instant minced onion
    1 cup commercial sour cream
    1 large cucumber, sliced thin

Gently fold caviar and chives into sour cream and pile into a bowl. Serve with cucumber slices for scooping up the mixture or offer crackers to dunk or spread.

And don't forget the salted nuts!

Certainly cooking will sometimes be a bore, a fatigue, and a burden. But it would be much more burdensome without knowledge and practiced judgment. And because you are involved in a subject where there is always something new to learn, it can have constant fascination. The reward—as with all education—the more you learn, the more you gain in assurance and in ease.

Finally, should a young son criticize your efforts, smilingly realize that someday, somewhere, he is going to say to his girl: I wish you could cook like my mother.

Happy Feasting!
HELEN WORTH

New York City

Potpourri of Cooking Aids

Nutrition Information

Advances in this science, which is wedded to cooking, are making international good health miracles possible. The cooking methods given throughout this book encompass the most recent techniques for conserving food value. In most foods good looks are related to high food value. Because the sparkle of vitality comes in part from a good diet, you too will benefit when you are as concerned with what you eat as you are with what you wear.

Following are daily food requirements. Add others as needed to complete meals and to provide additional food energy and other food values.

BASIC DAILY FOOD REQUIREMENTS

MEAT GROUP	*2 or more servings* Beef, veal, pork, lamb, poultry, fish, eggs (4 a week). *Alternates:* Dry beans, dry peas (their food value is increased when a small amount of any of the above companions them), nuts.
DAIRY FOOD GROUP	Adults: 2 cups milk (16 ounces). Children: 3 to 4 cups milk (1 quart). (Cheese, ice cream, or other foods containing these may be substituted.)
VEGETABLE–FRUIT GROUP	*4 or more servings* A citrus (or other) fruit or vegetable important for Vitamin C; a dark-green or deep-yellow vegetable for Vitamin A at least every other day.
BREAD–CEREAL GROUP	*4 or more servings* Whole grain, enriched, or restored. (Their food value is increased when milk companions them.)

Cooking Utensils–
Necessities and Gadgets

Mouth-watering meals on the table are, of course, the happy ending in cooking. But realize that any job, no matter how glamorous, is composed of some part drudgery, and that practiced efficiency and the right tools and equipment, kept in excellent condition, speed the performance of onerous cooking chores. For instance, it's easier to peel potatoes with a blade peeler, quicker to chop onions on a board with a chef's knife or cleaver, simpler to cut celery with scissors.

A kitchen overstocked with useless gadgets is no aid to cooking and an overflow of things to store hinders housekeeping. However, like good pots and pans, there are many gadgets that, valuable as well as multipurpose, simplify life.

In addition to the following, throughout these chapters are descriptions of other utensils you will bless.

SUGGESTION: Because it won't rust, whenever possible choose stainless steel.

NECESSITIES

Utensils	Use
BOWLS, MIXING	Preferably oven proof so they also may be used for baking. Pouring lips are helpful.

Utensils	Use
CAKE RACKS	For cooling cakes, icing petit fours, etc.
CLEAVER	For chopping, as with a chef's knife. Its weight makes it easy to use and the wide surface provides a scoop for foods after chopping. Also used to flatten veal for scaloppine, chicken breasts, etc.
COLANDER	For draining large foods, washing vegetables under running water.
COOKY SHEETS (measure oven because at least 1 inch of space is needed between cooky sheet and sides of oven)	Also for baking powder biscuits, hard meringues.
CUTLERY DIVIDER	To make order out of chaos.
CUTTING BOARD (hardwood)	Protects other surfaces; eases chopping.
FORK, LARGE 2-PRONGED	For handling large objects.
FUNNEL	Avoid spills when pouring.
GRATERS (choose those that fit over a pan to catch the grated food)	For potatoes, cheese, fruit rinds, etc.
HOT PAD (asbestos, metal, etc.)	To keep heat low, and in a pinch for toasting bread.
ICE PICK	To judge tenderness of foods, break apart cubes in ice bucket, puncture metal cans, dislodge stuck corks, etc.
KITCHEN SCISSORS	To cut fresh herbs, bacon, celery; cuts through bones, scales fish, etc.
KNIVES (stainless steel are harder to sharpen than other metals, but hold their edge longer)	For paring, carving, chopping, etc.
MEASURING CUPS	
Dry	Level surface insures accurate measure.
Liquid	Has a pouring lip, and 1-cup mark placed about ½ inch below top of cup prevents spills.
MEASURING SPOONS	Level surface insures accurate measure.
MIXER, ELECTRIC (preferably with metal bowl)	Choose a model with attachments such as can opener, knife sharpener, puréer, grinder, etc.
OPENERS	
Beer can	Handsome, sturdy ones are best.
Bottle	A beer and bottle opener combination is most practical.
Can	Choose the type you prefer (see Mixer).
Jar	Grips screw tops for easy twist-off.

Utensils	*Use*
Lid lifter	Lifts vacuum jar tops.
Permanent key	For cans such as coffee, shortening, anchovies, etc.
Waiter's corkscrew (be sure it has 5 grooved spirals)	Opens wine and soda bottles, has blade for cutting capsule on liquor bottles.
PASTRY BRUSH	Spreads melted butter, beaten egg; bastes, etc.
PEPPER MILL (wooden mills won't break, glass mills call attention to need for refilling)	To grind whole peppers (peppercorns)—an imperative for cooking and table use.
REAMER	For citrus fruit juice.
ROLLING PIN (hardwood)	The best have half-round handles and ball-bearing construction.
ROTARY BEATER	For beating eggs, whipping cream, etc.
SIEVES (small, medium, and large; choose extra-fine screen in small sieve)	For draining and straining; also sifting flour.
SPATULAS	
Flexible metal (long, narrow)	For frosting cakes, removing cookies from cooky sheets, etc.
Pancake turner	Also turns fried foods—eggs, hamburgers, etc.
Rubber	For creaming, folding, removing last drop of batter from bowls, sauces from pans, etc.
Spreader	Speeds buttering of bread and spreading of sandwich fillings.
SPOONS	
Long-handled	For stirring quantities of food. Choose handles that will stay cool.
Slotted	To remove solid foods from liquids: meat from gravy, fruit from sirup, etc.
TIMER	The best registers both from 1 to 6 minutes, and up to 1 hour.
TONGS	To remove hot foods from water or oven, turn chops or steaks, test artichokes for doneness.
WIRE WHISK	Facilitates making of gravies, sauces, custards.

GADGETS

Utensils	*Use*
APPLE CORER	Easier to use than a knife.
BLADE PEELER	To peel vegetables, fruits, core apples, cut lemon peel for drinks, make chocolate curls.

Utensils	*Use*
BLENDER	A gadget that fast becomes a necessity. **To** purée, liquefy, grate, etc.
CAKE TESTER	Also for testing cooked fruit and vegetables for tenderness, for cleaning sieves (forces out any stuck food particles).
CHOPSTICKS	For real enjoyment of Oriental food, learn to eat with them. For cooking, hold as fork or spoon. Except for serving or stirring, they're more effective and have same non-heat-absorbing advantages as wooden spoons.
EGG CUTTERS	
Slicer	For perfect egg slices.
Sectioner	For perfect wedges.
ELECTRIC HEATING SURFACE (Table type is most convenient)	To keep cooked foods serving-temperature hot, thus eliminating last-minute preparation and solving the problem of having all foods ready at the same time.
GRAPEFRUIT KNIFE	To section grapefruit, hollow tomatoes, or scoop crumbs from rolls, cut petals for radish roses.
ICE CREAM SPADE OR SCOOP	Those enclosing a liquid chemical cut through the hardest ice cream like butter.
LADLE	To serve soups, ladle doughs or batters into pans.
MELON BALL CUTTER (Although metal measuring spoons may be substituted, they are not as sturdy.)	Also makes potato balls, removes "choke" from artichokes.
MORTAR AND PESTLE (preferably porcelain)	To crush garlic, herbs, seeds.
NUTMEG GRATER	To grate whole nutmeg.
SCOOPS, COFFEE MEASURING SPOON	Keep with flour, sugar, coffee and use as measures.
SIFTER (Choose a single sifter with rotating handle; flour rarely requires multiple sifting and the three screens of a triple sifter are difficult to wash.)	To sift flour, confectioners' sugar, etc.

Tables of Weights and Measures

WEIGHTS AND MEASURES

A few grains	Less than 1/16 teaspoon
A dash	Less than 1/8 teaspoon
21 drops	1/4 teaspoon
1 teaspoon	1/6 ounce
3 teaspoons	1 tablespoon
16 tablespoons	1 cup
1 tablespoon liquid	1/2 ounce
2 cups	1 pint
2 pints (4 cups)	1 quart
1 quart	32 ounces
4 quarts	1 gallon
8 quarts	1 peck
1 pound	16 ounces

EQUIVALENT WEIGHTS OF SPECIFIC FOODS

BREAD

1 slice (1/2 inch thick)	1/4 cup crumbs†
3/4 cup bread crumbs	1 cup cracker crumbs†
1 pound loaf	12 slices, 1/2 inch thick†
	(1/3 pound creamed butter for spreading; 1 quart sandwich filling for spreading)

† Owing to variables, these are approximations.

238

CHEESE	
6 ounces	1 cup grated†
1 pound	2⅔ cups cubed†
1 pound cream cheese	2 cups
COFFEE	
1 pound beans	5 cups ground†
CREAM	
1 cup heavy cream	2 cups whipped†
DEHYDRATED FOODS	
1 part dehydrated	3 parts fresh†
FLOUR	
1 tablespoon all-purpose flour for thickening	½ tablespoon cornstarch, arrowroot, potato flour, or rice flour
NUTS	
2 pounds in the shell	1 pound nut meats; 3–4½ cups†
SOLID SHORTENINGS	
1 pound	2 cups
¼-pound stick	8 tablespoons
⅜ inch of a ¼-pound stick	1 tablespoon
½ ounce	1 tablespoon
SUGAR	
Granulated *or* Very Fine:	
2 cups	1 pound
2 tablespoons	1 ounce
Confectioners':	
2¼–2½ cups	1 pound
Brown:	
2–2¼ cups, packed	1 pound

MEASUREMENTS FOR ALCOHOLIC BEVERAGES

1 quart	32 ounces
1 fifth	25.6 ounces
1 pint	16 ounces (2 cups)
1 split (½ quart)	16 ounces
½ bottle (⅘ pint) wine	12.8 ounces (3–4 glasses)
1 jigger	1½ ounces (3 tablespoons)
1 pony	1 ounce (2 tablespoons)
1 barspoon	1 teaspoon

CAPACITY OF LIQUOR GLASSES

Liqueur	1 ounce (2 tablespoons)
Sherry	2½ ounces (5 tablespoons)
Wine	4–7 ounces

Cocktail	3–4 ounces
Punch	5 ounces
Old-fashioned	6 ounces (¾ cup)
Large highball	10 ounces (1¼ cups)

SUGGESTION: The 7-ounce all-purpose (*vin du pays*) glass may be used for any wine or beer, cocktails, brandy, etc.

ICE FOR DRINKS

1 ice cube	1½–2 ounces (about 4 tablespoons)
Crushed ice for 1 drink	1½ tablespoons

NOTE: Calories in alcoholic beverages are determined by proof. The proof equals the number of calories per ounce (1 ounce of 86-proof liquor equals 86 calories).

Cooking Guides

OVEN TEMPERATURE DESIGNATIONS

Very slow	250–275° F.	Hot	400–425° F.
Slow	300–325° F.	Very hot	450–475° F.
Moderate	350–375° F.	Extremely hot	500–525° F.

CHART FOR COOKING CEREAL

Cereals differ in age, length of storage time, and grind, and because some people prefer their porridge thin and others like it cooked to a heavy mass, consider the following chart a guide.

1 cup Cereal	Water	Salt	Time	Servings
Barley (pearled)	6 cups	2 teaspoons	1 hour	6
Cornmeal	4 cups	1½ teaspoons	30 minutes	4
Farina	5 cups	1½ teaspoons	30 minutes	6
Hominy grits	5 cups	1½ teaspoons	30 minutes	6
Oatmeal, cut (whole grain)	3½ cups	1½ teaspoons	1½ hours	4
Oatmeal, quick-cooking	2 cups	1½ teaspoons	5 minutes	4
Wheat, cracked	2 cups	1½ teaspoons	20 minutes	4

GUIDE FOR COOKING MEAT BY DRY HEAT

Roasting

Cut	Temperature	Approximate Time
BEEF		
Standing Rib Roast	300° F.	Rare—18 minutes per pound
		Medium—22 minutes per pound
		Well done—26 minutes per pound

Cut	Temperature	Approximate Time
Tenderloin (Whole Filet)	450° F.	Rare—45 minutes in all Well done—60 minutes in all
VEAL		
Breast	300° F.	30 minutes per pound
Leg		25 minutes per pound
Loin		30 minutes per pound
Rack (rib or loin)		30 minutes per pound
Saddle (double loin including tenderloin)		25 minutes per pound
Shoulder		25 minutes per pound
Boned and rolled		Add 10 minutes per pound to above
LAMB		
All cuts except neck are suitable for roasting	300° F.	Rare—18 minutes per pound Medium—20 minutes per pound Well done—25 minutes per pound
Boned and rolled		Add 10 minutes per pound to above
PORK (fresh)		
Fresh ham	350° F.	30 minutes per pound
Whole loin (12–15 pounds)		15 minutes per pound
Center loin (3–4 pounds)		35 minutes per pound
Loin ends		45 minutes per pound
Whole shoulder (12–14 pounds)		30 minutes per pound
Boned shoulder (4–6 pounds)		40 minutes per pound
Pork butt (4–6 pounds)		45 minutes per pound
Spareribs		2 hours in all
PORK (smoked)		
Whole ham (12–14 pounds) Quick-cured	300° F.	25 minutes per pound
Half ham (6 pounds) Quick-cured		30 minutes per pound
Ready-to-eat ham (Roasting improves texture and flavor)		18 minutes per pound
Whole loin (12–15 pounds)	350° F.	15 minutes per pound
Center loin (3–4 pounds)		35 minutes per pound

Broiling, Pan-Broiling, Frying

To pan-broil or fry cuts over 1 inch thick, after browning, cover, reduce flame, and cook gently until done.

Cut	Temperature	Approximate Time
BEEF		
Steaks:	Medium-high flame—450° F.	
1 pound,		Rare—8 minutes
1 inch thick		Medium—12 minutes
		Well done—16 minutes
2 pounds,		Rare—12 minutes
1½ inches thick		Medium—16 minutes
		Well done—20 minutes
Hamburgers and		Rare—6 minutes
Filet Mignon:		Medium—8 minutes
1 inch thick		Well done—10 minutes
VEAL		
Scaloppine,	Frying only	10 minutes
¼ inch slices		
Steaks, Chops	Frying only	20 minutes
and Cutlets:		
¾ inch thick		
LAMB		
Steaks and	Medium-high flame—450° F.	Rare—8 minutes
Chops:		Medium—12 minutes
1 inch thick		Well done—16 minutes
HAM		
1-pound slices:	Low to medium flame—250–	15–30 minutes
½–1 inch thick	350° F.	15–25 minutes
Tenderized ham		Cook in half this time
slices		
CANADIAN BACON		
Slices		10 minutes—turn once
VARIETY MEATS		
Liver slices,	Medium-high flame—450° F.	Rare—6 minutes
¾ inch thick		Medium—8 minutes
		Well done—10 minutes
		(Cook pork liver well done)
Kidneys,		Rare—6 minutes
whole, split,		Medium—8 minutes
or cubed		Well done—10 minutes
		(Cook pork kidneys well done)
Heart, cubed		5–10 minutes

GUIDE FOR COOKING MEAT BY MOIST HEAT

Braising

Cover and simmer on top of range or in a 250–350° F. oven.

Cut	Approximate Time
BEEF	
Brisket, chuck (shoulder), flank, round, rump, sirloin tip, short ribs	Whole—2½–3½ hours Small or cut small—1½–2½ hours
VEAL	
Blade, breast, neck, round, rump, shoulder, shank	Whole—45 minutes–1½ hours Small or cut small—45 minutes-1¼ hours
LAMB (usually cubed)	
Breast, neck, shank, shoulder	45 minutes–1½ hours
PORK	
Chops (loin, rib, shoulder), tenderloin (sliced), shoulder (usually cubed), spareribs	35–45 minutes
HAM	
Slices, 1–1½ inch thick	15–30 minutes
VARIETY MEATS	
Kidneys, cut small	10–20 minutes (Cook pork kidneys well done)
Liver, 1–2-pound piece	45 minutes–1 hour (Cook pork liver well done)
Heart, whole	1–2 hours

Water-Cooking

Cover and simmer on top of range or in a 250–350° F. oven.

Cut	Approximate Time
BEEF	
Brisket, flank, plate, rump	3 hours
BEEF (cut small)	
Flank, rump, shin, short ribs	2 hours
VEAL	
Heel of round, shank	¾–1½ hours
LAMB (usually cut small)	
Breast, shoulder, flank, neck	¾–1½ hours
PORK (fresh)	
Shoulder, pigs' feet or knuckles	2–3 hours
SMOKED HAM (water-cook in skin, then peel)	
10–12 pounds	25 minutes per pound

Cut	*Approximate Time*
Over 12 pounds	20 minutes per pound
Half ham	30 minutes per pound
Tenderized whole or half	Subtract 5 minutes per pound from the above
Fully cooked or canned	20 minutes per pound for heating
Picnic shoulder	45 minutes per pound
VARIETY MEATS (whole)	
Heart	1½–2½ hours
Tongue	3 hours

Vegetable Chart

Fresh vegetables vary considerably in age, size, and variety, so consider this chart only a guide. Because fuel and utensils add to the variables, the cooking time given can vary by about 5 minutes in either direction. Obviously, cutting vegetables small will shorten their cooking time.

Amounts per serving depend upon the size of the vegetable, its place in the menu, and appetites. The quantities given are for fresh (uncooked) vegetables.

Approximately ½ cup cooked vegetables makes 1 serving.

Storage Code: 1—Store in a cool dry place.
2—Refrigerate.
3—Refrigerate, covered, either in pliofilm bags or transparent plastic wrap.

French (Globe) Artichoke

SELECTION

Available: October to May
Peak season: March, April
Compact heads heavy for size

QUANTITY AND STORAGE

1 medium per serving
2

PREPARATION

Pull off discolored outer leaves. Remove stem at base with sharp knife. If desired, cut leaves about 1 inch down from top. To speed cooking cut lengthwise in halves, quarters or eighths. Then if desired remove choke (inner thistles) by cutting under it with sharp knife. Leave "heart" intact.

French Artichoke (cont.)
Test doneness with tongs: outside
leaf pulls off easily.

COOKING TIME

Boil whole 25 min., quarters 10 min.
Oven-braise whole 45 min., quarters
30 min.
Burner-braise whole 30 min.,
quarters 20 min.

Asparagus

SELECTION

Available: March to June
Peak season: April to June
Close, compact tips. Firm, tender
stalks, green almost entire length
(puncture with nail to test tenderness). More costly bought in
"bunches" but stalks will be uniform.

QUANTITY AND STORAGE

4 stalks per serving
2

PREPARATION

Peeling or scrubbing unnecessary
(grittiness usually due to soil char-
acteristics). Break stalks at woody
portion. To boil a quantity, tie stalks
in bunch and stand upright in about
2 inches boiling water. (To make a
deep pot, invert top of double boiler
over bottom.)

COOKING TIME

Boil whole 10 min., tips 5 min.
Oven-braise 20 min.
Burner-braise tips 5 min.

Beans, Lima

SELECTION

Available: March to January
Peak season: July to October
Well-filled, dark green pods; tender
beans. (Test with fingernail.)

QUANTITY AND STORAGE

3 pounds in the pod; 1 pound shelled
makes 4 servings.
Pods 2
Shelled 3

Beans, Lima (cont.)
PREPARATION

Shell just before use by cutting thin
strip from outer edge of pod with
scissors.

COOKING TIME

Boil 15 min.
Oven-braise 20 min.
Burner-braise 10 min.

Beans, Snap

(Green or Wax)

SELECTION

Available all year
Peak season: May to August
Formerly called "string" beans; new
varieties are stringless. Choose fairly
flat beans that snap sharply.

QUANTITY AND STORAGE

1 pound makes 5 servings
2

PREPARATION

Cut off tips and if desired "French"
by cutting slanting slices.

COOKING TIME

Boil 10 min.
Oven-braise 20 min.
Burner-braise 10 min.

Beets: Young

SELECTION

Available all year
Peak season: June, July
Firm with unwilted leaves

QUANTITY AND STORAGE

1 medium per serving
2

PREPARATION

Unpeeled: Remove all except 1 inch
of tops and leave root on. Rub skins
off after cooking.
Peeled: Cook whole, slice, dice, or
cut strips.

COOKING TIME

Boil 15 min.
Oven-braise 45 min. if whole, 30 min.
if cut.

Beets: Young (cont.)
Burner-braise 20 min. if whole, 10 min. if cut.

Beets: Old

SELECTION
Available winter
Smooth velvety skins

QUANTITY AND STORAGE
1 medium per serving
1

PREPARATION
As for Young Beets

COOKING TIME
Boil whole 1½ hours

Beet Tops
(See Greens)

Broccoli
(See Special Vegetables*)

SELECTION
Available all year
Peak season: October to March
Small leaves, firm stalks, compact heads and buds
Available green or purple

QUANTITY AND STORAGE
2 stalks fresh make 1 serving
3

PREPARATION
(See Asparagus)

COOKING TIME
Boil 20 min.

Brussels Sprouts
(See Special Vegetables*)

SELECTION
Available: August to March
Peak season: October to December
Firm, compact. Avoid worm-riddled leaves.

QUANTITY AND STORAGE
3 to 4 per serving
3

Brussels Sprouts (cont.)

PREPARATION
Cut stem at base, remove wilted leaves.
To speed cooking, make 2 deep cuts (X) in stem ends.

COOKING TIME
Boil 15 min.
Oven-braise 25 min.
Burner-braise 15 min.

Cabbage
(See Special Vegetables*)

SELECTION
Available all year
Peak season: May
Young: Loose rather than compact head
Mature: Solid head fairly heavy for size, stem cut close to base, few wilted leaves.

QUANTITY AND STORAGE
1 medium head makes 6 servings
3

PREPARATION
Discard wilted outer leaves.

COOKING TIME
Boil whole 20 min., wedges 10 min.
Parboil 5 min. to remove leaves for stuffing
Oven-braise wedges 25 min., shreds 15 min.
Burner-braise wedges 15 min., shreds 5 min.

Carrots

SELECTION
Available all year
Smooth, firm, well-shaped, bright orange for food value. Avoid thick leaf stem at point of attachment.

QUANTITY AND STORAGE
1 small makes 1 serving
8

Carrots (cont.)

PREPARATION

Remove tops—they take moisture from the roots and cause wilting.

Raw: Peel only if discolored. Peel for cooking if not to be strained and discarded.

To boil: Cut halves, sticks, dice, or rings, or boil whole and rub skins off after cooking.

COOKING TIME

Boil whole 20 min., cut 10 min.

Oven-braise whole 45 min., cut 20 min.

Burner-braise whole 30 min., cut 10 min.

Cauliflower

(See Special Vegetables*)

SELECTION

Available all year

Peak season: October, November

Firm heads, heavy for size. Closely united flower clusters, fresh white curd. (Leaves growing through curd affect appearance only.)

QUANTITY AND STORAGE

1 medium head makes 4 servings

3

PREPARATION

Remove stem and discard outer leaves.

To speed boiling whole head, make 2 deep cuts (X) in stem end.

COOKING TIME

Boil whole 20 min., flowerets 10 min.

Oven-braise flowerets 25 min.

Burner-braise flowerets 10 min.

Celery

SELECTION

Available all year

Fresh green leaves. Avoid cracked discolored stalks.

QUANTITY AND STORAGE

3 stalks make 1 serving

3 (wash and drain before storing)

Celery (cont.)

PREPARATION

Use fresh (or dried) leaves for salads, soups, stews, sauces. Scrape off any brown discoloration on stalks. Halve or quarter bunches lengthwise, or separate stalks and cut 1- to 2-inch lengths.

COOKING TIME

Boil 1- to 2-inch lengths 15 min.

Oven-braise 25 min.

Burner-braise 15 min.

Chard, Swiss

(See Greens)

Chicory

(See Greens)

Collards

(See Greens)

Corn

SELECTION

Available all year

Peak season: June to September

Well-filled ears, plump, shiny kernels, firm enough to resist pressure slightly. To examine ears for excessive worm damage, pull husks back only a short way, then replace.

QUANTITY AND STORAGE

2 medium ears make 1 serving

Unhusked 2

Husked 3

PREPARATION

Whole ear: Remove husks and silk just before cooking and remove (break or cut off) inedible ends.

Kernels (raw or cooked): Insert a skewer, stand ear upright on plate, and with sharp knife remove tips only. Scrape ear with sharp, then dull side of table knife.

COOKING TIME

Boil: Turn off flame as soon as water returns to a boil. (Keep second por-

Corn (cont.)
tions in covered pot on range.)
Oven-braise raw kernels 15 min.
Burner-braise raw kernels 5 min.
Fry Shallow Fat raw kernels 10 min.

Cucumbers

SELECTION
Available all year
Peak season: May to August
Firm, well-shaped, deep green

QUANTITY AND STORAGE
1 small makes 2 servings
2 (Wash and dry before storing)

PREPARATION
Bred for tender skins, so peeling
unnecessary.

COOKING METHOD
Boil slices or cubes 5 min.
Parboil 5 min. for stuffing.
Oven-braise slices or cubes 15 min.
Burner-braise slices or cubes 5 min.

Dandelion Greens

(See Greens)

Dried Vegetables

(See Special Vegetables°)

Eggplant

SELECTION
Available all year
Peak season: August, September
Firm, heavy for size, smooth glowing
skin, uniformly dark color

QUANTITY AND STORAGE
1 medium makes 4 servings
2

PREPARATION
Peeling, seeding, salting, pressing
with weight unnecessary. Halve,
quarter or cut in eighths if small;
slice if large.

COOKING TIME
Parboil for stuffing 20 min.

Eggplant (cont.)
Oven-braise quarters or slices 35 min.
Burner-braise quarters or slices 35
min.
Bake stuffed halves 40 min.
Broil small young 15 min., or until
brown.
Fry Shallow Fat slices 10 min., turn-
ing to brown both sides. *Deep Fat*
slices as above.

Garlic

(See Special Vegetables°)

Mushrooms

SELECTION
Available all year
Peak season: November, December
Moist, firm, clean, short thick stems

QUANTITY AND STORAGE
3 medium make 1 serving
Refrigerate stacked loosely in an
open pliofilm bag

PREPARATION
Remove woody portion of stem. Do
not peel or wash. Wipe with damp
paper towel if necessary. To slice,
make T-shaped strips.

COOKING TIME
Oven-braise whole 20 min., slices 10
min.
Burner-braise whole 10 min., slices
5 min.
Bake whole stuffed 500° F., 10 min.
Broil whole 8 min.
Fry Shallow Fat whole 10 min.

Okra

SELECTION
Available all year
Peak season: July, August

QUANTITY AND STORAGE
1 pound makes 4 servings
2

PREPARATION
Leave small pods whole, remove stem

Greens (See Salads*)	SELECTION	QUANTITY AND STORAGE
	Generally available all year. Young, green with no seed stems. Press or twist stalks gently to determine tenderness.	3
Beet tops	Available: Nov.–Aug. Peak season: Mar.–Apr.	1 lb. makes 4 servings
Chicory, curly	Peak season: June	1 medium head makes 4 servings
Collards	Peak season: Dec.–Jan.	1 lb. makes 4 servings
Dandelion	Peak season: Mar.–June	1 bunch makes 4 servings
Endive, Belgian	Peak season: Winter	1 root makes 1 serving
Escarole	Peak season: Oct.	1 medium bunch makes 4 servings
Kale	Peak season: Dec.–Feb.	1 lb. makes 4 servings
Lettuce	Peak season: June	1 medium head makes 4 servings
Mustard	Peak season: Jan.–Mar.	1 lb. makes 4 servings
Spinach	Peak season: Mar.–June	1 lb. makes 3 servings
Swiss chard	Peak season: June–Oct.	1 lb. makes 4 servings
Turnip tops	Peak season: Dec.–May	1 lb. makes 4 servings
Watercress	Peak season: Apr.–May	1 bunch makes 4 servings

PREPARATION

Discard roots, tough stems, imperfect leaves.

COOKING TIME

Cook gently 5 minutes, covered, over low flame, using only water clinging to leaves after washing.

Okra (cont.)
ends from large pods and slice rounds 1-inch thick.

COOKING TIME
Boil pods 20 min., rounds 10 min.

Onions
(See Special Vegetables*)

SELECTION
Bermuda—Peak season: March to June
Green—Peak season: May to August
Available all year

QUANTITY AND STORAGE
2 small white make 1 serving

Onions (cont.)
PREPARATION
Peel, cut, etc., as directed in recipes.

COOKING TIME
Boil small white 15 min.
Parboil large for stuffing 20 min.
Oven-braise small white 35 min.
Burner-braise small white 15 min.
Bake stuffed halves 30 min.
Broil slices or wedges 15 min.
Fry Shallow Fat slices 10 min., turning to brown both sides.
Fry Deep Fat rings 10 min.

Parsnips
(See Carrots)

Peas

SELECTION
Available all year
Peak season: April to July
Velvety, bright green pods of same size, neither plump (old age) nor flat (underdeveloped). Taste raw to judge sweetness.

QUANTITY AND STORAGE
1 pound in pod makes 2 servings
1 pound shelled makes 4 servings
Pods 2
Shelled 3

PREPARATION
Shell.

COOKING TIME
Boil 5 min.
Oven-braise 15 min.
Burner-braise 5 min.

Peppers, Sweet

SELECTION
Available all year
Peak season: July to October
Some varieties turn red when ripe. Thick flesh, deep color, no surface blemishes.

QUANTITY AND STORAGE
1 medium makes 2 servings
2

PREPARATION
Discard seeds and white membrane. For pieces, pull apart. For fine dice cut stacked strips with a sharp knife.

COOKING TIME
Parboil for stuffing 10 min.
Bake stuffed 30 min.
Broil pieces 20 min.
Fry Shallow Fat pieces 20 min.

Potatoes (White)
(See Special Vegetables*)

SELECTION
Available all year

Potatoes (white) (cont.)

QUANTITY AND STORAGE
1 medium per serving
1

PREPARATION
Peel, cut, etc., as directed in recipes.

COOKING TIME
Boil whole 30 min., cut 15 min.
Oven-braise whole 60 min., cut 40 min.
Burner-braise cut 15 min.
Bake 60 min.
Fry Shallow Fat dice or slices 20 min.
Fry Deep Fat sticks 10 min.

Potatoes (Sweet)
(See Special Vegetables*)

Radishes

SELECTION
Available all year
Peak season: April to July

QUANTITY AND STORAGE
3 make 1 serving
2 (Remove root ends and tips before refrigerating.)

PREPARATION
As directed in recipes.

COOKING TIME
Boil whole 15 min.

Pumpkin
(See Winter Squash)

SELECTION
Available: September to November
Peak season: October

Rutabagas
(See Turnips)

Spinach
(See Greens)

Squash: Summer (zucchini, patty pans, etc.)

SELECTION

Some varieties available all year, all interchangeable in recipes.
Peak season: June to August
Tender, fairly heavy for size. Puncture with fingernail to test tenderness.

QUANTITY AND STORAGE

1 small makes 2 servings
2

PREPARATION

If small, cook whole. If large, slice or cube. Peel varieties with tough skins. Do not seed.

COOKING TIME

Boil whole 20 min., cubes or slices 10 min.
Parboil for stuffing 10 min.
Oven-braise 20 min.
Burner-braise 10 min.
Bake stuffed halves 30 min.
Fry Shallow Fat 15 min.

Squash: Winter

SELECTION

Available: September to November
Peak season: October
Hubbard (large), acorn or Des Moines (small): Thick-skinned, heavy for size.

QUANTITY AND STORAGE

Hubbard: 1 pound makes 2 servings
Acorn (Des Moines): 1 makes 1 serving
2

PREPARATION

Halve small or dice large. Scrape stringy portion and remove seeds.

COOKING TIME

Boil peeled cubed 30 min.
Mash
Bake Brush with fat, 45 min.

Swiss Chard

(See Greens)

Tomatoes

SELECTION

Available all year
Peak season: June to October
Firm, plump, unblemished, smooth scarlet skin. Avoid if worm-damaged, puffy, watery.

QUANTITY AND STORAGE

1 small per serving
2 (rinse and dry before storing)

PREPARATION

Coring unnecessary.
Peel (see Blanching*) for cooking if not to be strained. To peel one or two, stick fork in bottom end, hold over flame, turning until skin loosens. Repeat with fork in blossom end. Slip skin off. To boil (stew): Peel and quarter. If not juicy, add just enough water to cover bottom of pan. After cooking, thicken liquid if desired.
To stuff: Remove thin slice from stem end. Scoop, leaving a ½-inch shell. Sprinkle inside lightly with salt and invert about 10 minutes to extract juice.

COOKING TIME

Boil (stew): Cover and simmer 10 min.
Bake in shallow pan 20 min.
Broil 15 min.
Fry Shallow Fat 1-inch-thick slices 10 min.

Turnips

SELECTION

Available all year
Peak season: October to March
Turnips are white. Rutabagas, sometimes called "Swedes," are yellow and stronger-flavored. Either should be smooth, firm, heavy for size.

QUANTITY AND STORAGE

1 small per serving
Young 2
Old 1

Turnips (cont.)

PREPARATION

Peel, leave whole if small. Halve, cube, or slice ¼ inch thick if large.

COOKING TIME

Boil 30 min.
Parboil for stuffing 10 min.
Oven-braise 25 min.

Turnips (cont.)

Burner-braise 15 min.
Bake stuffed 30 min.
Fry (see Eggplant)

Turnip Tops

(See Greens)

Fruit Chart

Fresh fruits vary considerably in age, size, and variety, so consider this chart only a guide. Because fuel and utensils add to the variables, the cooking time given can vary by about 5 minutes in either direction. Obviously, cutting fruits small will shorten cooking time.

Amounts per serving depend upon the size of the fruit, its place in the menu, and appetites. The quantities given are for fresh (uncooked) fruits.

Approximately ½ cup cooked fruit makes 1 serving.

Storage Code: 1—Store in a cool dry place.
2—Refrigerate.
3—Refrigerate covered either in pliofilm bags or transparent plastic wrap.

Apples
(See Special Fruits*)

SELECTION
Available all year
Peak season: Fall
Firm, unblemished

QUANTITY AND STORAGE
2 to 3 equal 1 pound

1 medium per serving; medium and small keep best
2 in crisper of refrigerator

PREPARATION
Peeling and cutting optional. Cook whole, halved, quartered, sliced, or cubed.

COOKING TIME
Oven-braise pieces 25 min.

255

Apples (cont.)
Burner-braise pieces 15 min.
Bake°
Broil slices 15 min. per side
Fry Shallow Fat slices 10 min. per side
Water-cook pieces 15 min. for *purée* pieces 15 min.

Apricots

SELECTION
Available: May to August
Peak season: June, July
Good color, slightly yielding.

QUANTITY AND STORAGE
2 per serving
8 to 10 medium equal 1 pound
2

PREPARATION
Do not peel. Halve and stone if desired.

COOKING TIME
Broil halves 10 min.
Water-cook whole 10 min.

Avocados (Calavos, Flavocados)

SELECTION
Available all year
Peak season: March, April
Slightly yielding; insert toothpick in stem end.

QUANTITY AND STORAGE
½ medium per serving
1 medium makes 1½ cups diced
Store unused portions unpeeled and unstoned.
2

PREPARATION
To separate, cut through to stone lengthwise all around, then gently twist halves between palms in opposite directions. Whack stone with paring knife, twist and lift out. Strip skin beginning at narrow end.

Bananas

SELECTION
Available all year

Bananas (cont.)
Peak season: Spring
Plump and yellow with brown flecked skin for eating; green *tipped* for cooking.

QUANTITY AND STORAGE
1 equals ¾ cup sliced or diced; ½ cup mashed.
Ripen at room temperature.
3

COOKING TIME
Oven-braise peeled halves 10 min.
Burner-braise peeled halves 5 min.
Bake unpeeled whole 15 min., halves 10 min.
Broil halves in skin or peeled 10 min.
Fry peeled halves 5 min. per side.

Berries
(See Special Fruits° and variety of berry)

Blackberries

SELECTION
Available: May to August
Peak season: June to August

QUANTITY AND STORAGE
1 pint (¾ pound) equals about 1¾ cups, makes 3 servings
2

PREPARATION
(See Special Fruits°)

COOKING TIME
Oven-braise 10 min.
Burner-braise 5 min.
Water-cook 5 min.

Blueberries

SELECTION
Available: May to September
Peak season: July, August

QUANTITY AND STORAGE
1 pint (¾ pound) equals about 1¾ cups, makes 3 servings
2

PREPARATION
(See Special Fruits°)

Blueberries (cont.)

COOKING TIME
Oven-braise 10 min.
Burner-braise 5 min.
Water-cook 5 min.

Cherries (Sweet and Sour)

SELECTION
Available: May to August
Peak season: June, July
Firm, shiny, stems attached

QUANTITY AND STORAGE
1 pound equals 2 cups
1 quart makes 2¾ cups after pitting
2

PREPARATION
Rinse in colander under running cold water. Pit with paper clip.

COOKING TIME
Oven-braise 10 min.
Burner-braise 5 min.
Water-cook 5 min.

Cranberries

SELECTION
Available: September to January
Peak season: October to December
Plump, shiny

QUANTITY AND STORAGE
1 quart (1 pound) makes about 3 cups cooked sauce, 6 servings
2

PREPARATION
(See Special Fruits*)

COOKING TIME
Water-cook only until skins burst, about 10 min.
Purée after water-cooking.

Grapefruit
(See Special Fruits*)

SELECTION
Available all year
Peak season: December to April

QUANTITY AND STORAGE
1 medium equals ¾ cup juice, 12

Grapefruit (cont.)
sections; 1¼ cups diced pulp.
2

PREPARATION
(See Special Fruits*)

COOKING TIME
Bake halves 20 min.
Broil halves 10 min.

Grapes

SELECTION
Available all year
Peak season: September to November
Tightly attached to stems (shake bunches gently to test). Cling skin for eating; slip skin for eating, juice, and canning.

QUANTITY AND STORAGE
2

Kumquats
(See Special Fruits*)

SELECTION
Available: November to April
Peak season: November, December

Lemons
(See Special Fruits*)

SELECTION
Available all year
Peak season: June, July
Yellow-green for acidity

QUANTITY AND STORAGE
1 medium equals 3 tablespoons juice, 1½ teaspoon grated rind

Limes
(See Special Fruits*)

SELECTION
Available all year
Peak season: June to August
Deep green for acidity

Melons
(See Special Fruits*)

Melons (cont.)

SELECTION
Available: February to December
Peak season: July to October

QUANTITY AND STORAGE
3

Oranges
(See Special Fruits*)

SELECTION
Available all year
Peak season: Winter

QUANTITY AND STORAGE
1 medium equals ½ cup juice, 10
sections, 1 tablespoon grated rind.
2

COOKING TIME
Bake halves 20 min.
Broil halves 10 min.

Peaches

SELECTION
Available: June to September
Peak season: July, August
Slightly yielding. Avoid those tinged
with green or with skin punctures.
Freestones—dessert, canning, general
use; clingstones—slicing, pickling.

QUANTITY AND STORAGE
4 to 7 equal 1 pound, make 4
servings, about 2¼ cup sliced.
2

PREPARATION
Peel if desired. Cook whole, halved,
or sliced. Peel a quantity by
blanching.*

COOKING TIME
Oven-braise whole 20 min., cut 10
min.
Burner-braise whole 15 min., cut 5
min.
Bake whole 25 min., cut 15 min.
Broil halves 15 min.
Water-cook whole 15 min., cut 5 min.

Pears

SELECTION
Available all year
Peak season: August to October

QUANTITY AND STORAGE
3 to 4 medium make 1 pound, 2 cups
cooked
2

PREPARATION
Peel if desired and cook whole, or cut
and core halves or wedges.

COOKING TIME
Oven-braise whole 40 min., cut 20
min.
Burner-braise whole 20 min., cut 10
min.
Broil halves 10 min.
Water-cook whole 20 min., cut 10
min.

Persimmons

SELECTION
Available: September to December
Peak season: October, November
Flabby—soft

QUANTITY AND STORAGE
1 per serving

PREPARATION
Eat whole or cut halves or wedges.

Pineapples
(See Special Fruits*)

SELECTION
Available all year
Peak season: March to June

QUANTITY AND STORAGE
1 medium equals about 2½ cups
diced, makes 4 servings
2

COOKING TIME
Oven-braise cut 20 min.
Burner-braise cut 10 min.
Broil rings 10 min.
Fry Shallow Fat rings 5 min. per side
Water-cook rings or cubes 10 min.

Plums and Fresh Prunes

SELECTION

Available: June to September
Peak season: July to September

QUANTITY AND STORAGE

About 15 medium equal 1 pound,
about 2 cups cooked
2

PREPARATION

Cook whole, or halve and pit. (Double
liquid and sugar for prunes.)

COOKING TIME

Oven-braise 20 min.
Burner-braise 10 min.
Water-cook plums 10 min., prunes 15
min.
Purée 15 min.

Quinces

SELECTION

Available: Fall and winter
Firm to hard, greenish to golden
yellow

QUANTITY AND STORAGE

3 to 4 medium equal 1 pound, make
4 servings
2

PREPARATION

Peel and core, halve or quarter
Allow 3 cups liquid, 3 cups sugar
per pound

COOKING TIME

Oven-braise 2 hours.
Burner-braise 45 min.
Water-cook 45 min.

Raspberries

(See Special Fruits*)

SELECTION

Available: June to November
Peak season: July

QUANTITY AND STORAGE

1 pint (¾ pound) equals about 1¾
cups, makes 3 servings
2

Raspberries (cont.)

COOKING TIME

Oven-braise 10 min.
Burner-braise 5 min.
Water-cook 5 min.

Rhubarb

(See Special Fruits*)

SELECTION

Available all year
Peak season: April to June

QUANTITY AND STORAGE

1 bunch makes 6 servings
1 pound fresh makes 2 cups cooked,
4 servings
3

Strawberries

(See Special Fruits*)

SELECTION

Available all year
Peak season: May, June

QUANTITY AND STORAGE

1 pint (¾ pound) equals about 1¾
cups, makes 3 servings
2

COOKING TIME

Oven-braise 10 min.
Burner-braise 5 min.
Water-cook 5 min.

Tangerines

(See Special Fruits*)

SELECTION

Available: November to April
Peak season: December, January
Loose skins

QUANTITY AND STORAGE

2

Watermelons

(See Special Fruits*)

SELECTION

Available: April to September
Peak season: June, July

QUANTITY AND STORAGE

3

Index